THE VALUE OF HAWAI'I

KNOWING THE PAST,
SHAPING THE FUTURE

BIOGRAPHY MONOGRAPHS

The Center for Biographical Research of the University of Hawai'i at Mānoa is dedicated to the interdisciplinary and multicultural study of life writing through teaching, publication, and outreach activities.

In addition to *Biography: An Interdisciplinary Quarterly,* published since 1978, the Center sponsors the Biography Monograph series; a chronological list of previous monographs follows.

Anthony Friedson, ed. *New Directions in Biography* (1981).

Gloria Fromm, ed. *Essaying Biography: A Celebration for Leon Edel* (1986).

Frank Novak, Jr. *The Autobiographical Writings of Lewis Mumford: A Study in Literary Audacity* (1988).

Mari Matsuda, ed. *Called from Within: Early Women Lawyers of Hawaii* (1992).

Alice M. Beechert and Edward D. Beechert, eds. *John Reinecke: The Autobiography of a Gentle Activist* (1993).

Donald J. Winslow. *Life-Writing: A Glossary of Terms in Biography* (2nd ed., 1995).

Koji Ariyoshi. *From Kona to Yenan: The Political Memoirs of Koji Ariyoshi.* Ed. Alice M. Beechert and Edward D. Beechert (2000).

Leon Edel. *The Visitable Past: A Wartime Memoir* (2000).

Ruth Nadelhaft, with Victoria Bonebakker, eds. *Imagine What It's Like: A Literature and Medicine Anthology* (2008).

Michi Kodama-Nishimoto, Warren S. Nishimoto, and Cynthia A. Oshiro, eds. *Talking Hawai'i's Story: Oral Histories of an Island People.* (2009).

Philippe Lejeune. *On Diary.* Ed. Jeremy D. Popkin and Julie Rak (2009).

For further information about the Center or its publications, contact the Center for Biographical Research, University of Hawai'i at Mānoa, Honolulu, Hawai'i 96822 USA; telephone/fax: 808-956-3774; biograph@hawaii.edu; www.hawaii.edu/biograph.

The Value of Hawai'i

Knowing the Past, Shaping the Future

EDITED BY

CRAIG HOWES

&

JONATHAN KAY KAMAKAWIWO'OLE OSORIO

A BIOGRAPHY MONOGRAPH

PUBLISHED FOR THE BIOGRAPHICAL RESEARCH CENTER
BY THE UNIVERSITY OF HAWAI'I PRESS
2010

© 2010 Biographical Research Center

Printed in the United States of America

15 14 13 12 11   6 5 4 3

Library of Congress Cataloging-in-Publication Data

The value of Hawai'i : knowing the past, shaping the future / edited by Craig Howes & Jonathan Kay Kamakawiwo'ole Osorio.

   p. cm. — (A biography monograph)

 Includes bibliographical references.

 ISBN 978-0-8248-3529-3 (softcover : alk. paper)

1. Hawaii—Social conditions. 2. Hawaii—Economic conditions—1959– 3. Hawaii—Politics and government—1959– 4. Quality of life—Hawaii. I. Howes, Craig, 1955– II. Osorio, Jon Kamakawiwo'ole. III. University of Hawaii at Manoa. Biographical Research Center. IV. Series: Biography monograph.

 DU627.8.V35 2010

 996.9—dc22

                    2010022651

University of Hawai'i Press books are printed on acid-free paper and meet the guidelines for permanence and durability of the Council on Library Resources.

contents

A NOTE ON THE TEXT AND ACKNOWLEDGMENTS

For ease of reading, all notes, documentation, and additional resources have been placed in a separate section at the back of this book.

The cover photograph is from the Hawai'i State Archives Collection.

Neither the editors nor the contributors are receiving any compensation for their contributions to *The Value of Hawai'i*. Any profits from this volume will be devoted to publishing more books about the politics, culture, history, and art of Hawai'i.

* * * * *

Many thanks to William Hamilton, Keith Leber, and Carol Abe at the University of Hawai'i Press, and to Puakea Nogelmeier, Kawaihuelani Center for Hawaiian Language, Hawai'inuiākea School of Hawaiian Knowledge, University of Hawai'i at Mānoa.

To Gaye Chan, who provided the striking and thought-provoking cover for this book.

To Stan Schab, of the Center for Biographical Research, University of Hawai'i at Mānoa, the editor and colleague who makes all things possible.

And of course, to this book's contributors, for their knowledge, their eloquence, their devotion to Hawai'i—and their ability to write to deadlines.

— *Craig Howes and Jon Osorio*

INTRODUCTION

CRAIG HOWES

The striking cover of this book brings into focus the themes and the ambitions of its contributors. The main photo shows a Hawai'i classroom, probably in the 1950s. Cut out numbers and the letters of the alphabet run along the walls just below the ceiling, but someone—probably the teacher—has written the word ALOHA in even larger letters on the blackboard. The two children are staging a display of Hawai'i's status as a separate place, with its own history, and as somehow part of the American union. The little girl holds up a silhouette of George Washington, who's looking backward, apparently at the approaching silhouette of Kamehameha, which the boy in the arts-and-crafts tricornered colonial hat has just finished making. (The scissors are still in his right hand.)

Neither of the children is looking at these iconic profiles. The little girl is gazing up at someone outside of the picture. "Is this what you want?" Lost in himself, the little boy isn't looking for understanding, or approval. He isn't looking anywhere. Gaye Chan, the cover designer, has also superimposed an open bankbook from the mid 1950s over part of the photo. In Hawai'i, this was a time of economic and social transformation that culminated in statehood, and it was also a time when people were intensively debating the price of paradise.

It's a striking cover because these somber, even bewildered children don't look anything like those beaming multiethnic young faces found in most statehood photographs. In fact, these children represent more accurately our current situation, which is forcing us to ask urgent yet uneasy questions about how Kamehameha and George Washington do see each other these days, if at all, and also about whether aloha is the most important thing in this scene, or just a scribbled-in afterthought.

* * * * *

Oscar Wilde once said "A cynic is someone who knows the price of everything, and the value of nothing," and the past generation of executive and legislative activity in Hawai'i could certainly stand as evidence that we have become a community of cynics. Governor Cayetano began his first term in 1994 by grimly announcing that we were in a disastrous budget crisis. Since then, we have lurched our way through a perpetual state of economic emergency. World and national events certainly played their part in creating this chaos. An economic recession covering the last half of the 1990s, followed by 9/11 and two wars, and concluded by the biggest economic collapse since the Great Depression have obviously affected tourism and the military, just to mention only the biggest drivers of our economy.

But if anything, Hawai'i itself has changed even more profoundly. Sugar and pineapple have disappeared, bringing to a close the large-scale agriculture that all but defined the islands for over a century. (Can you imagine what plantation owners—and plantation workers—would have thought in 1910 if you had told them that in 2010, only 1.6 percent of Hawai'i's population would be working in agriculture?) Perceptions of unions, those hugely formative forces on the course of twentieth century Hawai'i history, have shifted from the private to the public sector. In 1949, striking dock workers brought the territory to a standstill; in 2001, it was teachers and government and public employees.

What's frustrating about the current stagnation or decline in the quality of life in Hawai'i is that in certain areas we have traditionally done things much better. As our contributors point out, our healthcare provisions, our long-term commitments to environmental protection and historic preservation, our public and private advocacy for culture and the arts, our labor agreements that secured pension benefits, disability support, and a living wage, and our vigilant efforts to function as a productive, multiethnic, and equitable society have placed Hawai'i high on the list of comparatively progressive and peaceful places on earth. But as public debate and public policy have degenerated into an unending hunt for what we supposedly don't need or can't afford to provide ourselves, the daily news becomes indistinguishable from the equally depressing debates in California, or Illinois, or Washington, D.C. What's most troubling about the current public debates over education, social services, healthcare, the environment, and cultural preservation has been the expressed indifference, or even open antagonism, to any efforts at keeping these institutions from slouching toward total dysfunction. We deserve better.

There's been good news, and bad news. The balanced budget requirement in Hawai'i has prevented the bankruptcy disasters of states like California and Illinois. That's good. But in the past few years, the executive branch's refusal to raise state revenues at a time when expenses were steadily climbing has moved us toward what led California to disaster—rising costs for prisons, schools, universities, social services, and infrastructure, but an absolute inability, thanks to Proposition 13 and other constraints, for government to pay for essential services at a time when the self-inflicted collapse of the business sector has made them most necessary.

One of the strongest convictions that emerges from this collection is that letting certain services and institutions drop below a certain point is not only imprudent, but immoral. No one should be capable of walking out of negotiations to announce that the number of school days in a year will be dramatically cut. No one should be able to argue that the laws and mandates designed to keep government accessible, honest, and responsible don't apply to the executive or legislative branch, or can be bargained away. And no one should be able to argue for increasingly punitive law enforcement, long-term incarceration, and literal exile, while at the same time refusing to admit that the community has any responsibility to address the problems that contribute to homelessness or crime. This book can stand as a snapshot of sorts—a state of the State, compiled in early 2010. But its primary function is to provoke discussions of what is right—at first, in the period before the 2010 elections, but also into the future, as we keep our focus on what is valuable about Hawai'i to us, and how to care for this place that we love.

* * * * *

The idea for this book came just before dawn on October 26, 2009, as the co-editors were jogging through Mānoa Valley. We've done this roughly three times a week for years, and we run slowly enough so that we can talk the whole time. The conversation turned to the 2010 elections, and whether we could expect anything other that a continued gutting of the quality of life we cared about, and a sense of helplessness before the whims of economic and government forces that were all but defining these islands. Somewhere near the University of Hawai'i Press on Kolowalu Street, we started talking about a collection of essays that would talk about how we had gotten into this mess— we're both strongly convinced of the importance of history—and then would offer responses that didn't just focus on the bottom line. These would be essays about the value of Hawai'i, not the price.

We agreed that we needed to bring more people into the discussion, so we contacted Meda Chesney-Lind, Mari Matsuda, Neal Milner, and Deane Neubauer, because they were extremely familiar with sectors of the community that we weren't, because they have all been very public advocates for a better, more equitable Hawai'i, and because they all knew people who would be good potential contributors. We met briefly in mid-November, and batted around topics that might be covered, and the names of possible writers. We also agreed that we needed a brief—one paragraph—description of the collection to send along when we invited people to contribute.

There things stayed until late January, when we decided that if the book was going to appear well before the 2010 elections, it needed to happen now. So we met again in late January and early February, and came up with roughly thirty topics for essays, potential writers for each topic, and some backup names, in case the first person we approached said no. (Almost no one did.) We invited more than two dozen writers and asked them for an essay of about 3,000 words on the subject of their most passionate concerns. We asked them to describe how Hawai'i has arrived at the current state of affairs, and to include recommendations for addressing the problems. We wanted people to write for general, not specialist readers, and to have the essays done by March 29—a deadline of roughly seven weeks for most contributors, but an even shorter time for others.

Each contributor chose the approach and style that seemed most appropriate for the topic. Some essays are anecdotal and autobiographical. Some are highly schematic. Some have charts and graphs, others have photos. One has a recipe. We also asked each contributor to supply, if appropriate, a list of further resources, in addition to the ones quoted in the essay, for readers interested in finding out more about the essay's topic. The result is what you hold in your hands.

This book is not a repair manual. Although the writers propose solutions large and small to the challenges that face us, these essays encourage the entire community to enter into discussions about Hawai'i's future. Along the way, the essays also provide information about our past and present that can help inform these discussions—considerations often lost when people are under the budget-cutting knife.

This book is not a shared manifesto. The contributors are a diverse group. (We knew we were probably on the right track when some writers expressed reservations about other participants.) But they all really know what they are talking about—that's why we asked them—and they all share a concern about the current condition of Hawai'i, and a belief that our ways of thinking as a community have to change. We need to refocus, to remember, and to rededicate.

And though it's similar in certain ways, *The Value of Hawai'i* is not just an update of *The Price of Paradise*, Randall W. Roth's edited volumes of 1992 and 1993. The major differences are in timing, focus, and tone. *The Price of Paradise* appeared at the end of the Waihee years, with their booming revenues, major expansions of social programs, funding for virtually universal healthcare, and substantial increases in public employees salaries and benefits to make up for preceding years of neglect. A major theme of *The Price of*

Paradise was that government, and particularly state government, was too big and intrusive. "Normally," Roth writes in his introduction, "state and county governments are content to regulate businesses; here they compete with them."[1] What a change in less than twenty years! As many of our contributors point out, government now often does neither.

The perspective and method in *The Price of Paradise* were also different. "Most of the authors are economists," Roth wrote, "the others are journalists, lawyers, an educator's educator and a demographer."[2] The essays were also very short, and tended to deal with very specific topics—"Golf Courses," "Airport Expansion," and nine different essays on taxes. For the most part, our essays are somewhat broader in scope, and although they are still short, their writers had more space to inform and advocate. But perhaps the best way to describe the difference appears in *The Price of Paradise* itself. After granting that "there's more to 'quality of life' than just dollars and cents," Roth then expresses the hope that "environmentalists, sociologists, moral philosophers, and experts from other fields will continue and expand the dialogue."[3] *The Value of Hawai'i* grants this wish. Although two of our essayists also wrote for *The Price of Paradise*, the others represent the array of voices Roth suggests—and we have added social activists, nonprofit administrators, artists, and Hawaiian nationalists to his list.

Finally, as its subtitle suggests, *The Value of Hawai'i* assumes that we need to know how we got into the current state of affairs, and that we need to change attitudes as well as policies if we hope to restore, and to be directed by, what is truly valuable about Hawai'i. Roth notes that for economists, "the long run is more important than the short run."[4] We agree, but for our contributors, the short run is almost always a mistake, because "the long run" starts in the distant past.

* * * * *

Though many themes emerge from these pages, here are a few that show up repeatedly.

> I. Hawai'i will remain economically, socially, and ethically troubled as long as we refuse to come fully to terms with Hawaiian claims to land and sovereignty. Though the supposed reasons offered have changed with every decade, our government and judiciary have consistently delayed, avoided, and denied. Following this strategy of neglect, as a community we've withheld infrastructure funding, questioned the legitimacy of entities we have ourselves created to address the issues, negotiated agreements explicitly intended to prevent resolution, and most recently, actually proposed through legislation simply to sell

the contested lands as a one-time budget bailout. Until Hawaiʻi deals with this more than a century-old injustice, bad faith will continue to haunt everything that we do or don't do. That's why the current status of Hawaiians—not as a separate issue, but as a factor that must shape all decisions—is so important to so many of these essays.

II. The collapse of support for regulatory and service agencies has been disastrous for Hawaiʻi. The essay might be about the economy or water, about Hawaiian sovereignty or Hawaiʻi's forests, or about the arts, homelessness, or prisons, but the essayists all agree that the gutting of government departments and agencies, and the cutting of funds for the many organizations responsible for Hawaiʻi's arts, culture, and human services, have not only had obvious impacts—the growing numbers of the homeless, the virtual impossibility of our artists, social workers, cultural practitioners, and community organizers to sustain their work—but has also encouraged exploitive and destructive business and development practices to flourish. Especially in the last few years, the executive branch has seemed committed to a policy of destroying the government's ability to plan, preserve, nurture, or enforce. (Apparently the Superferry got the message that filing Environmental Impact Statements is for losers.) As many of our contributors point out, one surefire strategy for turning things around at least somewhat would be to demand that the government have the will, and expend the resources necessary, to enforce its own laws. For whatever reasons, it currently doesn't.

III. Partnerships between government and "the private sector" are essential—either one without the other is a recipe for disaster. We are the unfortunate heirs of thirty years of a national demonizing of government, and a knee-jerk faith in an unregulated private sector, that together have damaged all of us profoundly. And at present, Hawaiʻi actually seems to be out of sync with at least some national trends. The hardline combative approach to budgeting and taxation in the State's executive branch over the past few years seems to assume that in addition to children, the homeless, the troubled, and the disabled, all public employees, nonprofit workers, artists, and educators are basically welfare recipients. Gratitude for any support is the only appropriate response; furthermore, as dependents, these groups have no real right to express an opinion about their conditions of employment, or about the overall direction of Hawaiʻi, because their status as objects of charity makes them by definition self-interested. (It's not going too far to say that some people will reject out of hand many of the essays in this book precisely because the people writing them have spent years studying their subject.) This illusory polarizing of government and "the real world" of the private sector also makes possible some patent contradictions in general attitudes. Why for example is it a cardinal principle that you get what you pay for, unless you're paying for infrastructure, education, social services, and public protections, where it's assumed that more can always be done with less? Or to put it another way, how many businesses and independent contractors would accept the obligation to do 100 percent of the agreed upon work, or supply 100 percent of the products, for 40 percent of the necessary money, simply because times are hard for the purchaser? We need much more frequent and productive discussions of what infrastructure and services are essential for a decent society, and then we must accept the need to pay directly and consistently for them, regardless of economic upheavals, major or minor. Hawai'i has demonstrated repeatedly in the past that the people here value and are willing to support such services. Or as one of our contributors put it, "When I go to the all-candidates meetings, I'm going to ask 'Which of you is going to raise my taxes?' Because the person who says 'I will' is the one who will get my vote."

* * * * *

The confused little girl and boy on the cover are now likely in their late fifties, and if they still live here, they're probably still confused. But seeking approval from somewhere else, or escaping into our own thoughts, can't be options now. We have to grow up. The tools for breaking out of this malaise surround these children, and us. Education. A sense of the past—Hawaiian and American, for better or worse. And aloha.

Read the essays in this book, and you'll have a better sense of what some other people believe is important about Hawai'i. Much of what is valuable here we owe to those who came first—who cultivated this place, who preserved it, who came to know it in all the ways that humans have found to love where they live, and who still have undeniable claims to it that must be recognized. And we also need to value our distinctiveness today. The entire world recognizes this, even if only as a tropical fantasy, but we all need to remember to recognize it as well. To quote a bumper sticker, "This ain't da mainland." That's good, and it's also our greatest cause for hope. If nothing else, the writers in this collection demonstrate repeatedly that for all the impact of external economic and political forces, we can change course.

REINVENTING HAWAI'I

TOM COFFMAN

As we in Hawai'i start the next "X" number of years of U.S. statehood, most will agree the original invention is in trouble. We hear cries of pain throughout the state of Hawai'i, but we hear no real discussion of how we got to this pass or how we might find our way to better times.

Perhaps that is a possibility of this book—to get a group talking about the reinvention of Hawai'i. I'm not pretending to have the answers, but let me take my turn at the conversation.

As a marker in time, let us try to imagine the State's 2009 observance of the fiftieth year of statehood. For all who missed it—that would be almost everyone—the observance was held in that cold glass temple, the Hawai'i Convention Center. Most of the participants were under the gun to be there (literally, because the majority were National Guard personnel). The program was forced, the energy low. Audience participation in the breakout sessions was almost nonexistent.

Among the Hawaiians protesting outside, the venerable Dr. Kekuni Blaisdell was accidentally injured, surfacing inside the Convention Center with a painful black eye. That this thoughtful, gentle man would become an emblem of the Statehood Observance lights up the arc of the fifty-year subject. In 1959, when the sociologist Lawrence Fuchs was interviewing people for his book, *Hawaii Pono,* he said the only person who questioned statehood was Kekuni Blaisdell. Kekuni says that actually he was still brainwashed by American propaganda at the time, so Dr. Fuchs did not begin to get the full force of his dissent. Either way, you get the idea. Originally celebrated enthusiastically, statehood at year fifty was observed awkwardly.

While native Hawaiians have a way of illuminating and intensifying the public discussion, the need for a reinvention arises not only from their issues but our myriad of cascading problems: fiscal, educational, economic, etc. We have a resource management crisis, an energy crisis, and a crisis of leadership so pervasive in all sectors that it goes unremarked. (Quick. Name today's three great leaders of business. Name two great leaders of unions. Name one great leader of the legislature.)

Since we are arguably as well-intentioned as the statehood generation, how do we account for the present state of our State? As I attempt to find threads by researching Hawai'i's history, I am returned again and again to Hawai'i being a small, semi-separate outpost of American mass culture that is nonetheless original, distinctive, and vital. We twist in the wind between a hope that we are special and a fear that we are inconsequential. Our most familiar ways of expressing this dichotomy are "a subtle inferiority of spirit," on the one hand, and the power of the aloha spirit on the other.

How different are we? How different is our history? What other state of the USA began as a destination for Polynesian voyagers, evolved into multiple island chiefdoms, responded to Western contact by developing a unified constitutional monarchy, and then was illegally taken over and told this was a good thing?

Hawai'i was subjected to a territorial status longer than any geographic area that became a state of the United States—a possible clue as to our sense of being marginal. During the long territorial period, the essential point of contention was whether Hawai'i would be treated as an evolving community governed by constitutional principles, or exclusively as a military bastion governed by fiat. In response to the famous Massie case, the Navy admiral Yates Stirling argued for recognizing that Hawai'i's unique military importance required a unique military government, a government of Caucasian men "who are not imbued too deeply with the peculiar atmosphere of the Islands . . . by men without preconceived ideas as to the value and success of the melting pot."[1] Ironically, it was the crisis of World War II that tipped the scales in favor of democratic community-building, and it was with community-building in mind that the campaign for statehood took on a noble dimension.

Here was the upside: out of a determination that the sacrifices of war not be in vain, the statehood campaign was at the heart of a political strategy to create a novel multiethnic society, in which the rights of working people were to be secured and the colonial dominance of the Big Five corporations was to be curtailed. At the time, many people equated statehood with equality of citizenship—more fundamentally, an equality of being. With statehood, all became first-class citizens in the American democracy. From this widely shared viewpoint, statehood was a victory over marginalization and discrimination. It was goodbye to the Massie case, and the Fukunaga case, and English Standard schools.

Less obviously, the statehood campaign occurred in relation to the hot wars of the Cold War competition with communism—Korea in 1950, and the French colonial withdrawal from Vietnam in 1954. As an Asian Pacific state in which equality was an operative goal, the State of Hawai'i was greatly in the propaganda interest of an otherwise racially segregated United States. President Eisenhower said as much. Advocates such as the iconic man I first covered as a young political reporter, John A. Burns, similarly argued as much, and it was on a handshake with Burns in 1958 that the Democratic Senate Majority Leader Lyndon Johnson agreed to, and the next year delivered, the congressional votes for statehood.

Referring to the amicability of our race relations, the visiting President John F. Kennedy said, "Hawai'i is what the rest of the nation must become." Hawai'i led the country in the right direction. The combined Senate seats of Hawai'i and Alaska put an end to the Southern filibuster against civil rights legislation. Hawai'i's newly elected congressional delegation contributed substantially to the Civil Rights Acts of 1964 and 1967, to anti-poverty legislation, labor legislation, and Title IX of the Education Act, now known as the Patsy Mink amendment. The Republican Hiram Fong played a significant role in ending the Eurocentric bias of American immigration law, opening the door after 1965 to the second great migration of Asians to America.

The new State government prided itself on leading the way nationally in healthcare, labor legislation, streamlined state-county government, women's rights, and land use management. All occurred with astonishing speed—in less than a decade. It is little wonder that many people initially were exhilarated by statehood.

An economic development boom likewise happened quickly. We liked the income and the revenues but not the construction cranes and congestion. The impact of rapid development on people's lifestyle and on the landscape itself created the first big fork in the road of statehood.

In its first year, the State of Hawai'i had only 170,000 tourists—about one-thirtieth of today's visitor count. In that first year, there was a 42 percent increase. Thereafter tourism grew at 20 percent or more a year, and passed the one million mark in less than a decade. In ten years, the gross state product nearly doubled. The population of 605,000 grew 2 1/2 percent each year, compounded.[2]

In only a few short years, an intense political clash set in over development and growth. At the heart of the famous conflict between John Burns and Tom Gill was a dispute over the pace and scale of development—over transforming sheltered bays into destination resorts, and open spaces into subdivisions.

It is within the phenomenon of development shock that the story returns to native Hawaiians. Although most had previously lost their traditional land and water use rights, many still connected themselves to various small kuleana, to places in the country, streams, beaches, and near-shore waters—and these were being used up and closed off. I remember in the mid-1960s talking with Hawaiians in Nānākuli who previously had lived in Kaka'ako, or Kalama Valley, and who were thinking about moving on to Moloka'i, which not coincidentally became the cradle of the most vigorous Hawaiian protests. A mixture of active frustration and latent pride rose quickly to the surface and became more pronounced year by year, forming the basis of the Hawaiian movement. One of the sayings was, "We have to look back to go forward." Another was "Go back to get back." I vividly remember being summoned as a young reporter to the meeting hall of Queen Lili'uokalani Children's Center to write of the rebirth of the Hawaiian Homerule Party. Around that large table were the Kalahiki brothers, Alvin Shim, Winona Rubin, Georgianna Padiken, and the great Hawaiian writer of our time, John Dominis Holt, whose essay *On Being Hawaiian* had quietly sold a staggering sixty thousand copies.[3] Most of these extraordinary persons are gone now, but their challenge to the status quo lives on.

In her study of Hawaiian enclaves (kīpuka), the Hawaiian scholar Davianna MacGregor has most effectively described how the social and cultural roots of today's situation are not only political and national, but also tied inextricably to living space, lifestyle, and the sustainability of resources.[4] The clue was the combination of initial, almost reflexive anti-development protests and the much longer-term set of issues arising from the Hawaiian community around population, land, and water. In these terms, the far-reaching amendments of the Constitution of 1978 prescribed an idealized, self-sufficient, and environmentally sensitive approach to government that we have not been able to implement.

The shift from plantation agriculture to plantation tourism is a central reason. From statehood forward, the Hawaii Land Use Law was supposed to guide and control development on all islands. It resulted from a coalition of the ILWU, the Big Five corporations, and liberal Democrats. They boldly sought to protect prime agricultural land as well as the upland watersheds that replenish our aquifers, while encouraging compact urban growth and discouraging suburban sprawl.

Yet even as the public sphere struggled with mechanisms to achieve a sustainable existence, plantation agriculture was going down—plantation by plantation. The unions were blamed, but the underlying truth was more complicated. Sugar was always a substantially political undertaking, and in the mid-1970s, the federal government changed the quotas, subsidies, and tariffs that previously had supported the plantations. Think of the impact of high-fructose corn syrup and the making of ethanol from corn. In a sense, the plantation interests who wanted statehood to gain the security of the protected U.S. market were betrayed—and left to become land developers and seekers after urban zoning. The organizing basis of the statehood land use planning system progressively fell into disarray, and we now are fighting with one another over suburban sprawl across the entire ʻEwa plain of Oʻahu.

In the course of our population doubling, the original 117,000 acres of urban-zoned land has grown to nearly 200,000 acres. By almost any standard, the goals of compact development and the preservation of prime agricultural land have not been met.

In this history of eating land is a metaphor of our interrelated crises. We have been living beyond our means, our expectations conditioned by the economy of a nation that in turn lives beyond its means. We live on islands, but we eat the rich food of the continentals. In current jargon, we live unsustainably.

As a consequence of the national economic meltdown, the State budget is so out of balance, the programs of government cut so precipitously, that it will take many years to figure out how to mitigate the damage. We more than have our hands full. We might want history to leave us alone, but it won't. In the press for a system of reconciliation and redress for native Hawaiians, we will sooner or later establish a native Hawaiian governing entity. There will be a necessarily contentious negotiation of the associated issues of land and water—specifically those that belonged to the Hawaiian kingdom and the Hawaiian monarch. Resources and the monetary rewards of access will be at issue. The meaning of opportunity and equality will be debated anew. There will be many issues of governance, rooted in arguments as to the meaning of autonomy and sovereignty. The weight of all those other economic, educational, and political issues will be tugging at us, and from all of this will result a redefinition of what we thought of as the State of Hawaiʻi.

But God, we love Hawaiʻi. A recent national survey of the residents of the fifty states found that despite our problems we still ranked ourselves highest in our sense of well-being. So if we think about attempting a reinvention of ourselves, we can look to our abundant well-being as a starting point. As when we spoke optimistically about the noble possibilities of statehood, in that same spirit we can engage optimistically in a search for how a reinvented Hawaiʻi might work. The project called the State of Hawaiʻi in its present configuration is temporal, but Hawaiʻi is timeless.

HAWAIIAN ISSUES

JONATHAN KAY KAMAKAWIWO'OLE OSORIO

In her 1989 book *From a Native Daughter,* Haunani-Kay Trask said that the modern Hawaiian movement began when some fifty families living in Kalama Valley protested the eviction notices served by the Bishop Estate in 1967. Their resistance to a new suburban development, and the loss of one more productive working community, has grown over forty years later into a dynamic political, cultural, and social movement that has come to be a large part of the way that Hawai'i defines itself to the world.

It is difficult to identify any aspect of life in Hawai'i that does not reflect some part of the Hawaiian movement today: The resurgence of Hawaiian language has produced an outpouring of cultural productivity, from political demonstrations to State-supported Hawaiian language immersion schools. Consider contemporary fashions—even if they are mostly t-shirts—that articulate Hawaiian words that would have been unintelligible to the greater public a few decades ago. The word aloha will no longer suffice to represent an island identity. The history of the American takeover in Hawai'i, once a story repressed in Hawaiian families and ignored in public institutions, has spawned dozens of books, plays, video documentaries, lawsuits, music, and lately, slam poetry that have all brought this history into sharp relief in the public mind.

The physical landscape of Hawai'i has quite definitely been affected. Windward valleys on O'ahu are still agricultural communities because of the leadership of young Hawaiian activists in the early '70s, and there are areas in urban Honolulu where taro grows again, and students of the 'āina learn again how to protect water and land resources using technologies and values that we learn from a curriculum that is many centuries old. In fact, certain words and phrases like ahupua'a and mālama 'āina have crept into the popular lexicon, and may already be indispensable to anyone or any business that is practicing some *sustainable* activity.

And cultural heroes—outside of a few exceptions in the sports world— are Kānaka Maoli activists, cultural practitioners, and musicians who were also activists, or people who have identified themselves with Hawaiian causes.

I doubt that more than a few hundred people could name the boards of directors of any of the largest corporations in Hawai'i, while tens of thousands of people know Nainoa Thompson, George Helm and Kimo Mitchell, and Israel Kamakawiwo'ole.

But by and large, the Hawaiian sovereignty movement has been forwarded by thousands of people, faceless and unnamed, who have protested freeway and hotel construction over sacred heiau, grieved over the desecrated graves of ancestors, ended the military abuse of Kaho'olawe, demonstrated for prison reform and lobbied for health and education reform, proved that a Hawaiian diet prolongs life, translated nineteenth century Hawaiian language newspapers, and joined the rolls of Ka Lāhui Hawai'i.

None of this was predictable forty years ago, when it seemed that the story of modern Hawai'i was principally the story of the rise of Asian wage laborers and their descendants, and how they wrested fairer conditions, better lives, and opportunities from a society dominated by the plantation. Oddly enough, the values and principles that moved the labor unions and the Democratic Party to destroy the old haole race preferences in Hawai'i seem to have evaporated, as the Democrats and the tourism-driven economy have brought fantastical new riches to the Islands, and given unions and big landowners something to protect. When one turns to listen for the sounds of protests, or looks for the idealists who dream of a fairer and compassionate society, less destructive of nature, one sees Hawaiians.

This is something not lost on the old guard haole and malihini predisposed to think of rights and money as being indistinguishable from one another. For more than fifteen years a fairly small group of neoconservative activists have attempted to scuttle the Hawaiian movement, challenging government agencies that lay claim to revenues and land for Native Hawaiians, challenging the Hawaiian preference policy of a private school established by the will of a Hawaiian chiefess under Kingdom law, and insulting Hawaiian attempts to research and write their histories, reassert older spiritual values, and claim the right to live on as a people. That these objectors are unable to cultivate the same aloha for themselves as an almost homeless Hawaiian musician can with one recorded song is mostly a testimony to the stinginess of their agenda and the poverty of their beliefs. But it is also a testimony that some sense of pono, of justice, still resonates in the multiethnic and widely diverse society that Hawai'i has been for more than 160 years.

No one is really fooled that the conservative agenda is about civil rights, equal opportunity, or respect for property. Partly because of the Hawaiian movement, the public is much more aware of the extent to which the United States has ignored its own laws, and certainly the laws of a sovereign nation, to territorialize Hawai'i and take possession of nearly half of its property. People with long roots in the islands, and especially those who still remember life under the plantations, know very well that every political and economic reform was conceded grudgingly, and after more than fifty years of democratic reform, lo and behold, the plantation companies have held fast to the land and to economic power.

Though Hawaiian protest has resulted in protecting access to more public space, especially the shorelines, and has limited the ability of landowners to maximize their own profit at the expense of other landowners and the general public, these are precarious achievements. So too is the amazing revival of the Hawaiian language, which has important lessons to offer all residents of Hawai'i, so many of whom have lived through a time when their own cultures and languages were repressed, and when they were cast as inferiors, aliens, and even enemies. The Hawaiian cultural revival dignifies everyone except those who believe that there should really only be one culture, and demonstrates that identity is at least as important as economic opportunity. It is that lingering sense of justice denied, however, that makes Hawai'i's political and civil society a better place than it would be if the Hawaiian movement is silenced. Should that day come, the ideals of the neocon malihini and old guard landowners will dominate, and the signs of an island paradise for sale will be planted everywhere.

Maybe the most important achievement has been the way that Hawaiian rights—really multiple rights—in education, political standing, restoration of land, environmental protection, and religious freedom have all been asserted peacefully, consistently, and successfully for forty years. This should provide hope and confidence for all peoples that pursuit of dignity and cultural survival is not only possible, but perhaps the only really meaningful human endeavor left in a world that pursues consumer goods and security so mindlessly. Some people may say that Hawai'i will be a better place when Hawaiians no longer stand in the way of progress. But even these people must know that at that point, this will no longer be Hawai'i.

The sovereignty movement's political vulnerability has always been the issue of ancestry. Even the 1960s struggle over evictions in Kalama Valley was racially politicized when Bishop Trustee Richard Lyman attempted to portray the movement as led by haole, leading to a splintering of the Kōkua Kalama movement between Kānaka Maoli and the non-Hawaiian supporters of the valley's tenant pig farmers. When Ka Lāhui was formed in 1987, its constitution required voting citizens to have Hawaiian ancestry, and even required that half its legislature be elected by citizens with 50 percent blood quantum. Challenges that the Office of Hawaiian Affairs, the Department of Hawaiian Homelands, and Kamehameha Schools violate American civil rights laws may not be convincing to courts or to the general population, but residents of Hawai'i who are not Kānaka Maoli by descent do express uneasiness about where this movement is going, and whether they might, in time, face some kind of dispossession.

Recently, though, the movement has transformed from a purely native advocacy to a larger nationalist struggle to restore the nation-state that was invaded and occupied by American military forces in 1893. That nation, the Hawaiian Kingdom, was a multiethnic constitutional monarchy that treated with dozens of nations, and whose laws, at least until 1887, acknowledged that citizenship and civil rights were not related in any way to race. Restoration of the Hawaiian Kingdom has garnered more and more support over the past decade because it acknowledges the rights of nations under international law, and because it does not lead to the destruction of relationships among friends and families because of race.

Restoration, of course, would re-create a nation quite independent from the United States. Perhaps not ironically, then, the American government's responses to the sovereignty movement have been to insist that race *is* at the core of the political solution between Hawaiians and the United States. The 1920 Hawaiian Homes Act clarified that the U.S. owed some support to Native Hawaiians, and defined such natives by a blood quantum rule that articulates racist assumptions about human beings. In 1978, the new State Constitution set up the Office of Hawaiian Affairs to seek the betterment of native Hawaiians, and in 1993 the U.S. government apologized to the nation it had victimized a century before, but confined its apology to people of Hawaiian ancestry. Finally, since 1994, the congressional delegation from Hawai'i has tried to pass the Native Hawaiian Reorganization Act, which would allow natives to form their own government without addressing the non-Hawaiian Kingdom's subjects whose national identity was usurped as well. It is ironic that the only successful challenger to Hawaiian "entitlements" was a rancher named Freddy Rice. During his U.S. Supreme Court challenge to the voting procedures for the Office of Hawaiian Affairs, he made a public announcement that his ancestor was a Hawaiian Kingdom subject, and that he had the same right as any native to vote for an OHA trustee.

National identity and ancestry have been easily confused by a public generally ignorant about the standing of the nineteenth century Hawaiian Kingdom. Not many people in Hawai'i know that dating back to 1841, the nation had biennial elections conducted by a literate and well-informed electorate made up of native and non-native citizens, and that the voting franchise was offered with a liberality almost unknown in any other country of the world.

Rancher Freddy Rice probably knows that his ancestors' rights were protected, as were the rights of every other subject—native, Chinese, and African—under the laws of the Kingdom. In addition to the violence and humiliations that were done to the Hawaiian people since 1893, there have been the violations of law.

To ignore how law has been distorted to accommodate the American takeover may be easier for people who believe that everyone is much better off under American rule than we would be as citizens of a small island state thousands of miles from the major industrial centers that feed the global economy. And that brings one back to the central argument of this essay—that the sovereignty movement forces us to consider what it is we want this society to be.

At some point, it may be necessary for people to accept that independence from the U.S. is a logical and necessary step toward protecting the amazing society that matured in these islands, and which is now threatened by runaway land prices and an almost total dependence on the global market system for its survival. This assertion would have been considered an absurdity less than two decades ago, and its growing traction in the movement is not simply a result of a better understanding of the history of the takeover. In fact, it may have more to do with a blossoming disaffection with global modernity and the international consumerism that drives it.

The problems, not just for native people but for communities in the Pacific, are not simply related to climate change or environmental degradation. The overarching problem is that Pacific Islanders are less and less in control of our own destiny as we become more integrated into the global economy. That this is true for everyone, including the ordinary citizens of large industrial nations, does not make it any more palatable for islanders. Careful conservation, sharing resources, cooperation and consensus, honoring ancestors, protocols that demonstrate respect for one another, and a definition of wealth that is indicated by family relations, healthy lifestyles, and community connections along with monetary security—these are all Pacific Islander cultural hallmarks that have been assaulted by a Euro-American ethos of individual achievement and profit, and a reliance on the marketplace not just for trade, but as the foundation of its values.

The near collapse of the largest banks in America, and the economic crises that emerged from the mortgage-backed securities failure in 2008, have not led Americans or some Hawai'i residents to question the reliability of an unchecked capitalist society. In fact, Hawai'i's sudden vulnerability has not spurred a call for a diversified economy and more careful management of our resources, but a kind of panic in the governor's office and the legislature that created furlough Fridays in the public schools, a level of unemployment that was unimaginable three years ago, and a public that seems convinced that returning to the high point of seven million tourists a year is the only thing that can save the economy. In February of 2010, the House finance committee actually considered a bill that would set a minimum price of three quarters of a billion dollars for the sale of several properties controlled by the State. These specific properties are part of the Ceded Lands—Hawaiian Kingdom and Crown Lands—whose ownership has been contested politically and in court by the Hawaiian sovereignty movement, and the sale of which this very same legislature had agreed to impede in legislation a mere two months before.

Some of these lands are contested, most notably Mauna Kea, which houses thirteen large, multimillion dollar telescopes built on lands that the state leases out for one dollar a year. Hawaiian cultural practitioners have protested the presence of these telescopes for years as a desecration of sacred and environmentally sensitive areas of the mountain. The State seems to believe that it is easier to sell these lands off to meet this year's budget deficit through one big yard sale, than to do the hard work of really managing these lands—which would mean working with native cultural practitioners, astronomy practitioners, and the academic community to create a working relationship that could provide reasonable revenues, protection of the land, and a protocol that respects native religious and cultural beliefs.

No one would argue that this is not a difficult and demanding task. But consider this: in the ancient days, that is precisely what konohiki—the chiefly land managers in the Hawaiian ahupua'a—did. They managed human and natural resources by knowing everything about the land division over which they were responsible. Some of today's lawmakers may be able to read a spreadsheet, but they have practically no understanding of how to make the land really productive again.

Kānaka Maoli still know how to make the land a treasure and how to give people a chance to work productively. In taro gardens and fish ponds, young people from charter schools and expensive private schools are taught how to maintain an 'auwai, plant and harvest taro, inventory and utilize the resources of a shoreline, build and navigate a canoe using traditional methods, and harvest fibers that can be used for cords to thatch a house or create an intricate work of art. Perhaps we could call it basket weaving with a vengeance—young people returning to a kind of personal and purposeful creativity which may just save us all. But for that to happen, a form of subsistence and land management will need to be protected by the most powerful government agencies from real estate speculation, zoning that requires urbanization, large-scale agribusinesses that create their own protective infrastructures, the transfer of water from an agricultural watershed, and ultimately, from a market system that would require a profit. What we need is a puʻuhonua from the market system, and it needs to be large enough and capitalized enough to give people the opportunity to live a life directly nourished by the land.

This is what the pig farmers in Kalama Valley were trying to do in 1967, and what the taro farmers in Waiāhole and Waikāne were trying to do in 1974, and in the end, it is what the sovereignty movement is really about. We have seen what determined guerilla mahi ʻai (farming) can do to resurrect taro in urban places like Kānewai and Ānuenue, and to rebuild fishponds along the Molokaʻi shores, where the only government assistance required was that it not prosecute mahi ʻai for growing taro on public lands. Imagine what a partnership between government, the Bishop Estate, and people who want to grow food and live where they work might produce. Imagine homelessness addressed by a vigorous back-to-the-land movement, with training and housing and employment all located in ahupuaʻa that were naturally designed for growing taro and harvesting fish.

The Hawaiian sovereignty movement has also been about challenging our assumptions regarding the ways we live with one another by continually asserting a culture of sharing and interdependency with all of the life around us. This is why we must end the military occupation of Hawaiʻi, not just because military use poisons our lands and waters, but also because the mission of the armed forces so fundamentally opposes our values of inclusion and aloha ʻāina. It defends a very particular definition of a people, and we Kānaka Maoli are focused on a much larger society than the American nation. Indeed, we have nurtured and will continue to uphold a community that is larger than humanity itself.

It would be fitting that a movement begun by tenant farmers, idealistic twenty-year-olds, and Kānaka Maoli elders, all drawn to remember and recount the knowledge of their ancestors, might actually be the key to saving us all.

THE ECONOMY

SUMNER LA CROIX

THE ROAD AHEAD

In the decade after statehood (1959–1969), Hawaiʻi's economy boomed, with real per capita output (GDP) rising at an annual rate of 4.1 percent. From 1969 to 1989, per capita GDP continued to grow, but at the slower rate of 1.7 percent. The last twenty years have not been as kind, with per capita GDP increasing annually by just 0.3 percent. The slow growth has led to numerous economic problems. State and County governments have struggled to provide services desired by Hawaiʻi residents or mandated by federal legislation. College graduates have struggled to find jobs in Hawaiʻi that pay salaries commensurate with their skills and credentials. Hawaiʻi's businesses have struggled to remain competitive in a small market in which relatively high shipping costs raise the cost of capital and imported raw materials.

While there are no easy, off-the-shelf solutions to fix the slowdown in Hawaiʻi's economic growth, Hawaiʻi's policy-makers and citizens have a reasonably good understanding of the factors that are the proximate cause of growth. However, public policies enacted to promote increases in the quantity and quality of these factors—K-12 public education, for instance—have in many cases worked poorly. Other public policies that were enacted to achieve highly valued goals were either not evaluated with respect to their effect on economic growth or this effect has just been ignored. Even if the effect of a particular policy on growth is small, the aggregate effect of thousands of policies can be quite large.

These results are unsurprising, as Hawaiʻi's State and local governments lack the institutional infrastructure to evaluate changes in public policies prior to their adoption (or rejection) and after their enactment. Unless we gain a better understanding of how and why proposed policies have worked or failed in other states, we run the risk of adopting policies that worked well in other states but will not work in Hawai'i unless we adjust certain features to fit our island economy and society. Discussions of major policy initiatives—an appointed or elected school board, a tax on a barrel of oil, or a change in the top income tax rate—take place with little prior study of their expected effects.

TWO COMPETING EXPLANATIONS FOR SLOW GROWTH

Why has Hawai'i's growth rate been so low for two decades? There are two competing but potentially overlapping explanations. The first focuses on those factors that determine current output—physical and human capital, available production technologies, and the rules governing individuals, firms, and markets. Economic growth occurs over time when (1) firms provide their workers with *more physical capital*; (2) students enrolled in private and public schools receive an education that provides them with *more human capital*—i.e., an individual's health, skills, knowledge, and motivations—than previous generations; (3) firms use *new lower-cost production technologies* and introduce *new products*; (4) rules governing firms and markets change to provide *more effective incentives* to conduct business in Hawai'i efficiently; and (5) State and County governments provide *more public infrastructure* that increases the productivity of business firms. Slow growth or stagnation of any of these factors slows overall economic growth, but effective public policies that increase the growth rate of a slow-growing factor can increase overall economic growth.

The second explanation focuses on the difficulties an economy faces when its leading industry is in decline and other industries are not emerging fast enough to take its place. Various factors may be restraining growth in new industries: (1) public infrastructure that is inadequate or complements the declining industry rather than emerging industries; (2) a shortage of labor with the skills needed for emerging industries; (3) outdated, incomplete, or burdensome laws and regulations for emerging markets and firms; (4) imperfections in regional capital markets that increase the cost for firms in emerging industries; and (5) the small size of Hawai'i's domestic market.

BASIC BUILDING BLOCKS OF GROWTH: ARE THEY IN PLACE IN HAWAI'I?

The Hawai'i economy is seriously deficient in a number of the basic building blocks of economic growth, including (but not limited to) human capital formation by Hawai'i's youth, public infrastructure provision, and the legal and regulatory frameworks that support markets.

The services provided to students by well-functioning K-12 private and public schools (and by their parents and other involved community members) complement students' own efforts to learn, and allow them to attain a level of understanding and achievement that facilitates future learning as well as investment in highly specialized skills valued by the job market. When the average student in a high school class graduates with a higher quality education than the average student in last year's graduating class, then this group of students has a bigger and better tool kit for conceptualizing and solving problems, organizing and prioritizing their work activities, and just plain producing more in a set time period. In other words, increases in the quality and quantity of an average worker's K-12 education should, if the employer provides a set of clear incentives to the worker, increase output per hour of an average worker, raise worker wages, and in the aggregate contribute to economic growth. A higher quality workforce will attract firms to Hawai'i that offer higher paying jobs, and if some graduates still end up on the mainland, the sons and daughters of Hawai'i will still be earning more and living a better life because of their quality education.

Unfortunately, Hawai'i's public schools have not been providing average students with a good high school education. In a widely publicized joint statement issued on January 31, 2010, three former Hawai'i governors observe that Hawai'i's public school students rank near the bottom of the states in standardized test scores; they fail apprenticeship exams administered by construction unions; private employers and the U.S. military find them deficient in the basic skills required for entry-level jobs; and the University of Hawai'i requires many public high school graduates to do remedial work in math and writing. The governors' statement rejects many commonly offered excuses for the poor performance, such as low funding (per pupil funding ranks among the top fifteen states), a large percentage of special need students (Hawai'i's percentage is below the national average), a large percentage of second language students (many states have a much higher percentage), and unionized teachers (many states with unionized teachers also have much higher test scores).

The three governors argue that the public school system is plagued by a lack of accountability for poor student performance. To remedy this, they join many other politicians and analysts in proposing a Governor-appointed rather than an elected Hawai'i Board of Education. Whether this will be the key ingredient in reforming Hawai'i's public schools remains to be seen, but clearly, a mechanism is required that either provides students in poorly performing schools with more educational choices, and/or triggers rapid changes in the quality of education offered by those schools. Hawai'i has in fact been reforming public education for the last two decades, with school principals now controlling a much larger proportion of school budgets. The payoff could be large for the general public if the decentralization policies work: increased economic growth as graduates enter the workforce and college with far better skills, knowledge, and motivation.

But the decentralization reforms have generally avoided policy changes that are opposed by the massive State education bureaucracy or the unionized teachers or the unionized principals. How will the system work if some of a school's problems stem from the principal's poor leadership and decisions and it is still difficult to replace a school's principal? This raises a more general question: Are the reforms sufficient to achieve the desired results, or are they still missing key ingredients? Ongoing reforms to education in Hawai'i have been diminished by this problem. A key role of the next governor is to ensure that after all the politics of crafting legislation has been completed, a mechanism for bringing good schools to all Hawai'i neighborhoods is still in the legislation.

Now consider another basic building block of economic growth: the legal and regulatory framework that provides "a rules of the game" for consumers, producers, and workers participating in a complex market that generates costs or benefits to third-parties (e.g., a Continental Airlines flight from Honolulu to Houston generates noise for families eating dinner at their homes in 'Ewa Beach); that is a natural monopoly, in which one firm serves the market at less cost than two firms (e.g., electricity distribution—but not necessarily electricity generation); and that produces and exchanges common property resources (e.g., the State forests in which various groups legally and illegally engage in gathering forest resources).

Hawai'i's legal and regulatory frameworks have four problems that greatly reduce their effectiveness in many cases, and cause the systems to be dysfunctional in other instances. First, they are often outdated in their general approach to regulation. Consider the Public Utilities Commission, the State agency that regulates or monitors some firms in the energy, petroleum, transportation, telecommunications, and waste water industries. Its case-oriented method of conducting business has changed little since statehood. The three-member Commission has few resources to either review its own methods or to analyze whether regulatory techniques pioneered in other states could be productively used (with some modifications) in Hawai'i. A full review of the Commission's structure, responsibilities, and resources is long overdue, and could eventually lead to more efficient operations in the industries that it regulates, or a change in the set of regulated industries.

The second major problem with Hawai'i's legal and regulatory frameworks is that we rarely study how proposed regulations could affect future economic growth, and whether actual regulations have affected economic growth. For example, the three-decade-long battle over developer provision of low- and middle-income housing ignores economic analysis that highlights the inefficiency of housing set-aside policies. The Hawai'i State Tax Review Commission has regularly found that industry tax credits are inefficient methods for stimulating new firms to enter an emerging or established industry. In both cases, more efficient tools are available to achieve desired results. It is striking that the Hawai'i State Government does not have more explicit mechanisms in place to flag and revise problematic bodies of regulation.

Third, Hawai'i's legal and regulatory frameworks often provide few incentives for public agencies or regulated firms to "get the prices right" on their products. Agencies are often reluctant to utilize pricing methods that allow public infrastructure to be used more intensively in some cases and less intensively in others. For example, University of Hawai'i classrooms are used less on Fridays and between 3 p.m. and 5 p.m. By offering tuition discounts for classes held at under-utilized times, UH could hold more classes in the same number of buildings—a big consideration, since so many classrooms need repairs or replacement. Prices that are set uniformly low (e.g., the congested H1 highway never charges a toll) often produce revenue streams that make it difficult to maintain existing infrastructure or to initiate such projects as rail transit on a sensible scale and in a timely manner. Rush hour pricing on the H1 could also reduce traffic congestion substantially, reducing the need to expand highway capacity. More careful pricing of renewable natural resources, such as water, could delay the date when we will need to build costly desalinization plants. The list goes on, and could produce substantial savings in the amount of public infrastructure required to produce some public services.

Finally, the State of Hawai'i has not devoted nearly enough attention to implementing a regulatory framework to ensure that the vast natural resources of Hawai'i are properly managed and conserved. Starved for funds, the Department of Land and Natural Resources struggles to manage effectively the lands and resources under its stewardship. In the absence of effective systems of management and regulation, private users of Hawai'i's public resources take actions that diminish their value. Moving quickly to implement modern systems of regulation and management is vital if the resource waste is to end. It should be a top priority of the next governor.

PAST AND FUTURE SOURCES OF ECONOMIC GROWTH IN HAWAI'I

Over the last two hundred years, decreasing transportation and communication costs have integrated Hawai'i's product, labor, and capital markets with global and national markets. Market integration typically raises the income of a small economy, because it allows places like Hawai'i to specialize in products where they have a competitive advantage, and to import products that are costly to make. The persistent decline in shipping costs during the nineteenth century, for example, was a major reason for the rise of Hawai'i's sugar and pineapple industries. Strong federal aid for Hawai'i sugar cane—first via a special exemption from high U.S. tariffs, and later via generous U.S. agricultural price supports—made it the leading industry through the 1950s. But over the past fifty years, sugar and pineapple have faded away, due to increasing foreign competition, declining federal price supports, and the rising value of land in alternative uses, such as tourist resorts and residential housing.

In 1959, U.S. airlines began to use jet planes to bring tourists from the U.S. mainland to Hawai'i. The transformation of Hawai'i into a global tourist destination was dramatic, as the 296,000 visitor arrivals in 1960 rose to 6,723,000 in 1990. The last twenty years stand in sharp contrast. Visitor arrivals have been very volatile due to war and recession. In addition, inflation-adjusted visitor expenditures have registered substantial declines. If we detach ourselves from tourism's cycles over the last two decades, and consider only longer trends, it's clear that the decline of this industry has been a major cause of the fall in average economic growth.

The two-decade decline of tourism will not necessarily continue. Drug violence in Mexico and a strong yen may bring more tourists to Hawai'i over the next couple of years, and planned upgrades of Waikīkī hotels, the opening of the new Disney resort, and an increase in cruise ship visits could bring more tourists over a medium run of two to five years. Over ten years, new waves of tourists from Korea (now under the U.S. visa waiver program) and China (now allowing tourists to book group tours) could stabilize, and perhaps even expand the industry. Or perhaps the wave of Chinese tourists never materializes. The industry's uncertain prospects and its sharp decline in 2008–2009 have once again prompted residents to ask whether there are less volatile industries that could be induced to locate in Hawai'i.

The search for new industries to complement the state's leading industry dates back to the mid-1970s. After ten to fifteen years of breakneck property development, Hawai'i's residents in the mid-1970s became somewhat uncomfortable with an ever-expanding supply of resorts located on beautiful beachfront lands and offering an array of jobs (janitors, maids, parking attendants, front desk clerks) with limited opportunities for large wage gains and fast promotion within the organization. Residents asked where their children would work when they graduated from the University of Hawai'i. During the late 1970s and 1980s, the State of Hawai'i responded by creating numerous quasi-public entities to foster start-up high technology firms, such as the High Technology Development Corporation, the Hawaii Information Network Corporation, the Office of Space Industries, the Hawaii Innovation Development Program, the Hawaii Strategic Development Corporation, and the Research and Development Industry Promotion Program. During the 1990s, many companies affiliated with these programs—think AdTech, Pihana Pacific, and Digital Island—grew into bigger ventures before then showing a shocking lack of gratitude and relocating to the U.S. mainland.

The deterioration of the Hawai'i economy in the 1990s, and the mediocre performance of its quasi-public high technology incubators, pushed the Hawai'i State government to switch policy gears. Instead of providing direct services to firms in targeted industries, in 1999 the State Legislature passed a non-refundable tax credit for Hawai'i residents investing in selected Qualified High Technology Businesses, such as computer software, biotechnology, sensors and optics, ocean sciences, astronomy, and non-fossil fuel energy-related technology industries. In 2001 the Legislature allowed investors to transfer tax credits under the same regulations that monitored transfers of federal Low Income Housing Tax Credits, and increased the credit to 100 percent of qualified investment, claimed over a five-year period. This far outstripped other states' credits; only a handful offered investment tax credits amounting to 50 or 60 percent, and most refunded 25 percent or less of qualified investment, and placed binding caps on the overall volume of credits that could be claimed in a given tax year. Beginning in 2004, the Hawai'i Legislature reined in Act 221's incredibly generous provisions by passing Act 215, which limits the transfer of tax credits among investors. In 2009, Act 178 ended the practice of allowing Hawai'i investors to make two-to-one claims of tax credits against their State income tax liabilities.

Through fiscal year 2009, high technology business investment tax credits had already cost Hawai'i an estimated $657.5 million in foregone tax revenues. Act 221 will expire at the end of the 2010 fiscal year—a fortuitous sunset date that should end a deeply flawed subsidy program. Consider some of the problems. The tax credit program had little bang for the buck, creating very few jobs in its favored industries. Enforcement provisions in the federal housing tax credit legislation had been stripped from Act 221, inviting its abuse. And because the law's allocation exception initially provided incentives for equity in the tax credit allocation partnership deals sold to non-Hawai'i investors, control of these highly subsidized firms frequently shifted to these investors, who sometimes responded by moving the firm out of Hawai'i.

There are several lessons to be learned from Hawai'i's experiment with tax credits. First, large incentives for emerging firms can lead to wasteful rent seeking. Second, subsidizing potential "winning" firms to promote new industries and economic growth cannot substitute for supporting a well-functioning public education system or the other basic building blocks of economic growth. Third, picking the industries of the future is a perilous enterprise, and there is no reason to expect that bureaucrats, legislators, and representatives of vested interests will combine to make the right choices.

THE ROAD AHEAD

Is it possible to identify and develop a set of public policies that promote the basic building blocks of economic growth? Yes, the big issues facing the State have workable solutions. The challenge for the next governor is to ensure that the State focuses its reform efforts on the basic building blocks of growth. It's not that complicated.

TOURISM

RAMSAY REMIGIUS MAHEALANI TAUM

What is the future of this thing we call "tourism"?

According to the United Nations World Tourism Organization (UN-WTO), tourism is the world's fastest growing economic sector, is a major player in international commerce, and has become a main source of income for developing nations.[1] This global spread of tourism outproduces other industries like oil, food, and auto production. It is credited with providing economic and employment benefits in related industries like construction, agriculture, and telecommunications, while being touted as a source of greater wealth and success. The question is for whom?

In the five decades since statehood, tourism has grown to become Hawai'i's primary industry. It generates billions of dollars for the state economy each year. However, declining visitor counts and expenditures in 2008 and 2009 produced numerous negative economic impacts, including reduced tax revenues, mass layoffs and workforce reductions, business closures, bankruptcies and home foreclosures, as well as losses and reductions in critical social, community, health, and education services.

Are these recent economic challenges signs that Hawai'i's current corporate-driven tourism may be in trouble, and like the banking and auto industries is in need of an overhaul? Despite signs that the economic slide is slowing and that a return to better days may be near, the long-term future remains uncertain.

Advances in air and sea travel have made the world smaller, and destinations like Hawai'i easier to get to. What took days or weeks can now be achieved in hours. As a result, tourism has become a source of economic prosperity on the one hand, and a threat to cultural and community identity on the other. This phenomenon is not exclusive to Hawai'i alone, but is part of a global experience being felt worldwide.

To accommodate expanding appetites for exotic leisure and business experiences and destinations, tourism has become a development tool for multinational corporate interests and investments in transportation and municipal

infrastructures that transform natural, political, social, and economic landscapes. Consequently, decisions about the destination are being made in
boardrooms thousands of miles away. Local and indigenous communities
tend to be impacted most by these decisions, as the demands for greater access to cultural and natural resources lead to local populations being displaced
and converted into cheap sources of labor.

EGGS IN ONE BASKET

The full impacts of global tourism may not be fully understood, but what is
evident is that Hawai'i continues to be heavily dependent on the industry for
its economic well-being. According to the Hawaii Tourism Authority (HTA),
in 2008 visitor expenditures made up 19.5 percent of the State's tax revenue,
and contribute significantly to the State Gross Product (16.8 percent) and
overall employment (17.5 percent), which until recently has been taken for
granted by many.[2]

With the losses experienced in the sugar and pineapple industries still
fresh on our minds, we must acknowledge that our eggs are clearly in one basket. Can we afford to ignore the reality that as we import tourist dollars we
also import over 85 percent of our food and more than 90 percent of our fuel?
We should be seriously concerned about our sustainability and survivability
"when" not "if" we experience another natural disaster or shock to the market like H1N1 in 2009, influenza-A "bird flu" in 2006, SARS (Severe Acute
Respiratory Syndrome) circa 2002 and 2003, and the 9/11 terror attacks on
New York City before that.

We should be more mindful about adopting policies that enhance our
self-sufficiency while resisting the practice of relying too heavily on an industry whose success is tied to global economic forces we have little influence
over. Additionally, we need to reverse policies and practices that allow the
fruit of our labor to leave the economy to be returned to offshore foreign interests that own, manage, or control our travel infrastructure.

In its "Hawai'i Tourism Strategic Plan (TSP): 2005–2015," the HTA acknowledges that

> Sustainability and the preservation of the cultural landscape is the new model
> of global tourism. . . . Such a model is more sustainable because it preserves
> the goodwill of the host by celebrating the place and maintains the market
> value of the destination by preserving its cultural uniqueness.[3]

Arguably, much of the success the tourism industry enjoys can be attributed
to Hawai'i's natural beauty, moderate climate and temperature, white sandy beaches, and inviting blue oceans. The industry also owes some of that

success to the history, traditions, practices, and presence of Native Hawaiians (Kānaka Maoli) and their rich island culture, a culture that continues to host others despite challenges to its own existence. While Hawai'i's physical and natural attributes continue to draw and attract visitors to her shores, it is the culture of Hawai'i's native people that defines its essence.

The prevailing mass tourism business model is contributing to the bimodal distribution of wealth that is creating an ever-widening gap between the rich and poor. Despite the wealth generated from the integration and use of Maoli culture in the promotion and marketing of the islands as a premier destination, very little of that wealth directly reaches host communities or their cultural practitioners. In short, the mass tourism approach is responsible in part for creating a "disconnect" between the host and the visitor, and for experiences that are artificial, contrived, and inauthentic, which benefit neither host nor guest.

HTA not only acknowledges in the TSP that a "disconnect exists in the relationship between the visitor industry and Native Hawaiian community," but it took steps to address the disconnect by establishing a Hawaiian Cultural Strategic Initiative, with its stated goal being "To honor and perpetuate the Hawaiian culture and community." Through its Hawaiian Cultural Initiative (HCI), HTA also acknowledges that

A key aspect that separates Hawai'i as a globally unique visitor experience from all others is the highly valued Native Hawaiian culture. By focusing on the Native Hawaiian, the intent here is to properly emphasize the importance of the Native Hawaiian culture and community to the quality of life of Hawai'i's residents as well as to the quality of Hawai'i's visitor experience.[4]

That said, however, comments in the draft Maui County Tourism Strategic Plan 2006–2015 reported the following:

Better education of visitors and residents is necessary to ensure the Hawaiian culture is preserved and protected. Of Maui Island residents, 44 percent surveyed thought "*Tourism has worsened* the preservation of *native Hawaiian culture.*"[5]

In short, tourism is a double-edged sword. On one edge, tourism continues to dominate the economic landscape as a primary source of revenue. The other ingratiates us to a relationship with an industry that has globally demonstrated a preference towards urbanization and the systematic displacement of local and indigenous communities from their natural, cultural, and social resources, effectively reducing local self-sufficiency while exploiting human and natural resources.

HOW DID WE ARRIVE AT THIS CONDITION?

Perhaps equally important questions to ask are "what can we do about it" and "what do we have to look forward to" if we ignore signs that we no longer face a set of problems that can be solved by throwing more money at them. Instead, we are confronted with a multifaceted predicament that cannot be resolved by applying the rules of engagement, practices and policies, or decision-making criteria that brought us to this condition.

Albert Einstein warned that insanity is linked to the practice of expecting new results from the same methods and behaviors that created the condition you are trying to change. We may need to take a new approach that will require rethinking, reframing, and redefining what tourism is and what it means to us and our collective well-being.

Equally important, we may need to explore more deeply who we are as a community, what we value for ourselves and for future generations, and what behaviors and practices we must adopt to get there. By neglecting this opportunity to define what "there" looks like, we could easily find ourselves in a conversation that confuses the industry as the "ends" and not the "means," and end up focusing solely on the health of the delivery system rather than the product, the place, and its people.

THE FUTURE IS IN THE PAST

The Hawaiian 'ōlelo no'eau "I ka wā ma mua, ka wā ma hope" speaks to the idea that the future and the past are intimately connected. This Hawaiian proverb embraces an understanding that in order to move forward it is necessary to know where one comes from. An appropriate place to begin may be in taking a closer look at the genealogy and evolution of the prevailing "service industry" business model.

A standard mantra in business is "the Customer is always right." A quick survey of any room would demonstrate that most people with work experience have heard this preached on more than one occasion, have read it in an employee manual, or have been reminded sharply by customers who not only believe it to be true, but expect to be treated accordingly, whether their behavior warrants it or not. The survey would likely reveal that while most have heard the mantra, they also don't believe it to be true. Instead, there seems to be a universal understanding and agreement that the customer is NOT always right, but regardless, the person behind the counter is expected to accommodate the customer even at the risk of suffering personal embarrassments and indignities.

Where does this attitude of entitlement come from? Consider the root word "custom" in the word "customer." In earlier times, it was "customary" to respect and honor the "customs" of the place one was visiting as well the customs of those hosting. Over time, the customer has become accustomed to customized experiences that favor the needs and customs of the visitor *over* those of the place and host. Unfortunately, this is a practice that continues to be perpetuated by the market place, and is largely responsible for some of the "disconnects" mentioned previously.

ROYAL TREATMENT

There is also a deeper thread that should be followed to understand from where these foundational attitudes evolve. For that, we look to a time preceding mass tourism and the conveniences that have made leisure travel so popular and affordable.

Historically people have traveled for any number of reasons, starting with the most basic, such as the search for food, shelter, health, romance, and spiritual enlightenment. Others make war on their neighbors, who in turn flee their homelands to seek safety and comfort elsewhere. Leisure travel however was something few could afford either in time or money. The elite few who could were usually of royal lineage or high social and political status.

As a social group, "royals" were less likely to do their own housekeeping or cooking, relying instead on slaves or servants. When traveling, they would pack up their servants with their belongings, or enlist temporary ones upon arrival. When visiting other royals, they would enjoy the "service" of their host's servants, who no doubt would always deliver the "royal treatment"!

As access and affordability to transportation and accommodations have changed over the years, so has the profile of the traveler. Leisure travel is no longer reserved for royalty, and neither is the expectation of being treated as such. Regardless of one's station in life, every visitor expects to be treated like a king or queen. Consequently everyone else is a "servant." While most who work in the service industry do not consider themselves servants, nor do they behave that way, many of them would agree they are often treated that way by guests as well as employers! At the risk of oversimplifying the matter, the industry evolved from an elitist history that favored the well-being of the guest over the host.

MOVING AWAY FROM VISITOR CENTRICITY

The treatment of these issues is not intended to demonize tourism or diminish the value of exceptional customer service. There is no question that quality service and customer care reaps benefits and rewards in customer satisfaction and loyalty, which translates to a strong financial bottom line. Instead, it is an attempt to shed light on two things. The first is that it is hard to expect an unhappy host to delivery a happy experience, and second, that the prevailing customer-centric focus may be an unsustainable one. In the case of tourism, simply replace "customer" with "visitor."

In a society where consumer choices appear to be unlimited and there are an equal number of providers ready to accommodate those choices, the modern consumer has placed greater expectations on the market place. In response, the industry adopts practices, policies, and procedures to deal with finicky customers. This is particularly true for chain and brand operators who cater to preferred customers. These Standard Operating Procedures (SOP) insure the delivery and management of services while providing predictable quality experiences.

It also means that at great expense, a person can travel long distances to arrive at a destination that looks and behaves exactly like the one he just left. Too often the SOP results in the place and its host population being transformed and altered for the guest's benefit. Hosts become servants, and unique places become no place because they look like every other place. My good friend and fellow industry advocate Peter Apo of the Peter Apo Company refers to this phenomenon as "placelessness."

STAGED VS. GENUINE

In an effort to better manage the experience, authenticity actually gets managed out of it, to be replaced by formulaic templates and time-sensitive programming. Staged authenticity replaces genuine experiences in pursuit of a healthy bottom line. Cultural experiences eventually become calculated and contrived.

Consider the idea of an "authentic commercial lū'au!" Packaged and canned, the experience that began as a gathering of friends and family celebrating one another and the milestone moments of their lives has been turned into a well-choreographed dinner show for strangers who have no connection to one another, the place, or those who feed and entertain them.

Even the act of lei giving has begun to lose meaning. Some companies actually refer to the practice as the "ring toss." In the absence of a genuine "host," professional greeters can be hired to deliver lei flown in on a commercial carrier very much like the one the lei's recipient arrived on just a few days earlier. Could anyone have imagined fifty years ago that lei intended to express love, affection, and friendship would one day be produced by strangers in a foreign land, so they could be delivered by strangers to other strangers who flew in to visit no one?! Strange as it sounds, it has become our reality.

SCRATCHING THE SURFACE

As harsh as these examples may be, they only scratch the surface of what the commercialized mass tourism experience has become. They are offered in the interest of raising awareness about the kinds of business practices that may be creating unwanted effects. At a gathering of industry stakeholders and marketing partners, the Hawai'i Visitors and Convention Bureau (HVCB) reported that its research findings of West Coast travelers revealed that "they feel that Hawai'i is a been-there, done-that destination."[6]

At this same meeting, it was reported that while the China and Korea markets showed future promise, Japanese travelers didn't think there was enough diversity in the cultural experience in Hawai'i, and were choosing to go elsewhere. Unfortunately, those remarks were neither surprising nor unexpected.

Under new leadership and armed with a new strategic plan, HTA's vice president of brand management announced that the agency would renew its focus and commitment to support and promote Hawaiian culture, acknowledging that "Because we're a mature market, we need to take advantage of some of the experiential things we have available to us, especially with culture." Despite the rhetoric, Hawaiian culture has continued to be treated as a "value added"—like condiments rather than the entrée. The time has come to elevate culture to a more prominent place on the menu of offerings, and in doing so strengthen the product, its identity, and the Hawaiian "sense of place" that makes our island home the unique place that it is.

SENSE OF PLACE

Sense of place may be defined as the characteristics, qualities, and features that help distinguish one place from another.[7] Every place, every destination, has a story, a persona, customs, and traditions. Likewise, every place has a sense of place that helps the visitor judge his or her experience.

As sensual beings we formulate memories based on sights, sounds, smells, tastes, temperature, and climates. If the experience is a good one, we share it with others; if not, we don't! Sense of place, the new SOP, helps to define the relationships we have as hosts and guests, as well as how we treat one another and our surroundings.

The built and natural environments are only part of the equation. Eventually it comes down to the people and the atmosphere, the "hā"—the spiritual essence and ambience of the place that reflects the way people relate to one another and their surroundings. Consistently, the spirit of aloha and the people of Hawai'i rise to the top of the list of what makes a visitor experience in Hawai'i memorable and worth coming back for.

In the end, our economic well-being may depend on our spiritual well-being, and not the other way around. We may need to start reinvesting in the social, cultural, environmental, and spiritual banks of Hawai'i if we hope to rebuild and strengthen the cash ones. In the pursuit of money, we should be investing in the mana of aloha!

And what is aloha?

ALOHA is . . .

> More than a greeting, a salutation, a slogan, pitch line, or monogram.

> It is an overarching principle, condition, way of life, mind set, and attitude.

> A spiritual principle that conveys the deepest expression of one's relationship with oneself, creative and life-giving forces, family, friends, community, and strangers.

> A natural response of respect, love, and reciprocity, and not a contrived series of motions or expressions that have been rehearsed and perfected for economic gain.

AGRICULTURE

CHARLES REPPUN

Here are the global and the local problems: a growing population, increasing urbanization, degraded farmland, and destruction of important ecosystems for more farmland. On a global and a local level, we need to control population growth, or at least not encourage it by pushing urbanization, especially of farmland, and we need to farm in more sustainable ways. The old slogan, Think Globally, Act Locally, is still relevent. See and understand the big picture, how we are part of it, and work for changes at a local level.

In 2008, when a middle school class came to our farm, the current world economic problems were just starting to get noticed. So how does all this economic stuff relate to agriculture? Well, there is a big push to get the housing market going again, but that will just put us back on the same path we have been on for a long time. Since 1970, the U.S. has been losing farmland to urbanization at the rate of 2 acres a minute, or a bit over a million acres a year. The Central Valley of California, which grows one-quarter of the nation's produce, is losing 15,000 acres a year to development. Sustainability? During the Waiāhole water case, we found out that the State does population projections based in part on what our main economic drivers need to keep growing. In other words, the State promotes population growth to keep the construction industry healthy, even though State and County plans call for limiting population. In the late 1990s, when Hawai'i's economy was down, population growth was at zero for the first time. Construction workers went to places like Las Vegas in droves because of the demand for housing by a population growing at the rate of 50,000 a year.

"Luckily" another housing boom in Hawai'i started. So this is what is going on in the U.S. Keep the population growing. Build more and bigger houses—from 1982 to 1997 the U.S. population grew by 17 percent, but the amount of land urbanized grew by 47 percent. Buy food from all over the world. The U.S. became a powerful nation in large part because it has the most good agricultural land in a favorable climate zone. Unfortunately, while the industrial agricultural model can produce copious amounts of food, it has been equally good at degrading our environment through pollution of our water resources from excessive fertilization and the loss of valuable topsoil due to excessive tillage. There is of course much more about food systems, and Michael Pollan, Paul Roberts, and others have written about it very eloquently.

FOOD, GLORIOUS FOOD

Everybody's talking about food these days. We constantly hear that 85 percent of locally consumed food is imported. We also hear people talking about organic, local, additives, GMOs, corn syrup, sustainable farming, factory farming, frankenfoods—enough buzz words to confuse even an educated reader. So what's a kid to think?

Those students who came in 2008 were the inaugural class of "Roots—Where Do Things Come From and Where Do They Go," led by teachers Bob Tam and Emery Mitchum. Designed to trace the life cycles of everyday products, the class investigated topics like water, transportation, waste, and food. During the week devoted to food, students visited three supermarkets with different buying philosophies, and they came to the Reppun farm in Waiāhole valley, to see how food makes its way from the earth to the store shelf, and then into a mouth.

The students walked all over, sampling various fruits and checking out the more than seventy kinds of edible plants my brother Paul and I have stuck in the ground over the past thirty years, including corn, cacao, coffee, sweet potato, and taro. One boy said, "Gee, Mr. Charlie, there is a lot of food on your farm. So, how much is there?" "Well, knowing how much taro we get per square foot," I answered, "let's figure out how big this patch is and see how much we can get out of this lo'i." Evan proceeded to pace off the distances and Blaise did some quick mental math. "You can produce about 4,000 pounds of taro from just this one patch," he calculated. "How many people will that feed?"

Gradually a question emerged: could we feed everyone in the State with what is grown right here in these islands? Back in class the students went to work. Nutritionist and researcher Mae Isonaga from the Cancer Research Center of Hawai'i talked with the class about a person's nutritional needs—about 2,500 calories for the average adult male, with a variety of nutrients from across the USDA food pyramid. She helped the students come up with ingredients for a balanced diet for a single day. All the foods they picked had to be currently grown here—mustard cabbage, tomatoes, and papayas, for instance. The large bottom layer of the food pyramid consists of grains and other staples. Since wheat cannot be raised here, and rice is not currently grown, the students picked the historic staples, taro and sweet potato, and added sweet corn. The teachers put the results into a spreadsheet so the students could keep track of the calories as well as other nutrients such as protein and calcium. After some negotiations, the one-day diet was completed.

The spreadsheet columns grew when the amount of food for a day was multiplied by 365 to find how much one person needs for a year. Then came the big leap: when we multiplied what a single resident requires by the approximate population of 1.3 million to find the yearly demand of each food for everyone in the islands on that contrived diet.

The students then turned to the internet to find online resources about land use in Hawai'i. The National Agricultural Statistics Service (NASS) collects data from every state about land area in production, and the number of pounds harvested for each crop. The number of pounds per acre was simple to calculate, and the students used the yield to derive the land needed to feed everyone in the state.

	DIET FOR A SINGLE PERSON			CURRENT PRODUCTION		DIET TO FEED EVERYONE	
	cups/day	calories	lbs/year	lbs per year (millions)	acres	lbs per year (millions)	acres
FRUIT							
papaya	2	180	225	28.7	1,530	293.0	15,618
banana	2	400	362	20.0	1,000	470.8	23,541
VEGGIES							
tomatoes	2	64	290	14.7	700	376.7	17,936
broccoli	1	30	71	0.3	60	92.1	16,740
mustard cabbage	2	40	274	1.4	115	355.7	29,221
lettuce	2	10	58	1.2	120	75.3	7,533
zucchini	1	29	145	1.1	175	188.3	29,961
GRAIN/STARCH							
corn	1	177	132	1.8	350	171.6	33,364
taro	2.5	467	266	4.5	380	345.3	29,156
sweet potato	1	220	125	6.0	360	162.2	9,730
MEAT/NUTS							
beef* (oz.)	6	402	137	36.0	1,198,000	177.7	5,913,461
mac nuts	0.5	481	54	65.0	15,000	70.1	16,177
TOTAL		2,500			1,217,790		6,142,440

Total without beef = 228,979

*current beef production based on all cattle in Hawai'i staying in Hawai'i

FRUITS AND VEGETABLES

They first checked out produce. For everyone to eat one cup of broccoli a day for a year would require just over 92 million pounds. We now produce about 300,000 pounds on sixty acres. That means we need 16,740 acres in broccoli for us to be self-sufficient on the diet chosen by the students. How about papayas? If, following the diet, we all ate two cups a day of papaya, we would need 15,618 acres to feed everyone, instead of the current 1,530 acres. For all the fruits and vegetables in our diet to feed us for a year, we would need more than 140,000 acres in tillage. Of course we grow many more kinds of produce than those in the students' diet, some 11,000 acres in all. So we would need more than twelve times the current produce acreage to be self-sufficient.

ARE WE ANY BETTER IN STARCH?

No. In fact, starch production and our current eating habits could very well be the area of food security where we are the most vulnerable. Most food we import is in the form of starch—bread, pasta, rice, cereal, chips, cookies. It's a long list that shows our love and craving for a wide variety of tastes and foods. One cup of sweet potatoes per day, per person, for a year would require just over 162 million pounds. We produce now about 6 million pounds on 360 acres. That means we need more than 9,700 acres in sweet potatoes for us to be self-sufficient on the diet chosen by the students. For taro, with 1.3 million people we would need 28,776 more acres than the current 380 in production.

THE MEAT/PROTEIN ISSUE

The students chose to include beef in their daily meal, because cows can be reared in pasture land, while every other animal here depends on imported feed. At the current animal per acre rate, if all of the cattle in Hawai'i were used for beef production, we'd need nearly 6 million acres to feed us each 6 ounces of beef a day. That's a bit steep, considering that there are only 4.1 million acres of land on all the islands. Of course, the 25 million pounds of fish caught in Hawaiian waters are an important protein resource, and if that catch is sustainable, the acreage needed for beef could be reduced to closer to 5.5 million acres.

BACK TO CLASS

The students then discussed their research about the benefits of self-sufficiency. Why should we grow our own food? Blaise provided the most obvious answer: "Simple. Then we wouldn't have to depend on the mainland." John added, "We can help reduce the amount of gas that is used from ships to bring food here by trying to grow more crops." Alec then made this point clear: "Because gas prices are high, shipping from a farm on the Big Island will use much less fuel than shipping from Mexico." Megan had found out that "four hundred gallons of oil are used each year to feed one American, and 31 percent of that oil is devoted to producing the chemical fertilizers so plants will grow better. We don't need to hurt the environment by using artificial fertilizer. We can use natural fertilizers like mulch, manure, or compost." Katie then pointed out that growing our own food "can help Hawai'i's economy because the profits on the produce will go right back to the people of Hawai'i instead of going to a corporation on the mainland."

Mika talked about the quality of what we eat: "Our produce would be fresher. We could just go to a store and buy a tasty fruit or vegetable that has not been sitting in a container for days or even weeks." Another student had her eye on diversifying our employment base: "Farming opens up more job possibilities for the unemployed in Hawai'i, and offering college students courses for this occupation would ensure farming a safe place in tomorrow's economy."

These students learned a lot more than how to weed a taro patch.

ARE THE STUDENTS RIGHT?

When cover crops that take nitrogen from the air and put it into the ground to be used by the next crop, and animals, with their manure, were part of farms, two calories of food energy were produced for every calorie of energy invested. After World War II, the use of synthetic nitrogen and the industrialization of agriculture began, and today it takes ten calories of fossil fuel energy to produce one calorie of food energy. Synthetic nitrogen is made from natural gas. Its price has more than tripled since 2002, and the United States imports more than half its nitrogen. As soils become depleted of organic matter, farmers need to apply more and more nitrogen.

And how does nitrogen "hurt the environment," as Megan asked? Much of the fertilizer applied to fields never reaches the plants, but instead either leaches through the soils, with large amounts ending up in the water, or is volatilized into the air as nitrous oxide. Farming is one of the biggest polluters of our water systems, and nitrous oxide is a greenhouse gas three hundred times more potent than carbon dioxide. So both the soil and the atmosphere would benefit from going back to the old system of manure, cover crops, and compost.

HOW MUCH DO WE LOVE FRESH PRODUCE?

Mika thought it would be great to eat fresher produce. How many fresh fruits and vegetables do we eat? The recommendation is seven to nine servings, although a diet deficient in fresh produce is now the norm across the United States. If all of what Hawai'i produces is added to what we ship in, then we are eating less than one pound of fresh produce a day, compared to the almost three pounds called for in the USDA food pyramid diet. So eating the amounts of produce in the students' diet means that we need twelve times more land. That is not true for starch, the base of the food pyramid. We would need twenty-seven times the current acreage for sweet potatoes, and seventy-seven times the current acreage for taro.

While America's consumption of beef has been dropping—76.6 pounds per person in 1980 to 66.1 in 2004—our total consumption of all meat had increased to about 200 pounds in 2004. This is tied to eating fewer fruits and vegetables, and is one of the reasons for the steep rise in numbers of overweight people—nearly half of all adult Americans (31 percent of adults meet the criteria for "obese," as do one in seven children). We are replacing fresh produce with calories from more meat and starch.

WHO WILL FARM?

Finally, what about Megan's comments about farming as an employment opportunity? We are constantly reevaluating the ways that we work, trying to create a more sustainable farm. That work is, as Paul Roberts, author of *The End of Food* says, both intellectually intensive and labor intensive, which makes farming mentally and physically healthy.

Yet there are barriers to recruiting a new generation of farmers. Countless variables present daily challenges—especially the weather. Living on the farm helps farmers save money and keep tools, supplies, and crops secure, but many farmers cannot live on their leased agricultural land. Theft and vandalism in Hawai'i cost farmers 8 percent of their income in 2004. Nor, in our acquisitive society, is growing food lucrative: the 7,500 hired farm workers in Hawai'i earn on average only $25,094, and many farms rely on unpaid family members (there were over 1,100 non-paid agricultural workers in Hawai'i in 2002). That won't attract young people interested in material goods—not to mention needing to pay rent and buy health insurance. So, if Hawai'i wants to take significant steps towards food security, who and how many of us are going to need to grow food?

WHERE ARE WE GOING?

Those children came up to the farm almost two years ago, but globally not much has changed. Global warming from nitrous oxide, the continued heavy use of herbicides and pesticides, especially in foreign countries, that make farm work one of the most dangerous occupations—these and other external costs don't show up in the price of food. In 1929, Americans spent 23.4 percent of their income on food. Now it's just 9.8 percent. The world still eats mostly the four super crops—wheat, corn, rice, and soybeans—and animals consume one-third of production. Of course, we must have our sugar—about 100 pounds per person a year—and oil is still cheap enough that food can be shipped all over the world, helping poorer countries displace subsistence farmers with monoculture so that produce can be sold to high-end customers in high-end nations. This is also why a nation like Brazil is clearing 8,000 square miles of forest a year.

Does it make sense to pursue self-sufficiency in our island home? All of this information indicates that we must. Nainoa Thompson often talks about Hawai'i as a model for the world. When people finally realize that planet earth is a closed system, our "island mentality" can inform all. If the world is made up of many "islands," each "island" is in trouble when the food production and distribution systems they rely on are unsustainable.

Clearly, our global and local diets need to change, and that won't be easy, since the problem foods, high in fat and sugar, are also what we crave and love. The advantages to making the changes that the students came up with are enticing, and even compelling, and the journey in the direction of sustainable, self-sufficient agriculture, though fraught with difficulties, can be taken in small steps that will produce positive results immediately.

Organizations focusing on diet change and food security are springing up everywhere. There are more and more school and backyard gardens, which may provide one of the most important answers to the questions of who will farm, and how. We need to get good affordable food to lower-income families. We need to reduce synthetic nitrogen use, mitigate the external costs of conventional agriculture, and improve soils by using more organic matter. None of these will raise farmers' profits; in fact, they all translate into more labor. So maybe it doesn't work to have 1.6 percent of the population of Hawai'i doing agricultural production, and it doesn't work to keep bringing in poor people from other nations to do the work. Maybe we need to see how much of an agrarian society we can become again. That might just be possible in backyards, schools, and community gardens. Maybe building permits could be contingent upon putting in garden spaces. Maybe tax breaks could be given for gardens as well as for solar energy. After all, America now has 25 million acres of lawns. Green waste, now available at only a few sites, could be made available in every community. Many backyards could accommodate chicken-tractors and fish ponds—of course, restoration of some of the very productive historic Hawaiian fishponds has been underway for years. What about a fast-food restaurant chain with only local food? Healthcare providers could discount premiums based on steady weight reduction.

These are not really new ideas. Many have been tried before, but never before has the urgency to act been so great. The first people of Hawai'i took advantage of a very rich ecosystem, much of which remains. Their methods particularly suited to this ecosystem for cultivating an older brother who fed them well are legendary, but the older brother has been largely absent from most people's lives for too long. All of us who live here could benefit by his resurgence. Think Globally, Act Locally.

And just so there's some fun in this:

A (Healthy) Fast Food Recipe

> wash a raw sweet potato, don't peel
>
> grate it with a cheese grater
>
> add raw egg
>
> add chopped green onion, and or anything else, salt and pepper, and curry powder if you like
>
> form into a patty, pan fry in olive oil
>
> optional: add a piece of cheese on top, put lid on to melt it
>
> total time to prepare: less than 15 minutes

THE MILITARY

KATHY E. FERGUSON AND PHYLLIS TURNBULL

The U.S. military is the second biggest industry in Hawai'i. While the military has a lengthy history here, its growing presence over the last half century is due primarily to the enormous political influence of Senator Daniel Inouye. Born in 1924, and elected to the Senate in 1963, the man known simply as "The Senator" has been the primary promoter of all things military. Given his long incumbency, remarkable political skills, and iconic status as a war hero, it is highly unlikely that any other representative will be able to maintain a similar supply of federal resources to our state. As chair of the powerful Senate Appropriations Committee, Senator Inouye is able to bring home remarkable levels of federal funding: according to the Department of Business, Economic Development and Tourism (DBEDT), federal investment in Hawai'i in 2007 was over $14 billion. As Native Hawaiian and Wai'anae Harbor Master William Aila has remarked, "We have an artificial economy" because of the military's presence,[1] and we can expect about a 30 percent decline in federal funding when Inouye's career ends.

The military's investments here will soon become tenuous, because the training of troops can be done more economically elsewhere. For many decades, criticism of the military in Hawai'i has been the province of a small, hardy band of peace activists, environmentalists, and Native Hawaiians, whose critiques are often met with skepticism and patriotic outrage. The predictable decline of military holdings in a post-Inouye era will require a different approach. The ongoing environmental, ethical, and cultural controversies surrounding the military are therefore intensified by a looming practical consideration: since our second biggest industry is very likely to shrivel in the near future, what are we going to do?

HISTORY

The military came here in stages, starting with the arrival of the first U.S. warship in 1814, and the permanent rotation of warships in 1867. In the nineteenth century and for the first half of the twentieth, oceangoing ships were the only viable form of global transportation. During that time Hawai'i was an important coaling station for ships, as well as a handy launching point for other colonial endeavors in the Pacific. Pearl Harbor's deep-water port and repair facilities, as well as Schofield Barracks' extensive training and housing facilities, were consistent with this imperial strategy. But times have changed. Massive air freighters can move military technology and personnel rapidly around the world, lessening the strategic significance of fixed bases. Similarly, sophisticated virtual training methods do not require any particular geographical location.

The long history of military expansion in Hawai'i reflects the changing needs of military personnel and war-making technologies. The first permanent U.S. military garrison arrived in 1898, close on the heels of the overthrow of Queen Lili'uokalani in 1893 and the annexation of Hawai'i by the U.S. in 1898. Since that time, local authorities have worked closely with military leaders, making Hawai'i's land and water available for military use. The establishment of Forts DeRussey, Ruger, Shafter, and Armstrong in the first decade of the twentieth century reflected the military's need at that time for coastal defense and infantry units. Airfields at Bellows, Hickam, and Kāne'ohe established in the 1930s show the development of war-fighting capabilities in that era, while the creation of Barking Sands missile facility on Kaua'i during the Cold War reflected the expanding missile technologies of that time.

The transformation of the 2nd Brigade of the 25th Infantry Division (Light) into a Stryker Brigade Combat Team (SBCT) has caused the most recent expansion—the largest growth in military holdings since World War II. This transformation brings 291 Stryker urban assault vehicles to Hawai'i, requiring 25,663 additional acres of land on the islands of O'ahu and Hawai'i, as well as several thousand more soldiers and their families. As a consequence, according to the Environmental Impact Statement (EIS), overall military land holdings across the state thus increased by nearly 13 percent. The army considered and rejected the possibility of locating Stryker facilities on Naval Magazine Lualualei, which occupies 8,105 acres in central O'ahu, because "a possible hazardous material spill site" would pose very high "potential cleanup costs."[2] The EIS refrains from commenting on the source of this hazardous material, but it seems likely that the military occupation of that land since 1933 is the cause. As in Waikāne Valley, where land taken from Hawaiian farmers for military training was condemned because it was too riddled with unexploded ordnance to use and too expensive to clean up, Lualualei has been rendered unsuitable for the Stryker Brigade by past military use. Military efforts to mitigate environmental damage—to save some endangered species or preserve some land from maldevelopment—pale in comparison to its larger assaults on land, water, air, and ways of living.

And so on, and so on, and so on. The military has used Hawai'i's land and water as it has needed. When it no longer needs the state, it will leave.

BENEFITS OF THE MILITARY IN HAWAI'I

As reported in *The New York Times* on May 30, 2009, the nonpartisan citizen's group Taxpayers for Common Sense has named Senator Inouye "the last of the old bulls," referring to the band of aging Senators who have protected military projects from budget cuts.[3] The Senator brings nearly a billion dollars in earmarks to Hawai'i each year. DBEDT estimates that the federal government spends $10,957 per resident each year, making Hawai'i the fifth highest recipient of federal government spending. According to DBEDT, every billion dollars spent creates a billion and a half dollars in new business.[4] The military also creates more than 18,000 jobs locally, and receives over six billion dollars in Department of Defense (DOD) expenditures, ranking our state twenty-fifth among the fifty states in receipt of these payments. Half of this amount is paid in wages to military and civilian workers, while the rest goes to local businesses and institutions in the form of procurement contracts and research grants. Lawrence Boyd, a labor economist at the University of Hawai'i at West O'ahu, estimates that the military accounts for about 23 percent of the economy on O'ahu.[5] The direct and indirect economic dependence of many families in Hawai'i on military resources is unarguable. For this reason, it is all the more imperative that we recognize the contingent basis of these funds. Pretending that the military will always bring this much money into our state will not make it so.

COSTS OF THE MILITARY IN HAWAI'I

Promoters of the military, such as DBEDT and the Chamber of Commerce, usually fail to point out the accompanying costs of the various military investments. Hiding or minimizing the costs justifies the ill-conceived policy of desperately holding on to the military presence. On the other hand, if we foreground the costs of the military's activities, we are more likely to make the necessary plans to develop less damaging alternatives. Ironically, the post-Inouye military shrinkage that we are predicting also provides an enormous opportunity to reorganize our economy and protect our environment.

The most evident cost is environmental. Military training and its accompanying activities—building roads, transporting troops, washing and repairing vehicles, disposing of waste, live firing exercises, compacting the earth with the pounding of heavy equipment, washing silt into water supplies and onto reefs—cause enormous environmental damage. Water supplies are depleted, endangered species lose their habitats, unexploded ordnance renders land unusable, and toxic wastes leach into soil, air, and water. Hawai'i's vulnerable marine and island ecosystems cannot sustain this destruction.

Other costs of the military's occupation of Hawai'i often go unheeded. The continuing destruction of irreplaceable and ancient Hawaiian cultural sites is an assault not only on land but on a way of life. Educating the children of military personnel puts enormous pressure on our public schools, and federal impact aid is woefully inadequate to cover the expenses. The most recent data available indicate that impact aid to Hawai'i amounts to about 11 percent of the cost of educating students of military and other federal employees.[6] Despite the military's claims to take care of soldiers and their families, 3.5 percent of residents of Schofield Barracks, the army's largest base in Hawai'i, have incomes below the poverty level.[7] For these young soldiers and their families, Hawai'i is clearly a hardship post.

Competition for rental units with military personnel, many of whom receive housing subsidies, further restricts Hawai'i's tight housing market for local residents. Prostitution is likely fueled by steady military customers. Higher rates of family violence often accompany the psychological stress of frequent deployments as well as the straitened economic circumstances of the lower ranks. Economic and psychological investments in the military impose hidden opportunity costs: we avoid developing other economic initiatives because we depend on the military instead.

This dependence is perpetuated in many ways. Our major newspapers are saturated with upbeat military coverage, and their editorial pages evince near hysteria when activists protest military expansion. Our university is becoming increasingly dependent on military funding for research. Our schools and university host extensive military training programs, and our young people turn to ROTC and the Army Reserves to pay for college. As of January 26, 2005, according to the *Washington Post*'s Jonathan Finer, the Department of Defense indicated that per capita Hawai'i had more reservists called to active duty in the wars in Iraq and Afghanistan than any other state.[8] Since the Army Reserves provide working-class persons in Hawai'i with college tuition at the University of Hawai'i as well as a needed second or third job, these activated reservists are disproportionately from the least affluent ethnic groups, including Hawaiian, part-Hawaiian, Filipino, Samoan, and other Pacific Islanders.

WHAT CAN WE DO NOW?

The first thing that people in Hawai'i can do is to face the reality that sooner rather than later the military is likely to scale back, or even terminate, its extensive training here and its corresponding claims on land and water. It is foolhardy to face this huge change by holding blindly to the current situation rather than developing alternatives. When the military has withdrawn from other major training sites, such as those in the Philippines, it has left toxic environmental, economic, and social conditions behind. Planning for mitigation of these predictable consequences, and developing needed alternatives, cannot wait.

Second, we could listen to those who have carried on the analysis and critique of the military for many decades. The American Friends Service Committee (AFSC), Mālama Mākua, earthjustice, and others are our historians. We need to learn about the history of their protests, and to teach others. Mālama Mākua utilizes available legal tools to put continuing pressure on the military, resulting in small but significant improvements to the treatment of land and water. An earlier example of this approach is the Protect Kohoʻolawe ʻOhana, which insisted on cultural preservation and local control over the recovery of the damaged site. We must insist on generational planning, not limited five-year programs. We need to learn from past mistakes. William Aila, for example, stresses the importance of putting funds that may be forthcoming for the clean up of Mākua Valley into local rather than military hands, to limit waste and to provide employment locally.

Third, we could make better use of the procedures for Environmental Impact Statements (EIS) to contest ill-conceived expansion. We could insist on EIS's and refuse to accept waivers, as in the poorly handled case of the Superferry. Currently, EIS hearings are often contentious events where the military's plans are called into question, but they are poorly reported and most people pay little attention. Yet committed local groups often succeed in using the EIS process to delay military expansion, thus allowing them more time to articulate alternatives. For example, live fire training in Mākua Valley has been successfully curtailed by patient, persistent legal challenges. If local news outlets were less deferential to military interests and carried daily accounts of proposed changes, upcoming hearings, and relevant data, public involvement in the EIS process could be vastly expanded.

Fourth, we could make stronger use of parental authority to challenge military recruitment in the schools. Under a provision in the "No Child Left Behind" law, public schools that want to keep their federal funding must turn over the names, addresses, and phone numbers of high school students to recruiters. The local AFSC office has developed materials to support parents who want to remove their children's names from these lists. Concerned parents could organize larger, more public protests against this invasive outrage, and make more widespread use of their parental right to intervene. Like the EIS hearing, the "opt out" procedures are already in place; they do not have to be created, but they need to be more vigorously used.

Fifth, we could use the commitments of educational institutions to oppose discrimination toward women and toward gays/lesbians to put pressure on the military. Schools and universities usually have written prohibitions of discrimination, as well as programs to oppose sexual assault and abuse. These anti-discrimination provisions could be used to question and obstruct recruitment and ROTC/JROTC programs, since the military's "don't ask, don't tell" policy targets gay and lesbian service members. Similarly, the anti-violence provisions of educational institutions could be used to reveal and publicize the high rates of rape and sexual assault on women soldiers by their colleagues. While a 2006 Supreme Court decision (*Fair v. Rumsfeld*) upheld the military's right to recruit on campuses, it also upheld the rights of students and faculty to protest.

Lastly, it is vital for our state to develop economic alternatives to the military. We could invest much more substantially in clean energy, making use of our sunshine, wind, and waves to reduce our dependence on oil. We could develop sustainable agriculture, invest in food stuffs meeting local needs, and keep more consumer dollars within the local economy. We could explore the transformation of Pearl Harbor into a civilian shipyard, as was done at Subic Bay in the Philippines after the withdrawal of U.S. troops there. We could more fully explore niche tourisms that focus on environment, culture, or health, rather than the mass form with which we are familiar. We could invest in cleaning up and redeveloping land used and polluted by military activities.

We need a better future than the one that will no doubt come if we cling to the ways of life that our military dependence has fostered.

RACE / ETHNICITY

JOHN P. ROSA

Racial and ethnic relations in Hawai'i are good, but far from perfect. In the early twentieth century, Hawai'i was touted as a "laboratory of race relations," and since the 1980s, the islands have even been proposed as a "multicultural model" for the world. No single racial/ethnic group makes up a majority in the islands. The rate of interracial marriages outpaces that of anywhere in the United States. And oh yes, Barack Obama—the son of a white woman and an African man who met in Honolulu in the 1960s—is now President of the United States. "Race" does not matter in Hawai'i at all—right?

While many of the statements above might be true, touting Hawai'i as the Land of Aloha only gives us a superficial view of racial and ethnic relations here. As University of Hawai'i at Mānoa Ethnic Studies professor Jonathan Y. Okamura tells us, it is the category of ethnicity, not "race," that must be examined more closely. Inequality exists, and it is getting worse, precisely because we do not always acknowledge the link between ethnic difference and inequality in the islands.[1]

"ETHNICITY" VS. "RACE": WHAT'S THE DIFFERENCE?

Ethnicity—one's cultural background, ancestry, and traditions—is a more important marker of difference than race because it is the category that has been most often used as the basis for decisions regarding social interactions in the islands. People here more commonly identify as "Hawaiian," "Chinese," "Filipino," "Samoan," or even "haole," for example, rather than as one of the race designations found in Census 2000: White; Black or African American; American Indian and Alaska Native; Asian; and Native Hawaiian and Other Pacific Islander.

"Ethnicity" more commonly relates to ancestry, cultural background, or country of origin. "Race" is usually understood as a larger category related to perceived physical or biological attributes of skin color, hair type, facial features, and so on. To complicate matters more, the U.S. Census uses the general term "race" to keep consistent with standard federal reporting categories established by the Office of Management and Budget. Persons who identify as "Hispanic" can be of any race, for instance. Of course, the U.S. Census Bureau doesn't exactly keep the terms distinct either: "The categories are designed for collecting data on the race and ethnicity of broad population groups in this country. They are based on social and political considerations—not anthropological or scientific ones. Furthermore, the race categories include both racial and national-origin groups."[2]

In Hawai'i, people commonly accept and understand an individual's ethnic self-identification—recognizing a light-skinned girl with blond hair, blue eyes, and the last name of Kamaka, for example, as "Native Hawaiian." People in the islands do not automatically decide what a person's racial group might be on the basis of physical characteristics alone, as for example mistakenly assuming that an athletic, dark-skinned man is almost certainly a Pacific Islander. In our island society, residents are more likely to recognize—and act upon—a person's self-declared ethnicity than they are his or her perceived race.

We also need to recognize that interpersonal relationships (face-to-face interactions among people we often know or see routinely) are different from ethnic group relations (in which different groups might consistently, but unknowingly, treat other groups in prejudicial ways). Many of us can rightfully claim that we treat our neighbors-of-a-different-ethnic-group well, and that our families are indeed intermarried among a few or even several groups. These good interpersonal relationships, however, can obscure forms of institutional discrimination, in which different ethnic groups consistently receive unequal access to education, job opportunities, adequate housing, and avenues toward financial success.

In Hawai'i, for example, whites and older generation Chinese and Japanese might achieve higher education goals without being aware that their middle-class status and familiarity with college admissions processes makes their experiences relatively easy compared to those of Native Hawaiians, Filipinos, and Pacific Islanders, who historically have had lower rates of college attendance. When older, more established ethnic groups automatically expect newer minority groups to "pick themselves up by their bootstraps," they simply repeat patterns of subtle but damaging structural discrimination.

HISTORY

Hawai'i shares two characteristics with other geographically isolated locales. First, the islands experienced a rapid decline of the native population right after contact with the larger world, beginning with Captain James Cook's arrival in 1778. And second, the rapid transition of Hawai'i's traditional "fish and poi" subsistence economy to a capitalist society brought with it a wide variety of migrants to the islands—mainly from East Asia, Portugal, and Puerto Rico during the plantation era, but also from every corner of the globe when the tourism industry became the primary generator of jobs in the last third of the twentieth century. Since the late eighteenth century, Hawai'i has not been able to escape the world, its markets for cheap labor, and its consumer goods. The new economic order of capitalism has thoroughly transformed the islands.

We see these general features of Hawai'i's history in its historical and contemporary demographics. The arrival of Westerners brought rapid, substantial, and lasting change in the islands. Native Hawaiians decreased in number due to lack of immunity to newly introduced diseases. A census of 1872 recorded the islands' total population at its all time low of 56,897, indicating a drop of anywhere from 75 to 95 percent of the pre-contact population.[3]

Hawai'i's historical relationship with the United States has also strongly determined the ethnic groups that arrived. The expansion of the U.S. into the Pacific and Caribbean following the Spanish American War of 1898 made the immigration of Filipinos and Puerto Ricans in the early twentieth century much easier. Similarly, the reorganization of territories and their administration in the Pacific in the post-World War II period brought Pacific Islander immigration, starting with Samoans in the 1950s, and continuing with islanders from Micronesia from the 1980s to the present. When the Immigration Act of 1965 barred restrictions on the basis of nation of origin, newer groups began to arrive, such as Southeast Asians starting in the late 1960s due to the war in Southeast Asia, and also people classified as Latina/o or "Hispanic," who make up one of the fastest growing groups in the continental United States.

In addition to the impact of U.S. military policies and immigration law, a history of plantation and racial hierarchies has shaped Hawai'i. American sugar planters imported a range of immigrant workers throughout the second half of the nineteenth century and into the twentieth, as members of each successive ethnic group were eventually able to work themselves off the plantation. Once the bulk of Native Hawaiian, Chinese, and Portuguese workers left the fields or moved up to managerial *luna* positions, the mass migration of Japanese laborers began in 1885. Japanese made up a large portion of the work force for decades, but in the early twentieth century, the Hawaiian Sugar Planters' Association (HSPA) recruited Filipinos, Puerto Ricans, and others in order to keep wages low. Planters used a "divide-and-rule" strategy —hiring more recent immigrant ethnic groups at lower wages and keeping them in separate work camps. Fostering ethnic antagonism worked to the HSPA's advantage by keeping labor costs minimal and by discouraging strike activity. Workers of the early twentieth century were constantly reminded that they could be easily replaced by another ethnic labor group.

By the 1920s, the HSPA was what we might call today a collusion of agri-businesses, coordinating labor policies among themselves because they feared worker unrest and the potential political strength of the labor force that they had imported. Second-generation children of immigrants, after all, were U.S. citizens by birth and would eventually be able to vote in their adult years. The feared "Oriental vote," largely composed of *nisei* or second-generation Japanese, would not fully come into play until the World War II years and afterwards. *Nisei* veterans ("Americans of Japanese Ancestry" or AJA as they were called then) like Daniel Inouye returned to Hawai'i determined to break glass ceilings in various professions and to seek political office.

World War II and the 1950s changed everything. The ebb and flow of more than one million servicemen and defense workers from 1941 to 1945 into and out of Hawai'i nearly overwhelmed the territorial population, but it also spurred changes in racial and ethnic relations. Race relations between black and white servicemen stationed in Hawai'i, for example, could not follow the conventions of the Jim Crow American South.[4] The islands' multi-ethnic environment, combined with the exigencies of war, made Hawai'i an interesting cauldron to say the least. Local civilians (whether they were male bus drivers or female USO volunteers) often effectively demonstrated how their own local majority and familiarity with island ways could at times put them—non-white "Orientals" and "Natives"—in charge.

Nearly gone were the years of absolute military and federal domination. During the Massie-Kahahawai Case, for instance, a decade before the bombing of Pearl Harbor, the dictates of officials in Washington, D.C., had usually held sway. In that infamous case, in the fall of 1931, a naval officer wife named Thalia Massie had accused five "local" men of Native Hawaiian, Japanese, and mixed Hawaiian-Chinese ancestry of rape. The following spring, Thalia Massie's husband, mother, and two midshipmen were ultimately found guilty of killing Joseph Kahahawai, one of the accused, but territorial governor Lawrence McCully Judd succumbed to military and federal pressure, commuting the killers' prison sentences to one day. The outrage over this case gave voice to an emerging local identity—a communal identity in which Native Hawaiians, Asians, and other working-class residents of Hawai'i saw more clearly that their interests were very different from, and opposed to, those of the territorial elites, federal officials, and military personnel.[5]

After World War II, labor unions like the International Longshore and Warehouse Union (ILWU) forged ahead in organizing a multiethnic, interracial labor movement. In the Great Sugar Strike of 1946, more than 26,000 workers went on strike, shutting down 33 of the 34 sugar plantations in the islands for 79 days, effectively showing that the HSPA could no longer pit one ethnic work group against another. During the 1950s, the Big Five (Alexander and Baldwin, Castle and Cooke, C. Brewer, Theo H. Davies, and American Factors) also faltered, finding it difficult to compete with magnates like Henry J. Kaiser and multinational corporations that found Hawai'i to be a new place for business opportunities. In 1954, Hawai'i Democrats scored a significant number of victories in the territorial legislature, with sixteen AJA Democrats elected. In addition, five Republican AJAs were elected that year, thus displacing the old, Big Five-led Republican haole political elite for the first time.[6] Statehood in 1959 also accelerated investment from abroad, further dismantling the power of the Big Five, but also moving the islands more toward the service-oriented industry of tourism that continues to dominate our economy today.

CONTEMPORARY DEMOGRAPHICS AND ISSUES

Having briefly looked at the past, we must now look at the present more closely. Too many of us, myself included, have had misconceptions about Hawai'i's demographics, since as individuals, our assessments can be clouded by the interactions we have with our immediate family, coworkers, and small communities. For example, the most recent census figures indicate that for the islands as a whole, whites are the largest population group. Japanese—often criticized in the 1980s and 1990s for being a post-World War II bureaucratic elite—are no longer seen as dominating civil service jobs and political positions. Figures from Census 2000 also indicate that, whether census respondents indicated one group alone or in combination with another, the ranked order of the eight largest racial/ethnic groups in Hawai'i are: 1) White, 2) Japanese, 3) Filipino, 4) Native Hawaiian, 5) Chinese, 6) Korean, 7) Black or African American, and 8) Samoan. Furthermore, no group represents a majority.[7]

What goes on here in the islands is not like the continental U.S. We must orient ourselves differently, and take note that Hawai'i is, and should be, our Center of the World. Or as local poet Joe Balaz puts it: "Hawai'i is 'Da Mainland' to me."[8]

We must deal with three persistent contemporary issues.

ISSUE 1. Newcomers—usually whites, but basically anyone expecting Hawai'i to be like the continental United States—often initially feel uncomfortable, or decide they are the victims of "reverse discrimination" because they are not used to island ways and the racial/ethnic dynamics here. They might feel like an oppressed minority, but the U.S. Census tells us that whites are actually the largest group in Hawai'i.[9] Similarly, though older generations of Japanese and Chinese might still be perceived as running the islands, the ethnic hierarchies here are very much in flux.

ISSUE 2. Native Hawaiians still have high rates of health problems, incarceration, and poverty. These social ills are common to other indigenous peoples worldwide. The effects of colonization and occupation on Hawai'i's native people continue to this day. Though many might consider Native Hawaiians as a "race" in Western terms, we must also recognize they are a Lāhui—a People and a Nation—who collectively had their Kingdom taken from them in the 1890s. Regardless of which model will be achieved in the coming decades, sovereignty for Native Hawaiians is a matter of political status and self-determination. It is not an unfair "racial preference."

ISSUE 3. Recent arrivals routinely face the most difficult challenges when it comes to adapting to life in Hawai'i. Micronesians, for example, though experienced in the ways of the United States, are often discriminated against due to language barriers, lack of adequate employment, and the perception that they are a drain on social services. Latinos and other individuals considering themselves "Hispanic" (to use a federal Office of Management and Budget category) face similar patterns of discrimination.

WHERE DO WE GO FROM HERE?

Hawai'i has its own social and cultural values as an island society in the middle of the Pacific. Newcomers must realize that Hawai'i is a unique place that does not have to—and does not necessarily want to—be like where they came from. Whether newly arrived immigrants, military personnel, or folks from "the States," new residents must be open to adopting island ways. As many newcomers' guides point out, the best way to make waves here is to expect and talk about how "things are done better on the Mainland." But local born—whether Kānaka Maoli, older generation Asians, or kama'āina haoles—must be open to change as well. We must not do things a certain way just because that's the way they have always been done.

One guiding principle must be that both newcomers and local-born need to be willing to discuss, negotiate, and forge a new future in keeping with the values of our island society. Newcomers need to commit to changing to the ways of Hawai'i; kama'āina (those experienced in the ways of the land) must be open to suggestions for change. We must all think critically about our unique island society and act differently from the rest of the world.

There are no firm answers when it comes to solving racial/ethnic tensions, but we can commit ourselves to at least a few general goals:

GOAL 1. Avoid the myth that Hawai'i is a place of perfect racial/ethnic harmony. Recognizing the existence of race/ethnicity is healthy. We can never be "colorblind"—nor should we strive to be. Problems happen not only when individuals and groups discriminate against each other on the basis of their race/ethnicity, but also when they fail to recognize structural inequalities that are strongly linked to others' race/ethnicity.

GOAL 2. Educate ourselves as to what our history has been and where we are today. What are the large and small racial/ethnic groups in Hawai'i, and what are some points of historical and potential conflict among them?

GOAL 3. Find ways to overcome the social and economic inequalities that have historically been strongly correlated with ethnic difference in the islands. As former governor George Ariyoshi noted recently, we must strike a balance between the needs of newcomers and local-born residents in Hawai'i.[10]

In short, Hawai'i needs to have the courage to be what it wants to be. It does not have to try to be like anywhere else. The islands' geographic isolation, unique history, and ever shifting demographics encourage us to think of Hawai'i as a delicate ecosystem that, though changing, must be constantly kept in balance. The core of our past and current values have been Native Hawaiian in origin, and though we might not individually be Kānaka Maoli ourselves, we live here and can strive to be pono (harmonious) with one another and the land we care for. These values, after all, maintained a sustainable island environment for centuries before 1778.

LABOR

LOWELL CHUN-HOON

What does the mythical person on the street think of when she visualizes labor in Hawai'i? Angry construction workers in hard hats and torn T-shirts brandishing picket signs and obstructing traffic? Scowling backroom bosses pounding conference room tables with angry fists? Slothful government bureaucrats coddled by antiquated civil service rules? Quite possibly all of these images leap to mind.

Though perceptions like these are inevitably rooted in one's own experience and exposure, there is a forgotten and heroic history of labor in Hawai'i that shaped the fundamental contours of current society, and has the potential to do so again. Anyone seeking to understand modern Hawai'i and to address its future cannot comprehend either this evolution or potential without confronting this past. To some, this may seem to be a pointless excursion into a disturbing past that best remains buried and forgotten, but to others, it is an illuminating reminder of how much Hawai'i and the world have changed in a century and a half, and an indispensable foundation for searching for a better future.

Hawai'i's labor history is largely described by the successive arrival of different immigrant ethnic groups as plantation labor, the consolidation of these workers into working class labor organizations, and their dramatic success in achieving greater economic security and job protection. Between 1837 and 1868, sugar industry production in Hawai'i skyrocketed from only 4,286 lbs. to 17,127,161 lbs., creating an obvious impetus for labor recruitment. In 1852, 175 Chinese contract laborers first arrived, and earned a paltry $3.00/ month. In 1868, 153 Japanese sugar plantation workers commenced working on contracts paying $4.00/month. Koreans first arrived in 1903, and in 1907, the first 15 Filipino workers, or *sakadas,* were assigned to Ola'a plantation on the Big Island.[1]

The recruitment of agricultural labor to Hawai'i was also a part of a broader movement of workers from Asia to the American West. These new migrants were first welcomed in California and the West Coast as a source of cheap labor.

Chinese workers constituted a full one-half of California's farm labor by 1884. In the post–Civil War South, some entrepreneurs saw Chinese workers as replacements for freed black slaves. In 1869, the *Lexington Observer and Reporter* proclaimed that with the coming of the Chinese, "the tune . . . will not be 'forty acres and a mule,' but 'work nigger or starve.'"[2]

But the hospitality found in the editorial pages rapidly evaporated, leading to a period of episodic violence, racist stereotyping, and exclusionary legislation first against the Chinese, but later against other Asian immigrants. Various restrictive legislation followed, including the Chinese Exclusion Act of 1882, the first U.S. legislation to exclude any ethnic group by nationality, with modifications and extensions in 1888, 1891, 1902, and 1924. Concern over inroads made by Japanese into California agriculture, where crops they produced eventually were valued at $67 million dollars, or 10 percent of the state's total, prompted the passage of the Alien Land Law of 1913, barring Japanese from ownership of land. In 1922, the Cable Act stripped any American woman who married an Asian immigrant of U.S. citizenship, and in the same year, the U.S. Supreme Court ruled in the *Ozawa* case that naturalization laws did not apply to Asians. By 1934, the Tydings-McDuffie Act excluded Chinese, Japanese, Korean, Asian Indian, and Filipino immigration to the U.S.

In this national climate of exclusion, parallel incidents of labor violence and protests occurred in Hawai'i. At least in the eyes of some, Asian labor was merely a commodity that fulfilled economic need and was virtually devoid of human qualities. A representative of the Hawai'i Sugar Planters Association testified before Congress in 1910 that "the Asiatic has had only an economic value in the social equation. So far as the institutions, laws, customs, and language of the permanent population go, his presence is no more felt than is that of the cattle on the ranges."[3]

These dehumanizing and condescending attitudes did not remain unchallenged. In 1909, seven thousand sugar plantation workers struck, and protested the racial hierarchies imposed by the plantations. "Is it not a matter of simple justice and moral duty," they asked, "to give [the] same wages and same treatment to laborers of equal efficiency, irrespective of race, color, creed, nationality or previous conditions of service?"[4]

In 1920, three thousand Japanese and Filipino workers marched through downtown Honolulu behind a picture of President Abraham Lincoln as a symbol of freedom and equality. The demonstration prompted the *Honolulu Star-Bulletin* to respond: "Americans do not take kindly to the spectacle of several thousand alien Asiatics parading through the streets with banners flaunting their hatred of Americanism and American institutions and insulting the memory of the greatest American president since Washington."[5]

In 1924, sixteen Filipino sugar workers striking at Hanapēpē, Kauaʻi were killed by police. Others who survived were jailed or deported. In 1938, the Inland Boatman's Union and the International Longshore and Warehouse Union (ILWU) struck the Inter-Island Steam Navigation Company over the issue of a closed shop, or whether union membership was a prerequisite for obtaining employment. Some unionists were convicted of illegal possession of dynamite, and some charged these explosives were intended to blow up the Interisland ship the *Waialele*. When the ship sailed and arrived in Hilo manned by a non-union crew on July 22nd, longshoremen who had been working at other piers met the ship in protest, and were greeted by police with a tear gas grenade. Unionists and others urged the company to discontinue service during the controversy, but Hilo businessmen argued that shipping should be maintained, so the *Waialele* continued to sail. When it next arrived in port on August 1, 1938, 250 union members at the dock were met by 69 police officers and the Hilo Fire Department, which had deployed a truck with an 85 lb. pressure hose.

The jubilant mood of the crowd turned ugly when the police attempted to stop the demonstrators, and one police lieutenant stabbed a union leader in the shoulder after slapping him across the face with the flat side of a bayonet. As the crowd scrambled about, an order to fire was issued. Shotguns and conventional guns unloaded buckshot, birdshot, and .45 caliber ammunition, hitting some fifty unarmed people, including women and children. Though a grand jury was convened to allay the shocked territory, no one was indicted as a result of this incident, which became known as the Hilo Massacre. "A state of emergency existed on that date," the grand jury report concluded, but the "evidence is not sufficient to warrant an indictment against any person or group of persons."[6]

Though the strike accomplished little in terms of immediate specific gains, the legendary ILWU leader Jack Hall hailed it as a vital point of departure:

> When the strike began, many people expected the Hawaiians in the Union to hold out about four days. "The Hawaiians," they said, "are too easy-going. All they want is a little fish and poi and their liquor." This slander has been disproved by the strike. The Hawaiians demonstrated to the world that they share the determination and stamina of workers everywhere.[7]

In 1946, the ILWU led 21,100 sugar workers in the statewide Great Sugar Strike against the Hawaii Employers Council for seventy-nine days. In 1949, the Great Hawaiian Dock Strike lasted for six months in a successful attempt to win parity with mainland dock workers. In 1951, Art Rutledge formed the Hawaii Federation of Labor Memorial Association, which later became known as "Unity House." In 1958, the Aloha Strike by the ILWU engaged 13,700 workers from twenty-six plantations statewide. In 1971, the West Coast Dock Strike engaged 15,000 stevedores from the West Coast and Hawai'i for 134 days.

As organized labor grew in strength, it elicited attacks from McCarthyism. The House Un-American Activities Committee held hearings to expose Communism in Hawai'i. ILWU leaders were held in contempt of Congress for refusing to answer questions. In 1951, Hall and six others known as the "Hawaii Seven" were indicted under the Smith Act for allegedly being communists and advocating the overthrow of the government. In 1953, Hall and the others were convicted, prompting a four-day general strike in sugar, pineapple, and longshore industries, but that conviction was ultimately overturned by the 9th Circuit Court of Appeals in 1958. Hall was represented by Telford Taylor, the chief American prosecutor at the Nuremberg trials.

In 1954, with major assistance from labor, Democrats secured the takeover of both houses of the State legislature after they had been dominated by Republicans for fifty-four years. Under the remarkable leadership of men like Sen. Nadao Yoshinaga, Rep. Yoshito Takamine, and Justice Edward Nakamura, a comprehensive program of workplace reform and a social safety net that included workers' compensation, temporary disability insurance, unemployment insurance, and eventually prepaid health programs was established. The unions themselves grew to become an accepted part of the island's social and governmental structure. Charges of communism receded, and growing legislative strength lead to the passage of the Hawai'i Public Relations Act in 1970, which made possible the widespread organization of governmental public employees.

During the past two decades, union membership in Hawai'i has consistently been almost 10 percent higher a percentage of the work force than in the U.S. as a whole. In 2009, according to the U.S. Department of Labor's Bureau of Labor Statistics, 12.3 percent of the country's workforce was unionized, compared to 23.5 percent of Hawai'i's workforce, the second highest rate of unionization among all states, trailing only New York's 25.2 percent. In the preceding two decades, union membership in Hawai'i was at its highest in 1989, when it reached 29.9 percent.[8] In a less tumultuous but still litigious age, the rousing strikes of early years have yielded to a period of relative labor peace and stability. Disputes over individual discipline and contract interpretation are resolved by grievance filing and arbitration. While some complain about the impropriety of leaving wide-ranging wage increases in the hands of private arbitrators who are not elected by the public, arbitration is certainly a viable and less disruptive alternative to public employee strikes, such as the United Public Workers six week strike in 1979, or the Hawaii State Teachers Association's twenty day strike in 2001.

The accomplishments of the union movement in helping to transform Hawai'i from a narrow oligarchy to a pluralistic, multiracial democracy are by any reckoning deeply significant. But the very economic success of trade unionism, the dramatic increase in wages, the creation of a society in which public education was widespread, and the furtherance of social mobility created subsequent generations of union families whose children often became independent professionals, not blue collar tradespeople.

The legal landscape in which unions operate has also had a subtle but pronounced effect on their day-to-day operations in Hawai'i. One restraint on union action has been the imposition of the duty of fair representation, enunciated by the U.S. Supreme Court in *Vaca v. Sipes* 388 U.S. 171 (1967). Essentially this doctrine holds that unions owe their membership a duty to act in ways that are not arbitrary, discriminatory, or in bad faith. In *Vaca*, a union member sued his union over the failure to take his case to arbitration, when there was conflicting medical evidence of whether the employee's high blood pressure precluded him from working in a meat packing plant.

The doctrine serves an admirable and necessary purpose—to maintain institutional integrity and to preserve individual rights in the context of a union serving as the exclusive representative of those its represents. However, in practice, this doctrine has exerted a conservative force on union initiative as it necessarily compels unions to weigh the potential liability of their actions. While such considerations are absolutely necessary to protect and conserve union finances and ensure their long-term existence, the prominence of the duty of fair representation promotes a culture of risk avoidance that retards the kind of utopian and aspirational thinking that once made union organizations so potent, and which encouraged the emergence of charismatic leadership.

Political conservatives for years have denigrated trade unions as merely "a special interest group." But while labor is an "interest group," it is one that still represents almost a quarter (23.5 percent) of the working population in Hawai'i and adroitly wields major influence in the State legislature. One impressive recent example of this clout is the passage of SB 2650 through the efforts of the Hawaii Government Employees Association, which halted the reorganization of the Department of Human Services neighbor island offices, saved 228 jobs, and preserved direct personal services for welfare recipients. Though it is undoubtedly true that union members do not reflexively vote in favor of the slates recommended by political action committees, Hawai'i's unions possess an ability to generate campaign support for candidates that is still impressive. Neighbor Island union meetings where candidates seek endorsements are often gatherings of real excitement, and striking displays of real grassroots electioneering and elemental democracy.

In dire economic times, unions in Hawai'i rightly focus on "pork chop" issues—retaining jobs, fighting furloughs, minimizing cutbacks in wages, resisting increasing contributions for medical care plans, and preserving pension rights. These are the mundane but real issues that union memberships elect their leaders to protect and resolve, and any leadership that fails to address these matters jeopardizes its existence. Even today, the fundamental right for workers to organize a union is imperiled by naked managerial intransigence. In one noteworthy ongoing struggle, ILWU Local 142 has fought the Pacific Beach Hotel since winning a representation election in 2002, simply to obtain the Employer's recognition of the union, to achieve a basic collective bargaining agreement, and to reinstate five employees fired for union activism. On September 30, 2009, a federal administrative law judge ruled in favor of fifteen of sixteen unfair labor practices charged by the National Labor Relations Board and the ILWU, and on March 29, 2010, U.S. District Court Judge Michael Seabright enjoined the Employer from failing to implement the administrative law judge's ruling while it is on appeal.

The present moment is also one in which economic inequality grows more acute daily, and economic insecurity and basic joblessness abound. In his book *The Great Risk Shift*, Yale political scientist Jacob Hacker calculated that in 2003 the wealthiest 1 percent of U.S. households averaged over $800,000 in income, or more than eighteen times the average middle income household.[9] By contrast, twenty-five years earlier, the wealthiest 1 percent made less than twelve times the average middle income household. In addition, the instability and variability of before-tax family incomes was much higher in the 1980s than the 1970s; much higher in the 1990s than the 1980s; lessening during the boom of the late 1990s; but soaring in the first four years of the 2000s to twice the level of the 1970s across all levels of education.

Hacker notes that in most affluent countries a comprehensive welfare state exists to protect the economic security of its citizens. In the U.S., by contrast, less funds are spent on government benefits as a proportion of the economy, and far greater reliance is placed on private workplace benefits such as healthcare and retirement pensions, which are subsidized by tax breaks for employers. In recent years these same employers have successfully shed many of these responsibilities, shifting the risk of economic insecurity from themselves to workers and their families under the guise of promoting greater "personal responsibility."

In such times of economic turbulence, a receptive climate exists for unions to provide leadership and new ideas. Even as they struggle to retain hard-won gains, Hawai'i's trade unions can move to address the pervasive economic insecurity and reposition themselves on the forward edge of social change. They can convene a broad discussion from the perspective of average workers on what is necessary to restore the present economy, begin to reverse the tide of unfavorable labor precedents set by a Bush-dominated National Labor Relations Board, and move to prevent the disastrous recent failures of the nation's economic system. With the current legislative influence possessed by organized labor, it is not unrealistic to believe it can make a substantial contribution to reshaping Hawai'i's future both in the workplace and in the state's economy as a whole.

Over time, it may be that the union movement can also be reenergized and can recapture moral leverage, as well as attract the interest of younger activists and greater support from its female members by strategically addressing larger human rights issues such as human trafficking. Hawai'i is one of only eight states in the union that has not enacted an anti-trafficking statute, though our state was the first in the country to make sex tourism a crime.

On May 3 of this year, the State legislature passed and forwarded to the governor SB 2045, a human trafficking statute, but in the process a provision criminalizing labor trafficking was inexplicably removed from the proposed legislation, leaving only provisions regarding sex trafficking. This removal also seems illogical when Hawai'i is currently experiencing a major federal prosecution of labor trafficking at Aloun Farms, where two defendants, both corporate officers of the enterprise, this year pled guilty to trafficking some forty-four Thai laborers.

If labor is to recapture its role of advocating change on behalf of those who are excluded and voiceless, it should also strengthen its outreach to those groups of recent immigrants—Southeast Asians, Samoans, Tongans, and Micronesians—who have yet to achieve full integration into Hawai'i or educational and economic equality. Such groups are at the forefront of those needing representation and assistance, and can serve as new constituencies that will revitalize labor's rank and file support.

Another entirely separate effort worth expending is simple promotion of public service both for the state as a whole and for labor's own members. Programs within individual unions as simple as volunteer elder care, respite care for caretakers themselves, or medical transportation for the elderly would go far toward giving tangible meaning to appeals for solidarity, brotherhood, and sisterhood. The personal ties thus forged in mutual aid and support are an integral part of the larger task of building group cohesion and identity.

The specific initiatives suggested here may or may not be the ones that successfully unlock the full potential of organized labor. In general, the historical genius of Hawai'i's labor movement has been its ability to fuse workers' economic self-interest with altruistic social purposes, and to achieve these broader goals throughout all of society. The present growth of economic insecurity can create the urgency for action that in the past inspired decades of socially cohesive and committed reform. While the general public complains of governmental paralysis and an inability to solve fundamental economic and medical problems, the core values of unionism—teamwork and collective action, dedication to higher causes than one's narrow self-interest, the ability to have internal debate and reach common decisions that are acted upon—are central values of democracy that can overcome the present malaise. At its best, the kinds of commitment called forth by unionism also respond to central human needs for affiliation, identity, and purpose.

The constituent elements are thus present for organized labor to exert a major influence in the shaping of Hawai'i's future, righting those imbalances in the distribution of wealth that corrupt social decision-making and prevent the full realization of human potential. The time is right for labor to move toward restoring a society of equality, opportunity, and hope.

TRANSPORTATION

KARL KIM

Hawai'i has suffered from a serious lack of transportation planning. With projects such as the H-3 or the Superferry, and the repeated failed attempts to build rail transit in Honolulu, it is evident that there have been gross miscalculations, political machinations, and weak analysis of alternatives. The H-3 highway and fixed rail for Honolulu will have been the largest capital projects undertaken in Hawai'i. The current price tag on the rail system is $5.5 billion dollars. Ignoring cost overruns, this amounts to approximately $4,583 per person in Hawai'i. If paid on a per capita basis, a family of four could easily purchase a new car. Other new transit systems have been described as costing about the same as purchasing a new car for every passenger. Our system has set a new record: purchasing a vehicle for every household in the state! But do we really need yet more cars in Hawai'i?

Reviews of major transportation projects have displayed insufficient *systems thinking* and an alarming disregard for the public. Transportation projects in Hawai'i have been all about jobs and the connections between money, land, and power. There hasn't been sufficient scrutiny over who would be employed by these expensive capital projects, and the extent to which mainland firms and outside labor will be imported to complete them. It's been about winning or losing battles, rather than designing and building effective solutions for meeting the real transportation needs of communities.

How is it that we can be furloughing teachers, cutting welfare benefits, and downsizing vital community programs while still spending billions on fixed rail transit, financed largely by a regressive excise tax? We should use transportation policy to leverage positive social change. While transportation systems potentially provide an excellent opportunity to integrate land use, development, and economic growth, the mistakes of the past keep being repeated. While the rest of the nation and most of the developed world is focused on sustainable, context-sensitive, and participatory planning, in Hawai'i we appeared trapped in some kind of pathetic time warp in which the knowledge, tools, and advancements in transport planning are largely ignored.

A SYSTEMS VIEW OF TRANSPORT

Although transportation should be seen as a system, we tend to view such projects in utter isolation. Rational decision-making involves considering benefits and costs but also evaluating alternatives and incorporating probabilities, risks, and potential for losses. There has been insufficient consideration of multimodal travel behavior, in which walking, biking or driving, and travel by bus and rail are part of an overall system of ground transportation. We need to examine public and private options, including taxis and shuttle services. More careful study of travel behavior is also needed in terms of the locations of residences and jobs, and trip generators (school, shopping, recreational activities, etc.). Travel behavior varies by time of day, day of week, season of the year. It varies by age and other demographic factors. Travel demand is also dynamic. It changes as the population changes. We move from one home to another. We finish school. We change jobs. We age, marry, have children, retire, or move away. It's further complicated in Hawai'i because of our large military and visitor populations.

A narrow project orientation pushes us to consider bus *versus* high occupancy toll lanes *versus* light rail *versus* elevated rail. We should be considering *all* of the above, rather than limiting ourselves to comparisons between technologies which may be appropriate solutions in some areas and mistakes in others. A systems view would enable us to look across different technologies, and design solutions that are flexible, adaptable, and appropriate for particular neighborhoods. With H-3, Superferry, and the Honolulu High Capacity Transit Corridor Project (a.k.a., fixed rail), we've been boxed into a take-it or leave-it view of the project.

A systems view of transportation includes evaluation of land use plans and community development programs, as well as the economic and social needs of neighborhoods. This is important in older, established, built-up areas with many residents and attractors, such as restaurants, businesses, services, schools, and churches. Done the right way, transportation improvements increase mobility and accessibility, thereby supporting economic and social activity. Done improperly, a new transport system generates blight, noise, and vibration, and harms business both during and after construction. Worse case scenarios include technological failure, market failure, and irreparable damage to the environment. Other factors are outside the control of Hawai'i. Interest rates, global politics, international economics, and "wildcard" events such as natural disasters could have a profound effect on our economy, and therefore our ability to complete major projects. We should consider the opportunity costs associated with massive capital outlays. We have a moral obligation to consider who paid for the system, and who will benefit from the planning, design, construction, and operation of this expensive project. Finally, there needs to be a reckoning of the full costs and benefits of major capital projects, rather than treating them as yet another occasion for political sport.

IMPACT ASSESSMENT IS ESSENTIAL

The recent Hawai'i Supreme Court decision requiring the developers of Turtle Bay to prepare a new environmental impact statement before adding thousands of hotel rooms on the North Shore of O'ahu is a legal reminder of the importance of impact assessment. The court decision on the Superferry case also reaffirmed the need for alternatives analysis and measurement of environmental, cultural, and socioeconomic impacts associated with new projects. Government cannot simply exempt its way out of these legal requirements.

The outcome of both cases should not have been surprising. The natural environment is cherished in Hawai'i, and public sentiment towards environmental protection has increased. In places like the North Shore and on the neighbor islands, the increase in traffic, congestion, and urbanization is clearly visible. The desire to preserve natural areas and to limit new growth and development has been articulated and reinforced through community plans, sustainable development plans, and efforts to steer growth to other parts of the island. The public deserves assurances that significant environmental impacts have been identified and mitigated, and that new developments are consistent with community plans. Other jurisdictions have adopted robust procedures for considering the effects of climate change on projects, and the effects of projects on energy, transport, and greenhouse gases. Rail transit, unfortunately, is headed down the same track as H-3 and Superferry. We can expect lawsuits, challenges, delays, and wasted time and energy because not enough attention was paid to the assessment and disclosure of significant impacts.

Large transportation projects are more challenging than private development projects. With highways, transit, and public works, government acts as both the proponent and the accepting authority. Transparency and broad public participation are essential. Other complications arise when both federal and state environmental review processes are triggered. Federal concerns may not necessarily be the same as the state and local concerns, particularly in Hawai'i where there is such a rich natural and cultural environment.

PLANNING TO REDUCE RISKS

Because Hawai'i is vulnerable to natural disasters and isolated from other jurisdictions, major transportation projects should be designed to reduce the

risks of harm in the event of natural or manmade disasters. It may be necessary to transport large numbers of people from one part of the island to another. We may need to ship early responders, relief supplies, or workers on an
emergency basis from one island to another. We may need more waterborne
capacity than we currently have.

Transport systems should be designed to increase our resiliency—our
ability to absorb shock, recover from harmful events, and restore social, economic, and community systems so that health and safety and the quality of
life is preserved and improved. Transportation systems are increasingly vulnerable to a wide range of disruptions. If shipping lines were to be disrupted
or worldwide oil production were to decrease, not just ground transport, but
also air and sea transport would be greatly affected. We are running out of
fossil fuels. We are the most oil dependent state in the country, not just for
transport but also for power generation.

AUTOMANIA

In spite of the fact that Hawai'i is one of the most remote places in the world,
it has developed a transportation system with many of the same problems
as other communities in the United States. Surface transport is too dependent on the private automobile, not integrated with land use planning and
development, and harmful to our health.[1] According to 2000 Census data,
84.4 percent of workers commuted by automobile and only 6.3 percent of
Hawai'i's population used public transportation to get to work. The number
of people who walked to work was only 3.4 percent, and the proportion commuting by bicycle was even less.

Like other Americans, we have had a love affair with our cars.[2] We love
them so much that many of us have more than one. In 2000, there were approximately 724,000 cars and light trucks, plus another 20,000 motorcycles
in Hawai'i. The civilian labor force that year was only 595,000.[3] Motor vehicles are a technological marvel, from the initial development of internal
combustion engines to the deployment of power steering, cruise control, and
other innovations to make driving faster, easier, and more comfortable. Even
though we may be stuck in traffic, there are also in-vehicle amenities to help
us bear spending even more time commuting to town. Next to housing and
food, spending on motor vehicles represents the major expenditure category
for most households.

The investment in roadways, lighting, signage, and paving, as well as
parking spaces, gas stations, refineries, automobile repair and parts stores,
and other services and products related to ground transport make this an expensive component of our local, state, national, and international economies.

The side effects associated with automobiles (accidents, air pollution, noise, contaminated urban runoff, and disposal of used vehicles) further increase the true costs of driving. And since vehicles, parts, fuel, and other ingredients of the vehicle industry are imported from abroad, the economic benefits of the automobile industry are spread globally, while many of the environmental and social costs are borne locally.

The dangers associated with driving have not been adequately addressed. For most age groups, automobile accidents are the major cause of death and injury. Consider for a moment the number of people you know who have been killed or injured in automobile accidents. The growth in roadside memorials is a vivid, tragic reminder of just how many people have paid the ultimate cost of driving. The vulnerability to harm increases not just with exposure, but also with age. The fact that seniors are living longer, driving more, and becoming increasingly frail as they age means that more older adults are hurt and killed by cars. In Hawai'i, the situation is acute because the state has the third fastest rate of aging—behind Florida and Arizona—and there are few alternatives to driving.

Worldwide, traffic injuries are on the increase. It has become a major public health problem. Every year approximately 1.2 million people are killed, and more than 50 million people are injured in auto accidents.[4] That amounts to approximately 274 people killed every day—slightly less than the seating capacity of an Airbus 300 jet. While there is national attention every time a jetliner crashes, hardly a day passes without a similar level of death on our roadways. Why is it that we as a society are so complacent when it comes to traffic safety? In part, it has to do with the guilty pleasures we take from driving and our illicit love affair with the automobile. We are willing to overlook the risks, and the environmental and social costs, because our cars have become much more than just a means of transport. They are part of our identity.

THE SUSTAINABILITY TICKET

In the summer of 2008, the price of oil reached $140 a barrel. This occurred after UN Secretary General Ban Ki Moon declared climate change to be the "defining challenge of our age."[5] The UN Intergovernmental Panel on Climate Change (2007) reported that global warming was "unequivocal," and that "human activity was very likely the cause of rise in temperatures."[6] While there has been controversy over exaggerated estimates of glacier retreat in the Himalayas, it remains undisputed in the mainstream scientific community that motorized vehicles are major producers of greenhouse gases as well as particulate matter, which have contributed to the warming of the planet and increased extreme weather, including fiercer hurricanes, heavier rainfalls and flooding in some areas, and increased drought and wildfire in others. Upland wildfires are of particular concern in Hawai'i. According to a recent report, "93 percent of Hawaiian birds exhibit medium or high vulnerability to climate change," and both "increases in temperature and rising sea levels are expected to reduce natural habitats on islands."[7] Another threat to wildlife habitat is urbanization. Encouraging the development of dense urban centers as a strategy to preserve open space and natural areas is one of the central tenets of urban planning.[8]

Sustainability requires addressing environmental, economic, and community concerns,[9] and can be improved through vigorous transportation planning. Roadways are often the leading edge of development, so the decision to build (or not) transportation infrastructure can have long-term implications. There are opportunities to learn from cities that have implemented clean, green transport programs. These include Seattle and Vancouver, with their car-free days, and other cities throughout the world.[10] Boston's routine closure of major thoroughfares, for example, can remind us, in the words of Bernard Rudolfsky, that "streets *are* for people" and not just cars.[11] The Complete Streets movement emphasizes the use of streets by everyone.[12]

New York City has invested heavily in bicycle lanes, making it the eighth most bike friendly city in America.[13] Honolulu doesn't even make the top fifty. In 2007, Paris implemented a bold plan by placing more than 20,000 bicycles at approximately 1,450 stations strategically located throughout the city. This has radically changed and humanized Paris's streets, and promoted greater social interaction. The program is more advanced than the earlier bicycle-sharing efforts in cities like Amsterdam and Portland, Oregon, where the free bicycles were often stolen. The new systems require riders to make a deposit, and utilize clever pricing techniques. Renting a bike for the first half hour is generally free, but costs approximately $1.30 for the next half hour, and $2.60 for the third half hour. These programs make economic sense, and have improved the quality of the environment.

WHERE TO GO FROM HERE?

We can improve transportation planning in Hawai'i to increase the sustainability and resiliency of our communities. Here are some modest suggestions for improving both the processes and outcomes of transport planning.

First, adopt a systems view of transportation planning that integrates all of the different users, modes, facilities, needs, contexts, processes, and stakeholders in our island communities into the planning, discussing, debating, and deciding of alternatives. We need synergistic strategies for addressing not just transport needs, but also for improving societal welfare. Only from a systems view can we address the vexing relationships that involve justice, fairness, equity, and social conditions in Hawai'i. Transportation systems should be levers of positive social change. Our social welfare, including the positions of the poorest and weakest members of society, must be advanced through the implementation of massive capital projects. Proponents of big projects must demonstrate that we are better off by investing these scarce public resources.

Second, we need to establish environmental, economic, and community goals, so that we can measure the outcomes of massive capital expenditures. Transportation, fortunately, is a data-rich domain: measurable accomplishments can be readily tabulated. In addition to the reduction of pollution, rigorous economic analysis should be conducted to determine local benefits and multipliers to workers, businesses, and communities. Aggregate effects should be separated from localized costs and benefits. Hawai'i should not rely only on federal standards for impact assessment, but fully exercise State and local prerogatives to ensure disclosure of local costs and benefits of transport improvements.

Third, we need to adopt a "resilient communities" view when evaluating transportation alternatives. We must be attentive to the looming crisis of peak oil, and contend with climate change, global warming, sea-level rise, and the technological failures that can threaten the security of our communities. Transportation plays an essential role when it comes to disaster preparedness, response, and recovery. New transportation investments need to be measured against the yardstick of resiliency. Examples such as Wekerle and Whitzman's guidelines for safe cities abound.[14]

Fourth, we need to control the automobile. There is an adage that the automobile destroyed the American city. We also need to reduce the carnage on our roadways. It is unacceptable to have so many people killed and injured by motor vehicle accidents. Hawai'i can be a leader in traffic safety. We need to adopt a goal of zero fatalities on our roadways, similar to many other advanced nations. We also need to capture the true costs of driving, which include the public infrastructure and services necessary to support the automobile. The externalities associated with cars need to be more systematically studied, priced, and captured. This would allow for a more fair comparison with public transit, and will require real leadership, since it will be politically unpopular to charge people now for what they have been receiving for free— but our love affair with the car is ending.[15]

Finally, we need to invest in sustainability initiatives such as car-free days, walk to school/work programs, bike lanes, bus rapid transit (BRT), Complete Streets, traffic calming, context-sensitive design, ride-sharing, and other initiatives to make our transport systems cleaner, greener, less energy intensive, and more humane. Why can't Honolulu be one of the top twenty-five cities for bicyclists? These efforts are far less costly than highway and rail projects, are more broadly supported by the community, and provide a basis for building leadership, capacity, and commitment for the really big projects. If we can't build a track record of success with small projects such as bikeways and BRT, how can we possibly hope to implement a multibillion dollar rail system? Transport planning can be used from the ground up to increase the sustainability and resiliency of our neighborhoods and communities. Hawai'i should become a showcase for not just new technology, but for innovative planning and design, which will only increase our cachet as a thriving visitor destination.

PART THREE: *KE AUPUNI*

GOVERNMENT

CHAD BLAIR

HAWAI'I'S LEGISLATIVE AND EXECUTIVE BRANCHES

Political leaders have been fodder for ridicule for millennia, and Hawai'i's modern-day pols are certainly not exempt. But when the State Legislature and governor's office become punch lines on a near daily basis, as has been the case in recent years, something is wickedly rotten in Honolulu.

One of the sharpest observers of Hawai'i politics, columnist and blogger David Shapiro of the *Honolulu Advertiser,* has been milking laughs for a year or so now on how members of the Democratically dominated State House and Senate recently gave themselves hefty, salary commission-approved pay raises even as they postured to cut expenses and find revenue to meet a billion-dollar-plus budget shortfall. Shapiro has skewered the Republican governor and lieutenant governor as well, questioning their leadership skills, intelligence, and priorities.

It's all fair game—as with politicians everywhere, the bodies politic in Hawai'i have made their share of screw-ups. What makes residents today want to toss the bums out of office despite all the easy laughs is that the State is presently facing as serious a financial crisis as it has ever experienced. The Great Recession has cut drastically into government budgets. Hawai'i's response has been similar to other states: layoffs, furloughs, pay cuts, office closures, fund grabs, assorted tax increases, and reduction of essential services, including those that help our most vulnerable, powerless populations. All the while, a vicious flurry of finger-pointing and personal denigration has accompanied an almost universal inability of our leaders to accept responsibility for the consequences of their policies.

I say "almost," because there are local leaders from the governor on down who have stepped up, acknowledged the crises, and proposed solutions. They are not simply strumming ʻukulele while Hawaiʻi burns. And as ugly as relations are between the executive and legislative branches, it's a far uglier picture in many Mainland states, notably California, New York, and Illinois.

By the time this essay is published we will know the outcome of the 2010 Legislature and the governor's response to the budget and a slate of legislation. Maybe Hawaiʻi will get lucky and a huge pile of money will fall out of the sky. Kids will again go to school on Fridays, state workers will recoup lost wages and benefits (and once again anticipate raises), and the governor's cabinet and House and Senate leadership will join hands and sing "Hawaiʻi Ponoʻī" in the Capitol Rotunda—like the residents of Whoville after they awake to discover the Grinch stole Christmas.

I sure hope so. My guess, though, is lawmakers will only secure patchwork fixes, override most gubernatorial vetoes, and hold their breath until the state's top industry—tourism—springs back to life circa 2007 and replenishes the coffers of both the public and private sector. Our leaders will run for reelection or some other office, and come next session, they'll once again take up the same issue that has dominated recent sessions—where to find the money to run the state.

What follows is a look at several aspects involving the Legislature and the governor that I think offer insight into the current mess, and suggestions as to how both branches might better serve the common good. Some of these ideas are old, some are new, and some are upsetting. But I trust all will at least stimulate discussion and perhaps be of use.

CREATE A UNICAMERAL ASSEMBLY

We are one of the smallest states in the union, by population and geography, yet we have twenty-five State senators and fifty-one State representatives. We also have two U.S. senators and two representatives, a governor and lieutenant governor, four county mayors and three nine-member Councils (Kauaʻi has seven Council members), an elected Board of Education and Office of Hawaiian Affairs, and dozens of neighborhood boards.

That's a lot of people doing the people's work. Many of these elected officials have smoothly moved from office to elected office, learning the issues of different, though overlapping constituencies. One prominent example: Neil Abercrombie, a former Honolulu City Councilman, State representative and senator, U.S. Congressman, and in 2010, candidate for governor. Abercrombie also ran unsuccessfully for the U.S. Senate in 1970.

Does greater representation lead to greater government? That's debatable. But it's clear that Hawai'i's small size allows politicians to grasp the basic issues quickly, regardless of whether they actually live in the neighborhood. To wit: Ed Case, who formerly represented the State's 2nd Congressional District (rural O'ahu and the Neighbor Islands), sought election to the 1st Congressional District (urban O'ahu) in 2010. Colleen Hanabusa has run for both offices too, as has Mazie Hirono, a Honolulu resident who today represents Maui, Moloka'i, Lāna'i, Kaua'i, and Hawai'i Island in Congress.

Voters have not quibbled much with the pseudo-carpet-bagging. (To be fair, candidates like Case have lived in both districts.) Case, Hanabusa, and Hirono also all served in the Legislature, which acts as a tutorial of sorts on Hawai'i issues, and is often a successful launching pad for higher office. (Case and Hirono have both run for governor, and Hanabusa has thought about it.) But the presence of multiple unknown candidates for State House and Senate races may lead to confusion on Election Day, with name recognition from campaign signs posted at busy intersections a deciding factor in casting ballots. (Note: Before 1982, Hawai'i's Legislature had multimember Senate districts. Yikes.)

A unicameral Legislature could result in a stronger candidate pool, and fewer elected officials will make it easier for voters—with the help of the media and citizen advocacy groups—to keep track of their legislative records. Let's vote to keep either the House or the Senate, and then (I'm taking liberty here) turn the vacated chamber into a homeless shelter, seniors' center, or day-care facility.

ENACT OR ELIMINATE TERM LIMITS, AND TRY CAMPAIGN FINANCE REFORM

There are no term limits for the State House and Senate, yet terms are capped for governor and lieutenant governor and county mayors and Councils (Kaua'i voters this year are revisiting the matter of Council terms). Why the double standard? Is there something inherently superior about the Legislature that allows members a job security not enjoyed by others?

There are compelling arguments for term limits (new blood and ideas), and for no term limits (experience counts). And given Hawai'i's dismal voter turnout—the lowest in the nation—many State senators and representatives win reelection with only a handful of the district electorate supporting them. There is also the matter of home rule, which all four counties embrace. It makes sense for residents of each county to determine term conditions through charter amendment. (Seats in the U.S. Congress have no term limits, of course, and the president has been limited to two elected terms since

FDR.) One problem with no term limits, though, is that for many career State senators and representatives, political survival often trumps all other considerations. Entrenched legislators have the luxury of simply waiting until the next election to see who will hold power. Imagine, though, if they shared the same term limits—or none—as other leaders. It might motivate a lawmaker to work more closely with, rather than against, a governor and cabinet or fellow legislator, if they are all on similar clocks.

Hawai'i's Legislature is also part-time, as opposed to the executive branch, mayors, and Councils, yet it seems as if legislators sometimes treat the annual sixty-day session as something to do between campaign fundraisers. Campaigns for governor now cost upwards of $5 million, the largest chunk devoted to advertising and public relations. Which raises the issue of campaign finance reform, something most lawmakers have been loath to consider seriously. It's for a simple reason. The strongest indicator of a politician's ability to run successfully for office—and to get reelected in approximate perpetuity—is how much they raise and spend on campaigns. It's often not brains, nor experience, nor drive that prevails on Election Day. It's kālā.

There are those who argue that political contributions are examples of free speech, and that no one—not even companies and labor unions, according to the U.S. Supreme Court in a landmark 2010 ruling—should be denied the right to support financially a cause or candidate. But, as much as politicians may fervently deny it, it's hard to see how an elected official wouldn't take a phone call or meet in person with donors who just happen to want to talk about an issue of interest to them (or their business).

Hawai'i may want to look more closely at publicly financed campaigns, as have been adopted successfully in states like Maine, and as will be attempted on a pilot basis in Hawai'i County this election. Instead of forcing candidates to spend gobs of time raising cash and kissing the 'okole of all their contributors, publicly financed elections could help level the playing field and attract potential candidates who before would not have been able to raise the money needed to run. Candidates will then compete with—gulp!—ideas and not advertising paid in part through generous contributions from friends and aunties and calabash cousins—and also from banks, unions, and beer, cigarette, and oil companies.

HAVE NONPARTISAN ELECTIONS

Two offices with huge constituencies—the Honolulu City Council and Honolulu mayor's office—are nonpartisan. This has not necessarily resulted in smooth relations between the two; in fact, they've often been the opposite. Still, the point is that Honolulu's mayor and Council are able to govern an island of some 900,000 through public debate, consultation, coalition, and agreement, and not simply because Democrats or Republicans hold a majority.

Why can't the Legislature and governor's office be nonpartisan? Answer: They could, if Hawai'i decided so. (Nebraska's unicameral Legislature is nonpartisan.) Loyalty to political party has a deep tradition in Hawai'i, of course, and for Democrats especially it's been a matter of great pride for the past half century. Since the takeover of the Territorial Legislature in 1954, Democrats have held the most seats in the House and Senate, and dominated the governorship and congressional seats. I'll not address that history and its consequences here, except to say that it has produced notable milestones (mandatory employer-paid health insurance) and lingering failures (a lousy public school system).

But I will suggest that one big problem with one-party dominance is that the Democratic Party of Hawai'i believes its positions and values are not only the status quo, but are also the pono way to go. That effectively negates any contribution from the Hawai'i Republican Party, which is today so small and powerless that it does not even constitute a loyal opposition. The results of party polarization are clear when it comes to governance. There is rarely a serious challenge to Democrats getting their way at the Capitol.

But blind party loyalty also means many lawmakers adhere to the dictates of leadership rather than to their own beliefs or the views of the people they represent. Real decision-making is often done in caucus behind closed doors. (The Legislature conveniently exempts itself from the State's Sunshine Laws.) This pattern particularly weighs heavily on recently elected legislators, who come to the Capitol full of energy and ideas, but are quickly urged to fall in line by veteran lawmakers who feel they know better. (Joe Souki, the House speaker emeritus, has been known to refer to junior members in committee by their first names—as in "Representative Pono" or "Representative Jon Riki"—rather than their last names, as if to show who's in charge.)

It's no wonder, then, that the Legislature is seen as an "old boy network" that routinely turns new members into old ones, and ostracizes those that won't play along. Speaker Calvin Say has successfully resisted regime change by reform-minded House representatives like Scott Saiki and Sylvia Luke, while Senate President Colleen Hanabusa held her leadership in no small part by mollifying mercurial personalities like Donna Mercado Kim (who currently rules the Senate's most important committee, Ways and Means, following a listless stint as vice president) and Clayton Hee (whose tenure as Judiciary chair was controversial, but who seems to have hit his stride running the Water, Land, Agricultural and Hawaiian Affairs Committee).

Party politics can be a tremendous disservice, because most of the elected officials I have met and watched in action over the years are far more intelligent, thoughtful people (and that includes Say, Souki, Kim, and Hee) than the sometimes simplistic platforms they supposedly stand for would suggest. Indeed, lawmakers often hold certain positions that are the opposite of what might be expected from their party label. Four examples: Cynthia Thielen, a House Republican, is one of the most pro-environmental legislators around, while Norman Sakamoto, a Senate Democrat (and lieutenant governor candidate this year) is one of the most religiously conservative. Republican Governor Linda Lingle, meanwhile, has fought to help alleviate the growing problem of homelessness, while her predecessor, Democrat Ben Cayetano, incurred the wrath of public sector labor unions (much as Lingle has since 2002) as he sought to control spending in the 1990s.

To be sure, all of these politicians have demonstrated support for stands that are traditionally Democratic or Republican. But political parties can't solve Hawai'i's problems. It takes hard work, respectful argument, and ultimately, compromise. When a party controls twenty-three out of twenty-five Senate seats and forty-five out of fifty-one House seats, however, as has been the case in the 2009 and 2010 Legislature, might has usually made right, even when it sometimes has been wrong. Recent examples include meddling with powers that have belonged to the executive branch, such as agency appointments; removing oversight of the State Elections Office from the lieutenant governor; and trying to amend the Constitution so Supreme Court justices can stay on the bench past the age of seventy—or at least until a Democrat replaces a Republican on the Capitol's fifth floor.

STREAMLINE THE LEGISLATIVE PROCESS, AND CURB WASTE

The State Capitol has a terrific Web page (www.hawaii.capitol.gov) that allows users to search quickly for bills, submit and read testimony, find laws, and perform other tasks. Its Legislative Reference Bureau and Public Access Room make it easier for citizens to do their homework, and many legislative staffs are diligent at returning calls and emails, and answering questions about legislation.

In the past few years the State Senate has sought to go "paperless," reducing the costs and clutter associated with endless printouts, and the House would do well to follow this lead. Many committee meetings and floor sessions are also now televised and available online, making participation in the process a lot more accessible, particularly for folks who can't make the trip down to the Capitol themselves—or who just dread the awful parking. And both chambers have employed PR specialists to get the word out and to facilitate media and other requests via multiple lines of communication.

The governor's office has joined the twenty-first century too, and many departments have made it easier to access government online. There's room for improvement: the governor's home page, for example, is sometimes dated, and efforts to stream live press conferences and major announcements from the Fifth Floor have been a work in progress.

There's room for improvement at the Legislature, too. Possibilities include limiting testimony time, prohibiting submission of written testimonies that are word-for-word copies of others (it happens a lot), and not holding hearings on controversial issues that committee members have no serious intention of voting on. It's a neat tactic. By holding a hearing, lawmakers can say they are doing their job of listening to the people. It's usually deployed for hot-button topics like passing civil unions for same-sex couples, allowing physician-assisted suicide (a.k.a. "death with dignity"), legalizing gambling, or banning fireworks. Thousands turn up to testify, the hearings take hours, the media gives it tons of attention . . . and then there's a deferral, or a vote that was already known to lawmakers before the decision to hold the hearing(s).

When the economy is in the tank, a gambling measure might reasonably deserve renewed, and deep, consideration. Hawai'i is one of only two states that prohibit gambling, after all. But if lawmakers are not serious about changing the law, they shouldn't waste the energy and time. That was the case in the 2010 session, when lawmakers again dithered over perennial issues like gambling and prohibiting fireworks, but also deliberated at length over new measures that would allow flying U.S. flags in condominiums or would recognize the cultural value of the illegal "sport" of cockfighting. One of the most time-consuming and controversial issues in the last decade was the enactment of a cap on gasoline prices, which would later be nixed. It was a serious issue: Hawai'i drivers pay more at the pump than those in all other states. But what was problematic was whether the Legislature, which taxes gasoline sales, should also be in the business of consumer-price controls.

Then there are the dozens and dozens of nonbinding resolutions introduced and often passed by lawmakers during session. Examples in 2010 include measures recognizing February as Hawai'i-grown Cacao Month, proclaiming 2010 as the Year of Ethnic Studies in Hawai'i, changing Father Damien de Veuster Day (April 15) to Saint Damien de Veuster Day (May 10), designating the week of August 24 as Surf Week in Hawai'i, and urging the Board of Education to provide academic credit or "some other incentive or penalty to motivate students to take the adequate yearly progress tests seriously."

That last resolution brings this essay back to where it started: a governor, lieutenant governor, and Legislature that are considered jokes. And you may as well add the D.O.E., the B.O.E., and the Hawaii State Teachers Association to the list—as the *Advertiser*'s Shapiro has—as all were players in the Furlough Friday Fiasco that has been a tragedy at home and black eye for Hawai'i nationally.

These arguments are easy for me to make. I have never run for office, nor assumed such awesome responsibilities. And I accept that there are many knowledgeable people—namely, lawmakers—who could tell me why these ideas are unworkable . . . and while they're at it, point out how journalists and academics like me can improve upon their own lot.

Fair enough. But as a registered voter of the State of Hawai'i, I think it is our responsibility to help each other crawl our way out of our fiscal malaise. I hope this at least fosters constructive debate.

LAW AND THE COURTS

MELODY KAPILIALOHA MACKENZIE

Hawai'i has a unique legal system, a system of laws that was originally built on an ancient and traditional culture. While that ancient culture had largely been displaced, nevertheless many of the underlying guiding principles remained. During the years after the illegal overthrow of the Hawaiian Kingdom in 1893 and through Hawai'i's territorial period, the decisions of our highest court reflected a primarily Western orientation and sensibility that wasn't a comfortable fit with Hawai'i's indigenous people and its immigrant population. We set about returning control of interpreting the law to those with deep roots in and profound love for Hawai'i. The result can be found in the decisions of our Supreme Court beginning after Statehood. Thus, we made a conscious effort to look to Hawaiian custom and tradition in deciding our cases—and consistent with Hawaiian practice, our court held that the beaches were free to all, that access to the mountains and shoreline must be provided to the people, and that water resources could not be privately owned.

—William S. Richardson, Chief Justice,
Hawai'i Supreme Court (1966–1982)[1]

Hawai'i's modern legal history has been an attempt to reconcile our past with our present—to reconcile Hawai'i's status as an independent sovereign nation with our history as an American possession and territory; to reconcile our indigenous heritage with our immigrant and now western-dominated culture; and to reconcile a unique island worldview with a worldview shaped by national boundaries thousands of miles away across an ocean and a continent.

This essay examines the role of law and the courts in addressing the historical claims of the Native Hawaiian community to land and sovereignty. It suggests that, to a large extent, Hawai'i's people are engaged in a reconciliation process rooted in Kānaka Maoli values that seek balance, harmony, and aloha. That reconciliation process, however, has been hindered by the U.S. Supreme Court's narrow and constricted view of law and history. In this twenty-first century, political leadership grounded in aloha is crucial to continuing the reconciliation process.

LAW IN HAWAI'I

Not until after statehood, the point at which Hawai'i's people regained some measure of self-government, could Hawai'i begin to come to terms with its past. Thus, since 1959, Hawai'i courts have been more open to public claims and group rights, often drawing upon Hawaiian custom, tradition, and law as a basis. In 1968, for instance, the Hawai'i Supreme Court determined that pursuant to ancient Hawaiian tradition, custom, and usage, seaward boundaries described as "ma ke kai," or along the ocean, are located along the upper reaches of the wash of waves. In subsequent cases, the court has reaffirmed and refined the principles leading to public ownership and usage of Hawai'i's beaches, has applied these principles to property registered in the Land Court system, and has required the State to preserve the shoreline area for public use. In another landmark case, the court recognized that water in traditional Hawaiian society could not be privately owned, and concluded that the State, as successor to the Hawaiian sovereign, holds water in trust for the people. The Court has also held that lands created by lava extensions are owned by the State, reasoning that such land should benefit all of Hawai'i's people, with the State as trustee.

Hawai'i's courts have also opened the way for greater public access to both the administrative process and the courts. Beginning in the 1970s, the Supreme Court adopted progressive standards that allowed organizations and individuals to challenge land use decisions and to assert environmental and other important public rights. The 1978 Constitutional Convention and amendments approved by voters were crucial developments in Hawai'i's law. Among those amendments were provisions recognizing the right to privacy and the right to a clean and healthful environment. Another amendment declared that Hawai'i's natural resources are held in trust by the State for the benefit of the people.

RECONCILING OUR PAST

Probably the most far-reaching amendments, however, addressed long-standing claims of the Hawaiian community. These amendments were reparatory —they sought to redress historical claims, and to provide resources and a measure of self-determination to Native Hawaiians. They recognized the loss of sovereignty and land resulting from the 1893 illegal overthrow of the Hawaiian Kingdom, and they specifically dealt with the "ceded" or public land trust.

The public land trust consists almost entirely of the Government and Crown Lands of the Hawaiian Kingdom. In the mid-1800s conversion to private property, Kamehameha III set aside the Government Lands for the benefit of the chiefs and people. The Crown Lands, reserved as the King's private lands and made inalienable in 1865, provided a source of income and support for the Crown. After the illegal overthrow of the Hawaiian Kingdom in 1893, and with establishment of the Republic of Hawaii in 1894, the Republic merged the Government and Crown lands. In 1898, the Republic ceded approximately 1.8 million acres of these lands to the United States.

In 1921, the U.S. Congress passed the Hawaiian Homes Commission Act (HHCA) to address the deteriorating social and economic conditions of the Hawaiian people. Congress set aside 203,000 acres of the Government and Crown Lands, designated as Hawaiian Home Lands, for a homesteading program benefitting those of not less than 50 percent Hawaiian ancestry. The 1959 Hawai'i Admission Act transferred approximately 1.4 million acres of the Government and Crown Lands to the State. As a condition of statehood and as a trust responsibility, Hawai'i agreed to incorporate the HHCA into the State constitution and administer the Hawaiian Home Lands. The remaining lands, 1.2 million acres, were transferred to the State for five trust purposes, including benefitting Hawaiians as defined in the HHCA.

Thus, the 1978 constitutional amendments sought to strengthen the Hawaiian Home Lands program by ensuring sufficient funding. The amendments established the Office of Hawaiian Affairs (OHA), with a board of trustees elected by the Hawaiian people to manage resources and funds, including revenue from the public land trust. Another amendment clarified that the lands were held in trust for Native Hawaiians and the general public.

Other reparatory amendments mandated that the State promote the study of Hawaiian culture, history, and language, and provide for a Hawaiian education program in the public schools. The Hawaiian language was designated as one of two official languages of Hawai'i, and limitations were placed on the doctrine of adverse possession, which had played a major role in the dispossession of Hawaiians from their lands. A separate provision protected the traditional and customary practices of ahupua'a tenants.

Both the Executive and Legislative branches of State government have also taken reparatory actions to address historical claims. After years of illegal State use of Hawaiian Home lands, Governor George Ariyoshi cancelled Executive Orders that had improperly withdrawn lands from the trust inventory. Following a lawsuit and successful lobbying, the Hawai'i legislature passed a law in 1995 committing the State to pay $600 million over a twenty-year period to compensate the Hawaiian Home Lands program for past illegal uses of the trust lands. These funds have been utilized for infrastructure and new homestead development.

In 1993, the State took several important actions in recognition of the 100th anniversary of the Overthrow of the Hawaiian Kingdom, and in response to a consensus that reconciliation efforts must be renewed. The Legislature adopted a powerful statement of reconciliation in a concurrent resolution, upon which the 1993 U.S. Congressional Apology Resolution was based. The State also enacted other reparatory measures, including a commitment to hold the island of Kaho'olawe in trust for a future Native Hawaiian government.

HAWAI'I COURTS AND RECONCILIATION

Hawai'i's courts have been particularly sensitive to the claims of the Native Hawaiian community, furthering efforts toward justice and reconciliation. For instance, in a 1982 case, *Ahuna v. Department of Hawaiian Home Lands*, the Court drew the analogy between the federal government's relationship with Native American peoples and the State's relationship with beneficiaries under the HHCA, and declared that the State must adhere to the same duties as those required of a trustee. These duties include the duties to act solely in the interests of the beneficiaries and to exercise reasonable care and skill in dealing with trust property and, the Court decided, should be judged by the strictest fiduciary standards.

In two other cases, the Court has allowed beneficiaries on the Hawaiian Home Lands waiting list to pursue claims under a federal statute, holding that the beneficiaries had a property interest in the award of homestead lots, and liberally construed a law to allow claimants in an administrative process to proceed on claims in court against the State.

Similarly, in a series of important cases interpreting the constitutional provision on traditional and customary rights, and based on laws of the Hawaiian Kingdom, the Hawai'i Supreme Court has recognized that Hawai'i law ensures the continuation of Hawaiian customs and traditions, and adopted a test balancing the interests and harms involved in each instance where customary rights are at stake. Subsequently, the Court rejected the argument that when an owner wishes to develop lands, customary rights disappear, holding instead that the State is obligated to protect the reasonable exercise of traditional and customary rights to the extent feasible. These cases recognize that Hawaiian custom and usage continues in spite of the transition to a fee simple property system, reaffirm Hawaiian Kingdom law, and implement protections in the Hawai'i Constitution.

RECONCILIATION v. U.S. LAW

In 2000, the U.S. Supreme Court in the *Rice v. Cayetano* case soundly rejected Hawai'i's efforts at reparatory justice and reconciliation. Eighty-five years after the overthrow, the 1978 amendments establishing OHA afforded

Native Hawaiians an unprecedented measure of self-governance. For twenty years thereafter, Hawaiians elected OHA trustees to administer trust proceeds and programs benefiting the Hawaiian community. The U.S. Supreme Court determined, however, that restricting the voters for OHA trustees solely to those of Hawaiian ancestry was race-based and violated the 15th Amendment to the U.S. Constitution. The State, and many native and civil rights organizations, argued that the voting limitation was permissible based upon the political relationship between the U.S. and indigenous peoples, and the federal and state governments' history of special protections for native peoples. The Court, however, viewed OHA elections as solely State elections, distinguishable from elections of Indian communities, the internal affairs of quasi-sovereign governments.

In an opinion that minimized the importance of State and federal reconciliation efforts, including the 1993 Congressional Apology Resolution, and ignored the overwhelming vote by Hawai'i's multiracial citizenry to establish OHA, the majority in *Rice* distorted Hawaiian history. According to the *Rice* court, Native Hawaiians are a defeated people overcome by historical circumstance and civilization, a fate that must now simply be accepted.

RECONCILIATION v. U.S. LAW (REVISITED)

The Hawai'i Supreme Court and the U.S. Supreme Court's vastly different interpretations of the 1993 Apology Resolution highlight their conflicting views of history and law. In the Resolution, Congress apologized to the Native Hawaiian people for the overthrow of the Hawaiian Kingdom with the participation of agents and citizens of the United States. Congress also expressed its "commitment to acknowledge the ramifications of the overthrow . . . in order to provide a proper foundation for reconciliation between the United States and the Native Hawaiian people." Congress specifically recognized that the Government and Crown Lands were taken without the consent of or compensation to the Native Hawaiian people or their sovereign government, and that "the indigenous Hawaiian people never directly relinquished their claims . . . over their national lands to the United States."[2]

In a 2008 unanimous opinion authored by Chief Justice Ronald Moon, the Hawai'i Supreme Court placed a moratorium on the sale of public trust lands until Native Hawaiian claims to the land were resolved. In *Office of Hawaiian Affairs v. Housing and Community Development Corporation of Hawai'i (HCDCH)*, the Court reasoned that the Apology Resolution and analogous State laws gave rise to the State's fiduciary duty to preserve the trust lands until a resolution of Native Hawaiian claims. This duty, the Court believed, was consistent with the State's "obligation to use reasonable skill and care" in managing the public lands trust, and thus the State's conduct should be judged by the most exacting fiduciary standards.[3]

In summing up, the Court found it significant that

> Congress, the Hawai'i state legislature, the parties, and the trial court all recognize (1) the cultural importance of the land to native Hawaiians, (2) that the ceded lands were illegally taken from the native Hawaiian monarchy, (3) that future reconciliation between the state and the native Hawaiian people is contemplated, and (4) once any ceded lands are alienated from the public land trust, they will be gone forever.[4]

Notably, in placing a permanent moratorium on land sales, the Court recognized that the trust lands or 'āina hold unique cultural, spiritual, and political significance for the Native Hawaiian people—they are not fungible or replaceable:

> **Aina is a living and vital part of the [n]ative Hawaiian cosmology, and is irreplaceable.** The natural elements—land, air, water, ocean—are interconnected and interdependent. **To [n]ative Hawaiians, land is not a commodity; it is the foundation of their cultural and spiritual identity as Hawaiians.** The aina is part of their ohana, and they care for it as they do for other members of their families. For them, the land and the natural environment [are] alive, respected, treasured, praised, and even worshiped.[5]

Unfortunately, even though the legal issues were unique and best resolved in Hawai'i, in a controversial move that appeared to reverse the State's long-standing commitment to reconciliation, the State administration sought U.S. Supreme Court review. Given the U.S. Supreme Court's increasingly conservative views, as well as the opinion in *Rice*, the Court's March 2009 decision was no surprise. According to the Court, the Apology Resolution was merely conciliatory, and its findings had no operative effect and did not substantively alter the State's obligations.

The Hawai'i Court's views of the public land trust and claims of Native Hawaiians are in sharp contrast to those of the U.S. Supreme Court. The U.S. Supreme Court did not dispute the findings of the Apology Resolution. These findings, when coupled with the State's independent trust duties in relation to the trust lands, were clearly sufficient for the Hawai'i Supreme Court to make its determination. The Hawai'i Court examined both the legal and equitable issues involved, seeking to strike a balance. Although it declined to rule on the ultimate claims of Native Hawaiians, the Hawai'i Court sought to protect the trust lands until a political resolution could be achieved.

After the U.S. Supreme Court decision, most of the plaintiffs settled with the State, agreeing to dismiss the lawsuit without prejudice. The 2009

Legislature passed Act 176 implementing the settlement by requiring a super-majority legislative approval for the sale or gift of trust lands. Ironically, land exchanges, which require only a two-thirds disapproval of either house or dis-approval by a majority of the entire legislature, have often been a method to dispose of trust lands. Moreover, in the 2010 legislative session, only six months after Act 176 became effective, an effort was made to bypass the super-majority requirement and sell trust lands.

In the *HCDCH* case itself, one plaintiff, Jonathan Kay Kamakawiwoʻole Osorio, decided to continue on with the lawsuit. The State objected, arguing that because Osorio is of less than 50 percent Hawaiian ancestry, he could not pursue a claim. The Hawaiʻi Supreme Court disagreed, holding that as a Hawaiian and a member of the general public, Osorio might be injured by the loss of trust lands. Consistent with its earlier analysis on the relationship between the Native Hawaiian people and the ʻāina, the Court believed that Osorio could suffer cultural and religious injury if the lands were transferred in violation of the State's trust responsibility.

ALOHA

Controversies over trust lands and the contours of Native Hawaiian sover-eignty will continue to challenge us in the coming years. With the expected passage of a Native Hawaiian federal recognition bill and subsequent negotia-tions between the State and a native government, how we approach reconcili-ation is more important than ever.

Our laws and our courts have been instrumental in moving our commu-nity toward reconciliation. Sometimes that movement has been reluctant, sometimes the State has reneged on its promises, and sometimes reconcilia-tion has taken a back seat to expediency or the economy. Yet, to move for-ward as a community, we must recognize past injustice, and we must recom-mit ourselves to returning to balance and harmony through reconciliation. In doing so, we should allow our path to be guided by aloha, a foundational value of Native Hawaiian life, encompassing a way of living that promotes healing, harmony, compassion, and balance.

Political leadership in Hawaiʻi requires aloha. Our state law encourages legislators, judges, and policy-makers to apply the "Aloha Spirit":

> In exercising their power on behalf of the people and in fulfillment of their responsibilities, obligations and service to the people, the legislature, gov-ernor, lieutenant governor, executive officers of each department, the chief justice, associate justices, and judges of the appellate, circuit, and district courts may contemplate and reside with the life force and give consideration to the "Aloha Spirit."[6]

Recognizing that the aloha spirit was "the working philosophy" of Native Hawaiians, which was presented as a gift to the general community, Hawai'i law defines aloha as "mutual regard and affection" with "no obligation in return," and "the essence of relationships in which each person is important to every other person for collective existence."[7] Hawai'i's unique history and culture have resulted in a modern society renowned for its warmth and generosity of spirit. That spirit finds its roots in traditional Hawaiian culture, and it continues to infuse island life today.

In our continuing quest for reconciliation, we should take to heart the words from the Oli Aloha as expressed in Hawai'i state law:

Akahai, meaning kindness, to be expressed with tenderness;

Lōkahi, meaning unity, to be expressed with harmony;

'Olu'olu, meaning agreeable, to be expressed with pleasantness;

Ha'aha'a, meaning humility, to be expressed with modesty;

Ahonui, meaning patience, to be expressed with perseverance.[8]

Is aloha enough? Aloha is the foundation and base; it is a place to come from, a place in which to ground ourselves as we undertake the challenges of reconciliation. Aloha requires courage and perseverance, and ultimately, it requires principled actions. These actions may lead us down unknown paths, perhaps to restructuring our legal relationships and redefining Hawaiian sovereignty and nationhood in our laws and through our courts. Most importantly, without aloha, can we ever hope to reconcile our past with our present and live together as a community?

PUBLIC EDUCATION

MARI MATSUDA

SAVE OUR SCHOOLS[1]

Our sneakers were squishing in the mud as we followed our 7th grade science teacher up the Koʻolau ridge, hunting liverwort. Our assignment: situate liverwort in the scientific systems for classifying life on earth. The picture is held for a lifetime. Green, flat, branching fingers extending over a piece of rotting tree. Even though it had no leaves and looked like fungus, it was a plant, because it used photosynthesis. We decided this, because it was green.

I had no occasion to use liverwort knowledge until writing this essay, but it is an example of the thousands of bits of learning given to me by Hawaiʻi public schools that added up to a sense of myself as an educated person who is curious about the world, who has the habit of learning, who participates in the grand democratic conversation, bringing information and ideas to it. Without citizens thus educated, there is no democracy.

Thank you, Mr. Takeyama, for taking us on a liverwort hunt. Thank you, Miss Nebeker, for teaching me to play the cello. Thank you, Mrs. Minami, for making me read Faulkner. ("Mrs. Minami, I can't read this. It doesn't make any sense." "Yes, you can, try harder.") Thank you, Mr. Sonomura, for teaching acapella madrigals and entering us in the all-state competition. Thank you, Mr. Lowell, for finding me during a senioritis extended lunch break, and walking me over to the AP English test—oh, and thanks for making me read Dostoyevsky, which I used to ace the test. How did you know they were going to ask for an essay on a literary protagonist wondering about the existence of God?

I start with teachers because so much of the rhetoric surrounding public education blames the teachers, and their unions. The kids aren't learning, it must be the teacher's fault. No, it's our fault, and we can do something about it.

Mānoa Elementary 1967: art, music, and PE every week, a working kiln, an orchestra teacher and a full set of string instruments, independent learning projects. Elites sent their children to public school then. Children of university professors went to my high school. Trapido, Kefford, Boggs, Beechert, Simson, and Lindley were campus names at UH *and* at Roosevelt. Gill and Fasi —the big politico names—were at Roosevelt. Children of professional, college-educated parents studied alongside children of janitors and construction workers. The biggest rock and roll promoter, and thanks to the proximity of "Beverly Hills"—a.k.a. Papakōlea—some of the biggest names in Hawaiian music, also sent their children to our school. A wonderful mixing of race, culture, class, religion, and social practices coalesced in school in the late babyboom years. We had the odd and endearing custom of "cosmopolitan court," voting for the best looking couples of every ethnicity. There was stratification and conflict; there was interaction and intercultural competence. Everyone was pidgin literate, if not fluent. Everyone recognized the smell of model airplane glue and marijuana, and the different effects of those drugs. In short, we learned the entire social strata of Hawai'i nei, and developed the ability to thrive while negotiating interactions along that strata. That is something no prep school will ever teach.

The schools I went to were markedly better than today's. My heart breaks when I visit. No more orchestra, no glee club, no kiln. No auto body, no metals workshop, no school play. This is on the days there *is* school. Our depleted education system is now asked to bear the cost of global economic decline. Furlough Friday children fend for themselves, paying for our failure to raise adequate revenue to run our state.

How did this happen? In the postwar years, Hawai'i's economy was growing, and our tax system was relatively progressive, so that booming businesses and their rich beneficiaries paid a greater share. New Deal optimism, given a rocket boost by the cold war fear that we were falling behind the Soviets in science, prompted investment in schools. Unions were strong, and their members' interest in good schools placed pro-education politicians in the legislature. The reformers of Hawai'i's democratic revolution believed we could solve social problems by investing in public infrastructure. The very architecture of our public elementary schools—with a large public room that serves as cafeteria, gym, and auditorium—is a product of the New Deal. Thousands of these were constructed across the nation in an effort to move education into the modern age.

Teaching was a relatively good job. Teachers did not experience the wealth gap they do today. They could afford a house, a car, and a middle-class life style. No one asked them, as young teachers are asked today, "when are you going to get a real job?" Mr. Takeyama, who took us to hunt flora, wore a tie to work when he wasn't mucking in the hills. It was a respectable, professional job, and it was thus viewed by the community.

Starting in the 1980s, Reaganomics ascended. Instead of faith that public infrastructure benefits us all, the new mantra was "big government takes your money." The solution was cutting taxes and cutting government. This ideological shift succeeded for several reasons. First, it benefitted the powerful. The biggest tax breaks went to the top brackets, increasing wealth inequality in Hawai'i. Second, the "big government" story resonated. There was cronyism in the DOE, and as in any large institution, waste and inefficiency. All large operations (including private businesses) have inefficiencies. They also have economies of scale, and resource advantages that can improve quality. Rather than targeting waste, the "government is bad" ideology simply let the public sector die through attrition.[2]

As we reduced funding, schools were asked to do tenfold more. The federally-imposed mandate of special education was an important civil rights victory. Unfortunately, it came with a price tag. Special education swallows huge chunks of education funding in Hawai'i. Without the funding to build an excellent system of special education, the DOE has stumbled along, facing costly litigation. This is not intended to excuse any foot dragging on special education, but simply to note a significant cost strain.

The second, hidden "unfunded mandate" placed on schools is that they are the final repository of all social ills. Teachers in Hawai'i have told me of children who come to school with open, untreated wounds; of children who are chronically absent because "Mommy wouldn't get out of bed"; children who bring wet, torn homework sheets to school because it was raining last night and they live in a tent; children who move several times a year, going to new schools and never catching up; children who don't speak English and for whom no translator is available (anybody out there speak Kosraen?); children who come to school famished on Monday because without the free school meals they don't have a reliable source of food. Teachers are doing the best they can for these children, but they do not have the ability, training, or time in a crowded classroom to serve as nurse, social worker, psychologist, and translator, and they cannot provide what this child really needs to learn—a stable living environment. A large number of the children in the "underperforming" schools come from multiple social dislocations. The teachers know this. They are often the only witnesses, and we do not invite them to tell us what they see. Instead we blame teachers for the low test score of a hungry child.

Schools were asked to do more with less, and the landscape of social attitudes changed. The idea of the school as the public commons gave way to the market. If big government was bad, if the social safety net was wasteful, then citizens were left with survival of the fittest. Parents decided their children's future depended on private schools. In other places, this phenomenon was called "white flight." In Hawai'i, the flight was multiracial, but it was flight nonetheless. In talking to these parents, some are quite honest about trying to give their children an advantage in a winner-take-all world. At Punahou, one parent told me, his children meet the future movers and shakers and make the contacts they need to get ahead. Others talk about the computer lab, broadened curriculum, college counselors, things their children would lack in public school. A considerable cohort is simply protecting their children from harm. They speak of fear of physical assault, of overwhelmed teachers who will let a child slide by without learning. At least at the small religious school he chose, one father told me, his daughter "won't be able to hide." Other parents speak of the public school "trouble makers" who will suck up the teacher's time. The exodus to private makes it seem as though the "good" families have left, and your child will remain in Loserville. Not all the departing families are wealthy. Some make huge sacrifices, working two jobs, and saving nothing for college, just to send their child to a private school.

These parents are not irrational. Public school has gotten worse—although much more good education goes on there than is generally acknowledged, and a significant amount of boring conventionality is sliding by in private schools. What is the better way?

First, here is what does not work. Test-driven, rote curriculum does not work. It is embittering teachers and forcing them to abandon innovation to chase scores. Excellent schools aren't trying to move 1 percent above basic. They are teaching students to program computers and solve climate change.

Blaming teachers and their union doesn't work. We need teachers on our side to build better schools, and we face a coming shortage of teachers as baby boomers retire.

Shifting the deck chairs doesn't work. Proposals to break up the DOE, trading one bureaucracy for five, or for an appointed board, trading board politics for gubernatorial politics, will not work. Politicians offer restructurings because they are afraid to raise revenue to run schools well. Debating an elected vs. appointed school board ignores the real reasons schools are failing: long-term divestment from the infrastructure of good education; underfunded schools dealing with multiple, impossible mandates; underpaid, unsupported teachers; and elite flight.

What would a truly good school look like? I asked one of the best teachers I know. She described a classroom that the children own. No one tells children to sit still or be quiet. They move around the room attending to tasks they are responsible for. Their body language says "I own this place and I have important work to do here." Whether it is a science experiment or putting tools back in the right place in the cupboard, the good classroom has a culture of active responsibility for learning, emanating from the students.

I watched as a fifth grade teacher asked the class to help him figure out whether he could afford a leather jacket, on sale, 30 percent off $99.99. He begged for help, since he was single and needed to upgrade his look. He showed them the crumpled bills in his wallet. Raucous teasing about Mr. Leonard's wardrobe ensued, from students straddling the edge of adolescent romantic anxiety.

"Figure it out, but don't say anything," Mr. Leonard said. "When you have it, raise your hand, and when all the hands are up you get early recess." Some hands went up immediately. The ones who were stuck felt social pressure to catch up. The teacher feigned continued concern about the jacket, and indifference to recess.

"Did you remember I have to pay tax?" he asked, and some of the hands went down for re-calculation. Finally, one of the students who had the answer started an impromptu lesson on percentages.

"Remember? You can just move the decimal like we did last week and then you know what ten percent is. If you can get 10 percent, you can get 30, just add it three times."

"Or multiply," another chimed in. Somehow, through the magic of his relaxed joshing about the desperately-desired jacket, the teacher had left the students in charge. What could have been an exercise in humiliation for the "slow" learners, became a triumph of whoops and high fives when the last hand went up and everyone had the answer. We did it. In our classroom, with Mr. Leonard, this is how we do it.

In thinking about the student-owned classroom, I realized that if you add it three times, you get the good school. In the good school, the students, the teachers, and the parents own the school. This is our school, and this is how we do it. A parent picking up a child sees a discarded can on the ground. "Let's pick that up and take it to the recycling center." A student sees a visitor arriving with a hesitant look. "Are you looking for the office?" she asks. A teacher wants to build a catapult in the parking lot and has the students draw up plans to present to the principal, knowing that the first, reflexive response from the office is always "great, let's figure out a way to do this."

The good school district is one that supports the good school. It focuses on putting strong principals in place, paying them well enough to take on the hard jobs of forcing out the bad teachers and building a high-performing culture. Good principals will document the inadequacies of bad teachers and ease them out. No teacher's union, ever, has taken the position that bad teachers should have job protection. The union is used as an excuse for gutless management. It doesn't feel good to fire people, but we can pay principals well and tell them it is their job. Supported principals get their phone calls answered by a person with authorization power at the DOE, and the answer to whatever they are asking for is yes. A good superintendent makes this the culture of the school district, and we can put principals in charge of determining whether the superintendant is achieving this mandate. We can drill down to local control without restructuring the school board or the DOE, simply by demanding school-centered management practices.

Here are ten things we should do today if we are serious about saving public education in Hawai'i:

1. Raise teacher salaries to attract the best, at the same time that we raise requirements for entering the teaching profession.[3]

2. Fund schools at levels that will turn back three decades of divestment in Hawai'i, allowing us to reduce class size and bring back art, music, and PE.

3. Reward and recruit strong principals.[4]

4. Demand an end to unfunded mandates.

5. Introduce wrap-around social services to the schools. If families lack medical care, drug abuse counseling, violence intervention, food, or housing, the schools can help provide it.[5]

6. Provide quality early childhood education, investing where intervention reaps the biggest payoff: in the first five years.[6]

7. Create incentives for families to choose public school, and bring the social capital of elites back to public schools.[7]

8. Organize to vote out politicians who strip-mine public education, imposing furlough days on public schools while their children attend private academies.[8]

9. Use qualitative evaluation along with quantitative, measuring success by more than scores.[9]

10. Reward and replicate best practices.[10] There are good public schools and excellent public school teachers: grow more.

Naysayers will argue we can't afford these changes. The punitive No Child Left Behind Act is what we got from politicians who pretend we can fix schools for free. Look at the much admired private academies in Hawai'i, and note their multimillion dollar endowments, supplemented by steady fundraising. Good education costs, but it is worth it. More significantly, bad education costs, too. Our prisons are filled with citizens we failed to educate. Many never learned to read or write. Many had undiagnosed learning disabilities. Many were physically abused. One effective classroom could have caught that kid and changed the path from prison to productive citizen. We have boatloads of longitudinal data proving that early intervention works. A child who gets quality early childhood education is more likely to graduate, to get a job, to stay off welfare, to avoid teen pregnancy, to stay out of prison, to go to college, to stay off drugs. Just about any social ill you can name is increased by bad education and ameliorated by good education. Pay now, or pay later: failing to teach a child costs.

Furthermore, paying for education increases the general health of Hawai'i's economy. Teachers and schools spend money locally. A teacher told me recently that furlough paycuts meant she bought her daughter's prom dress at the thrift store. No shame in that, but when middle class workers stop shopping and eating out, our small businesses go bankrupt. A true economic stimulus, designed to build local economies, would flood the schools with funds. Bailouts for banks saved bankers. This did little to jumpstart our local economy. Local spending will do this, and schools are the logical place to start. Many small businesses in Hawai'i would benefit immediately if we reinvested in our schools, and educational spending has a long-term multiplier effect, generating future innovation and revenue.

The legacy of the ahupua'a system is a constant reminder that people once lived in these islands with an ethic of mutual care and mutual responsibility. No one went without food or shelter, all were expected to acquire the skills of useful work, all work was valued, there was no such thing as "dropping out of school." After Western contact, this legacy continued in the form of universal public education. Everyone was expected to learn, and as the written record shows, Hawaiians grabbed enthusiastically at literacy. Everyone read, from the barefoot newsboy on the corner of Fort and Merchant to the ali'i at the Palace. Auwe, what happened, that we let education become a privilege, and sent the brown-skinned, angel-faced newsboy to languish in prison, without the basic ability to read the paper?

Out of the darkness came all living things, including liverwort, in the taxonomy of the Kumulipo. You are holding this text, and following allegories of classification, because you are a reader. Education was a gift given to us. It is ours to bequeath. Whether by Linnaeus or He Kumulipo, things have their rightful place. The children belong in school, learning.

UNIVERSITY OF HAWAI'I

NEAL MILNER

WHAT WE NEED TO DO TO DEAL WITH THE UNIVERSITY OF HAWAI'I'S PERMANENT FINANCIAL CRISIS

To survive the present budget crisis and the lean years beyond, the University of Hawai'i has to deal successfully with two questions: (1) revenue—where is the money going to come from? and (2) reorganization—how can UH reorganize fairly and sensibly to deal with these new realities? For years UH has had trouble dealing with these issues. If these questions are not addressed properly, UH will offer less quality for more money. The answer to the revenue question will by default be "the students," while the answer to the reorganization question will be "there really is no sensible and fair way to do this, so we will make an ad hoc decision here and there and hope for the best."

WHY REVENUE AND REORGANIZATION ISSUES ARE SO SERIOUS NOW, AND WHY THEY WILL BE MORE SERIOUS IN THE FUTURE

In its recent analysis of national trends in college spending, the Delta Cost Project argues that the biggest threat to higher education "is a system of finance that will be hard to sustain in the current economic environment." Current here means well beyond the present recession. "To be sure, higher education has gone through hard times before," the authors of this report go on to say, "But looking at the economic and political horizon of January 2009, only the rosiest of optimists can believe what lies ahead is going to be similar to what we have seen before."[1]

Nationally, university revenues have dropped, and tuition has markedly increased. Even before the present crisis, universities were in serious financial trouble. Government appropriations to universities declined significantly from 2002 to 2005, and only partially recovered in 2006. The present fiscal crisis makes the situation worse, but the pattern of losing revenues and then only partially regaining them—never quite catching up—is well established nationally, as is the now prevailing wisdom that universities need to do more with less. This pattern of partial recovery and gradual overall loss is in the DNA of UH funding. The University of Hawai'i never catches up.

Tuition has gone up dramatically across the nation during the last few years, enough to trigger recent national student protests. The reasons for the increase are straightforward. The money replaces lost State general fund revenues, and raising tuition is a relatively quick and easy way to respond, or at least the most feasible under dire circumstances. As less money comes in from State general funds, and obstacles to raising revenue through gifts or grants continue, tuition increases become the fattest target. As the Delta Cost Project data show, nationally tuition increases have increased much faster than general spending per student. In other words, significant amounts of these tuition increases are being used to subsidize all other university functions, not just the amount spent on the students.

While the University of Hawai'i is going through the same pattern of response to a fiscal crisis as other universities, UH is in a particularly precarious position for two reasons. First, funding problems at UH are endemic to the place. The University of Hawai'i, primarily through its scientists, does an outstanding job of bringing in revenues through research grants. But it is impossible to increase these sources significantly in the short run, and extremely hard even in the long run, just as it is hard to get benefactors to donate large sums of money to UH. UH is a poor cousin compared to many other state universities when it comes to big benefactors. Second, there is a strong tradition in this state to keep tuition low. This tradition emphasizes that higher education is a collective good that should be funded by the collective.

TUITION RATES AND UH AUTONOMY: HOW, IN THE NAME OF UH INDEPENDENCE, TUITION HAS BECOME PURELY A FINANCIAL MATTER, AND WHY THAT IS WRONG

To understand how this pressure for tuition increases plays out in Hawai'i, it is necessary to understand the University of Hawai'i's autonomy problem. In 1986, the Hawai'i State Legislature passed Act 321, which grants UH a degree of autonomy. Because of the way the act is worded, and because of skepticism that UH could be trusted to play a more independent role in administering its affairs, actually getting this autonomy was a struggle. Primarily, this struggle has been a series of insurgencies wrapped in dry, technical, fiscal language that sounds like a bunch of CPAs talking to one another. Among supporters of UH autonomy, which it's safe to say includes most people who work at UH, the problem gets defined this way: the University has too little autonomy, and needs more to free itself from suffocating State bureaucracies and meddling political officials.

In fact, when it comes to getting out of this assets jam, UH has too *much* autonomy. Thanks to its newly granted autonomy, UH gets to set tuition rates and keep the tuition revenues, and that is good. But UH also gets more than it bargained for. Elected officials have used the autonomy argument as a way of passing the buck when they cut the UH budget and force the University to raise tuition. The prevailing attitude among political officials seems to be "You got the autonomy you wanted. Now use it to solve your budget problems."

Usually saying that something involving UH is outside of politics is good, but not in this case. Decisions involving the costs of education involve political questions, the consideration of which should involve the right kind of politics—one that recognizes that the way a public university like UH is funded raises a fundamental question that has disappeared from the public agenda: *To what extent do all citizens of Hawai'i have an obligation to pay for an individual's college education, and to what extent is it the responsibility of the individual him or herself?*

That question is about economics and social justice, and not one that the Board of Regents can or should answer. A proper discussion of it would bring out very different and of course often contradictory views about the role of the market, equality, individual responsibility, and privatization. Without such a discussion, the public takes a backseat—taxation without representation.

The Legislature needs to bring the question back by encouraging open, public, sustained discussions about it. Take the present tuition situation as an example. In 2006, Hawai'i students paid a smaller share of the costs of their college education than students anywhere else in the U.S. Because of the state's financial trouble, that piece of data alone trumps anything else. In desperate times it is tempting to let that happen, but doing so without discussing the larger question is shortsighted and undemocratic. I am not saying what tuition rates should be, but rather that we need a better process that examines the role of tuition in a broader, more political context. Political officials have an obligation to examine the question in this comprehensive way, but so do the rest of us. The issue is too basic and too complex to be answered indirectly by the Board of Regents, or by horse trading during the closing hours of a legislative session when basic policy questions are about the last thing on a beleaguered legislator's mind.

**ASSESSING AND REORGANIZING: WHAT UH HAS FAILED TO DO
IN THE PAST, ITS ATTEMPTS TO OVERCOME THESE FAILURES,
AND THE SHAKINESS OF THE RESULTS**

In this section I focus on the Mānoa campus because I know it so much better than the other campuses. When it comes to adjusting to budget cuts, UH has two fundamental problems, and both have been around long enough to be called historical. First, it does not have an established process for assessing its academic programs. Second, the organizational culture of the University is extraordinarily resistant to change. Consequently, UH Mānoa has no tested method for determining how to make cuts, and no proven way to implement the cuts after they are made. In the thirty-eight years I have worked at UH, the University has never implemented a fully operational plan that allows it to make such judgments about the quality of its programs.

These failures are a cultural problem, but not in the way we typically talk about culture in Hawai'i. The late David Yount's book *Who Runs the University?* is the best book ever written about UH, but it has significant flaws, especially when Yount talks about how culture affects the way UH Mānoa has been run.[2] Yount explains much of the turmoil in terms of local versus academic culture. The locals are the politicians as well as the UH administrators, who come from the same background. When it comes to UH, Yount argues, locals are more interested in maintaining old ties and what he calls "creature comforts" than they are in academic quality. The academics, primarily haole, on the other hand, are the rational, cosmopolitan sophisticates who are the true advocates of quality. Yount's view of culture is crude and simplistic. More significantly for our purposes, his view is wrong because it is overly optimistic.

The real problem at UH is not local culture. The cultural problem is wider and more encompassing than that. There is a prevailing, overarching culture of cynicism, pessimism, self-interest, and distrust that transcends any of the culture differences that Yount saw. This culture cuts across the entire university. All large universities are extraordinarily hard to change because, like UH, they are so non-hierarchical. Collective bargaining, which is typically a go-to villain when people discuss UH organizational problems, certainly reinforces the lack of hierarchy, but there is much more to the story.

The full story is too complex to tell here, but basically, it is this. The prevailing culture at the University is risk averse. This aversion is a response to the failures and dashed hopes people have encountered when they have tried to make changes. It is also based on a long-standing lack of trust that the University administration can effectively represent UH at the Legislature, and related to this distrust, an entrenched political process that rewards individuals at UH for circumventing UH and going directly to the Legislature when they want something. At this stage, there is no reason to believe that people working at Mānoa believe that the internal process will work fairly, or believe it will work at all. This skepticism is part of an informal process that is so entrenched because it serves a purpose.

A little over ten years ago, responding to a significant cut in its funding, the UH Mānoa administration made an unprecedented attempt at implementing a process that was supposed to target where cuts should be made, rather than taking the easy but ultimately harmful way out by cutting equally across the board. The objective of the two committees set up to do this was to identify and justify these cuts. *Star-Bulletin* reporter Helen Altonn (September 14, 1998) offers a nice summary of this tragicomic story.[3] The process turned out to be such a colossal dud that the administrator in charge tried to keep the final report from the public. The two committees involved in the process agreed on almost nothing, including what they were supposed to do and how they were supposed to do it. This came to light not at the beginning of the process, when it would have been possible to do something about the disagreement, but rather at the end, when the committees' respective reports were signed, sealed, and delivered. Members of one committee accused the other of simply being interested in defending their turf. One committee refused to consider more definitive action because the University took some of the programs, like athletics, off the table. The only important cut that both committees recommended, closing the medical school, never took place. In fact the opposite happened. Funds for the med school increased enormously.

This 1998 report is a dud that keeps on giving. It did more than just reinforce past skepticism. The story of this attempt became a beacon that highlighted and bolstered the prevailing view that UH could never do this well. No serious attempt to do comprehensive assessment took place for almost ten years after the 1998 failure. In 2007, Mānoa officials initiated a new process, which in fact is much better than the earlier one. It identifies programs that should be eliminated, reorganized, or enhanced. It is also deliberate and relatively transparent, with plenty of room for discussion and debate as the process moves forward. Still, at this juncture it is at best a work in progress. So far, the administration has used the process mainly as the basis for recommending the reorganization of four units. Two of these reorganizations are routine and uncontroversial. In the other two cases, there is much opposition both from within and outside of the University. Those two cases will be the acid test.

We are witnessing the beginning of an untested process in a distrustful, skeptical environment. It is certainly too early to tell whether the decisions made though this process will have any impact, because the organizational culture has not changed. It is realistic to assume that at Mānoa, desperation will make people less compliant, less cooperative, more skeptical, and more resistant. UH faculty and staff threatened by the assessment's recommendations will continue to go around the University and turn to the Legislature and to others in the community for help, as they have done for years.

Implementation is far from an automatic process. In fact, implementation never is, but in this case it is about as far from automatic as it gets. Because of the financial situation, UH has even fewer resources than usual to encourage people or groups to change, and given UH's non-hierarchical nature, it is not possible to impose changes from the top down.

Adopting the prioritization process was a big decision. In contrast, making the changes in the culture essential to making the policy work involves, as Randy Roth put it in his discussion of how to improve Hawai'i's public schools, "thousands of little decisions."[4] In a recent essay about university reform, Anthony Grafton, a Princeton humanities professor, noted that to make these kinds of changes happen, you have to "climb down to the local and personal."[5] Cultural change involves small-scale, everyday grunt work—persuading, reassuring, keeping in contact, and resolving conflicts. Success depends much more on soft power than on hard power.

In order to do this, the agents of change at UH must overcome three obstacles. First, the process itself is a very deliberate one. It is designed for long-term change, but is getting pressed into action as a partial guide for how to deal with imminent budget cuts. Nevertheless, the process is not likely to have much of an immediate impact. Second, few administrators have the skills, inclination, or time to climb down to the local and personal. Their jobs are not designed to give priority to this. Third, there is a false optimism built into the sense of accomplishment that has come from actually getting an assessment project off the ground. It is a big accomplishment indeed, but the pride and enthusiasm should not create blinders. Unfortunately the recent report by the Western Association of Schools and Colleges (WASC), the agency that accredits UH, reinforces this false optimism. On the basis of only a two-and-a-half day visit, the WASC site visitors felt that they could assess the organizational culture, which they did this way: "The [accrediting] team had the distinct impression of a sense of community across campus, a willingness to collaborate, to facilitate partnerships at all levels and a keen realization that this collegiality was essential to help weather the economic crisis."[6]

If only. There is no way on the basis of such a short visit that anyone can make confident conclusions about an organizational culture, much less conclusions that are so different from the way UH has worked—and the way WASC has said UH has worked—in the past. WASC's assessment of the UH community is more than inaccurate. It has the potential to lead the agents of change astray. People trying to make the prioritization process work are much better off assuming that the task is even harder than they think.

CONCLUSION: REVENUE AND REORGANIZATION— WHERE DO WE STAND AND WHAT MUST WE DO

I have two recommendations.

First, revenue issues need to become public, political issues that consider tuition in the broader context I described earlier. It is not the University's responsibility to do this. It is the broader community's, including, but not at all limited to, elected officials.

The second is definitely the University's responsibility, and the more those political officials avoid interfering with this responsibility, the better the chances of success. UH is responsible for making the new prioritization work. UH people need simultaneously to confront and appreciate the existing organizational culture. Just labeling this culture as a problem will not change anything. Making these changes requires time and an appreciation of low-level everyday change strategies that aren't sexy but are the key.

But there is also a large-scale and public strategy that UH needs to do better. In a recent essay on leadership in Hawai'i, Peter Adler described this strategy as leadership that creates "the atmosphere, tone, and sense of urgency that are required to bring about institutional change." Adler is very critical of public leadership in this state. In his opinion, the most effective political leaders in Hawai'i right now are military commanders, which Adler sees as "a backhand indictment of other local leaders. . . . Hawai'i politicians [today] simply cannot do bold things."[7] UH administrators need to do a far better job at this.

That is also precisely what many people say about the University of Hawai'i. It is a fair criticism as long as we understand that the creativity and courage that boldness requires need to be accompanied by a set of strategies that makes the bold ideas work. Without this combination, UH is doomed to continue down a path toward fragility, marginality, and mediocrity.

PRISONS

MEDA CHESNEY-LIND AND KAT BRADY

ENDING HAWAI'I'S IMPRISONMENT BOOM:
LET'S BE SMART ON CRIME, NOT SIMPLY TOUGH

The last decades of the twentieth century saw the United States embark on an unparalleled increase in the use of incarceration. As a result, the number of inmates in state and federal prisons increased nearly seven-fold. We incarcerated less than 200,000 people in 1970, but by 2008, we were incarcerating over a million and a half prisoners (1,518,559). An additional 785,556 are held in local jails, for a total of 2.3 million of our citizens under lock and key.[1] As the Pew Center on the States noted in 2008, we now imprison one out of every hundred of our citizens, giving us the dubious distinction of being the world's largest incarcerator.[2] With less than 5 percent of the world population, the United States houses nearly a quarter of its prisoners.[3] Commenting on this trend recently, Senator Jim Webb noted that "With so many of our citizens in prison compared with the rest of the world, there are only two possibilities: Either we are home to the most evil people on earth or we are doing something different—and vastly counterproductive. Obviously, the answer is the latter."[4]

Most criminologists reject the notion that this increase in imprisonment has much to do with the crime rate, particularly in recent decades. They note that from 1971 to 2000, the overall crime rate remained virtually the same, while the national incarceration rate went up by almost 500 percent (494 percent). A recent study by the University of Texas found that while the number of inmates has grown by over 300 percent since the late 1970s, growth in prisoner numbers is responsible for no more than 27 percent of the recent drop in crime. In fact, in states with the fastest growing prison populations, crime rates did not show the marked decreases one would expect if imprisonment "worked" to reduce crime. In West Virginia, for example, incarceration increased by 131 percent, but crime in that state dropped only 4 percent; in Virginia, incarceration rose just 28 percent, but crime dropped 21 percent.[5]

What accounts for most of the increase in prison population? Many believe that a number of legal and policy changes explain the phenomenon. The
passage of mandatory sentences, particularly for drug offenses; the adoption
of "truth in sentencing" provisions that require prisoners to serve most of
their sentences in prison; reductions in the amount of good time a prisoner
can receive while imprisoned; and more conservative parole boards have significantly impacted the length of stay. In a special study by the U.S. Department of Justice on truth in sentencing, between 1990 and 1997, prison admissions increased by only 17 percent (from 460,739 to 540,748), while the
prison population increased by 60 percent (from 689,577 to 1,100,850).[6]

Finally, many admissions to prison are actually re-admissions, because
individuals have violated a condition of parole, like failing a random drug
test. There has been a sevenfold increase in the number of parole violators returned to prison between 1980 and 2000. In states like California, an astonishing 67 percent of prison admissions are actually parole violators.[7]

This essay documents Hawai'i's involvement in mass incarceration over
the past few decades, and how these choices continue to impact other aspects
of our state's economy, including the provision of other much needed government services, especially vital social services and education. We hope that
the data presented here stimulate an important and overdue debate about
Hawai'i's response to crime—one that focuses on best practices and proven
results, rather than mindlessly tough and costly incarceration.

LOCK 'EM UP, DANNO: HAWAI'I'S IMPRISONMENT BOOM

Like the rest of the country, Hawai'i has dramatically increased its reliance on
incarceration in the last four decades. Hawai'i now imprisons roughly 6,000 of
our citizens (5,955 in 2008).[8] That is up from 5,053 in 2000—an 18 percent
increase (see Table One). Ironically, this increase occurred despite the fact that
Hawai'i has seen its crime rate decline to the lowest level in decades.[9]

Hawai'i's prison population has also increased at a faster pace than the nation as a whole, increasing since the turn of the century by 2.4 percent a year,
compared to a national average of 2.0 percent. California's prison population,
by comparison, increased by only 1 percent per year, and New York's prison
population actually decreased by 1.6 percent per year for the entire period.[10]

Hawai'i is unique among the states in its reliance on incarceration in
mainland facilities, most frequently in prisons run by the for-profit Corrections Corporation of America. Fifty-nine percent of Hawai'i's prisoners (on
the mainland) are housed in facilities run by CCA on the U.S. continent, making Hawai'i one of its biggest customers. Those prisoners doing time on the
mainland are far away from their families, incarcerated in states like Arizona

and, until recently, Kentucky. A review of Hawai'i's classification system reveals that 60 percent of our Hawai'i inmates doing time in mainland private, for-profit prisons are actually minimum or community custody, meaning they could be housed in minimum security or community custody beds in Hawai'i, instead of thousands of miles away from their homes and families.

TABLE 1: GROWTH AND DISTRIBUTION OF HAWAI'I INMATES, 1970–2008.

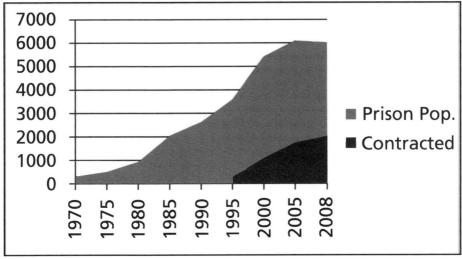

CHARACTERISTICS OF HAWAI'I'S PRISON POPULATION: RACE AND GENDER MATTER

Over-representation of people of color in the U.S. prison system has long been a problem. Nationally, more than 60 percent of those in prison are racial and ethnic minorities.[11] In Hawai'i, it has long been recognized that Native Hawaiians are over-represented among those under lock and key. A look at the data provided by the Department of Public Safety (PSD) reveals that while Native Hawaiians account for about 20 percent of the population, they constitute roughly 40 percent of those who are sentenced felons. Data from 2001 indicated that Native Hawaiian women were slightly more likely than their male counterparts to be over-represented: 44 percent of incarcerated women are Native Hawaiian, compared to 38 percent of men.

The Department of Public Safety also indicates that for many Native Hawaiians who are in prison, it is not their first time there. Consistent with other research on probation and parole as significant back doors to incarceration increases, only about a third of Native Hawaiians doing time are there for the first time.

PSD data also highlight the strain that returning ex-offenders can place on marginalized communities. On the island of O'ahu, a quarter of all Native Hawaiians released from prison return to one community: Wai'anae.[12] Given what we already know about probation and parole revocation, these data suggest that low income communities are hard pressed to provide the level of services, job opportunities, and drug and mental health treatment that those released from prison require. Without these services, they return to prison, often through the back door of parole revocation.

Research following those released on parole in 1996 found that in the next two to three years over half were returned to custody (53.9 percent), with only a quarter returned for new crimes, and three quarters for technical violations of probation and parole conditions—generally for drug relapse, another significant source of prison growth in Hawai'i and elsewhere. In Hawai'i, nearly half of the admissions of women to prison were the result of failed drug tests.[13] A January 8, 2009, memo to Senator Will Espero from Richard Yen of the Hawai'i Paroling Authority detailed the technical violations and the length of time given for 244 individuals whose parole was revoked between January and December 2008.[14] The total time given for these 244 revokees was 467 years: Maui, 18 revocations—27 years, 6 months; Hawai'i Island, 25 revocations—30 years, 6 months; Kaua'i: 4 revocations—12 years, 4 months; O'ahu: 197 revocations—396 years, 11 months. Nor was this year particularly unusual. Recent comparative research suggests that at nearly 50 percent, Hawai'i has the nation's fifth highest proportion of prison admissions due to parole revocation.[15]

The imprisonment boom has also meant increasing numbers of women are actually being sentenced to prison, a number that has increased by 4.2 percent for each year since the turn of the century—a rate roughly double the male rate of increase—until by 2008, women made up 12 percent of the total number of Hawai'i inmates. The majority of Hawai'i's incarcerated population are non-violent offenders, and this is particularly true of the women inmates, with 84 percent of the women, compared to 63 percent of the men, being nonviolent. As a result, 68.1 percent of females and 62 percent of males were classified as minimum or community custody, the least restrictive levels.[16]

While we do not have complete current data on the specific offenses of all women in Hawai'i's prisons, it is clear that a considerable proportion are doing time for drug offenses. In 1990, about one quarter (24.7 percent) of sentenced felons were incarcerated for these offenses; a decade later, it was 53 percent. Research on the characteristics of Hawai'i's imprisoned drug offenders found that in one two-year period (2003–2005), prisoners serving mandatory minimum sentences for drug offenses increased by 37 percent.[17]

Moreover, research conducted in 1991 indicated that during a two month period, 55 percent of the admissions to the Women's Community Correctional Center (WCCC) were probation or parole violators.[18] More recent data suggests that the percentage of women's admissions produced by parole revocation is likely the same or higher.[19]

Women held in facilities with male guards are also at increased risk of sexual abuse, a problem that has long haunted Hawai'i's women's prisons. This problem was dramatically illustrated recently when 168 Hawai'i women inmates were returned home from a private prison run by Corrections Corporation of America, Otter Creek Correctional Center in Wheelwright, Kentucky—one of that state's poorest districts. A total of twenty-three allegations going back to 2006 were being investigated, and at least five corrections officials at the prison, including a chaplain, had been charged with having sex with inmates in the last three years. Four were convicted. In addition, three rape cases involving guards and Hawai'i inmates were recently turned over to law enforcement authorities. The Kentucky State Police said another sexual assault case would go to a grand jury soon. Kentucky is one of only a handful of states where it is a misdemeanor rather than a felony for a prison guard to have sex with an inmate; in Hawai'i, these would have been felonies. According to Hawai'i corrections officials, the Hawai'i women had been incarcerated in Kentucky, far from homes and families, solely to save money.[20]

CLASSROOMS OR CELLS FOR HAWAI'I?

Speaking of money, let us not forget cost in this discussion of Hawai'i's imprisonment practices. Corrections spending has long been the fastest growing segment of state budgets. According to CBS News, taxpayers are paying an estimated $40 billion a year for prisons.[21] Feeding and caring for an inmate costs about $20,000 a year on average, and construction costs are about $100,000 per cell. Incarceration does not come cheap. The Pew Center on the States noted that between 1987 and 2007, the amount that states spent on corrections doubled.[22]

In Hawai'i, spending on incarceration has soared in recent years, despite the economic problems that have been haunting the state. Since the turn of the century, the corrections budget has increased by 87.5 percent (from $128 million in 2000 to $225 million in 2009). During the same time, the money spent to send prisoners to private prisons increased by 192 percent, from $20 million to $58.4 million. As it stands now, 26.0 percent of PSD's general fund operating appropriations goes toward incarcerating prisoners outside of Hawai'i; this is up from 15.6 percent in 2000.[23]

TABLE 2: HAWAI'I'S IMPRISONMENT EXPENDITURES, 2000–2011.

Where did the money that fueled Hawai'i's and the nation's imprisonment boom come from? Higher education has been a clear loser in the nation's choice to fund bars not books. The Pew study documented that between 1987 and 2007, corrections budgets rose by 127 percent (meaning
they more than doubled), while higher education funding increased by a far
more modest amount: only 21 percent.[24]

The State of California provides a fairly clear study of this budget shift
over time. In 1980, arguably the year that mass incarceration began, California spent 9.71 percent of its budget on public higher education and 2.83
percent on corrections. Fast forward to 2009, and the figure for higher education is 5.81 percent and for corrections 10.93 percent.[25] Proportionately,
corrections budgets quadrupled in California, recently prompting that state's
Republican governor to call for a shift away from those priorities: "spending
45 percent more on prisons than universities is no way to proceed into the
future."[26]

As the California data indicate, there are clear trade-offs here. Colleges
and universities, in turn, had to pass the cost of higher education along to
taxpayers, in the form of steep tuition increases. Consider that the University
of Hawai'i at Mānoa increased its tuition 20 percent for both in-state and
out-of-state students in 2006, achieving the dubious distinction of increasing
our tuition more than any other public university in the country that year.[27]

The public does not generally link corrections costs and college tuition, but it should, because every dollar spent on cells takes money from other important government services, including access to an affordable public university education. The nation also loses in this trade-off. At a time when our country clearly needs to invest in education for our citizens to face the challenges of a new century, including rising competition abroad, college educations have become increasingly unaffordable for average families in Hawai'i and elsewhere.

The good news is that a number of states, including California, are reconsidering these "choices." The Sentencing Project noted that in 2009, state legislatures in at least nineteen states enacted policies that have the potential to reduce prison populations and/or promote more effective approaches to public safety. A number of states like Minnesota and Rhode Island scaled back the scope of mandatory drug sentences; seven states amended probation and parole policies to expand good time and earned time programs resulting in reducing prison sentences; and two states, California and Illinois, created incentive programs for local jurisdictions to reduce probation revocations.[28] Prison admissions in the U.S. have also leveled off, growing at the slowest pace in this century.[29]

Unfortunately, Hawai'i's policy-makers and leaders have not taken such an innovative stance. There is talk, though, of building on the promising results of HOPE Probation, which provides probationers with access to drug treatment and emphasizes swift, short-term jail time instead of costly re-incarceration.[30] House and Senate Resolutions requesting the Hawai'i Paroling Authority to establish HOPE Parole have passed the 2010 Hawai'i Legislature. More robust challenges to the current reliance on costly and unproductive incarceration should be tops on any new Governor's agenda. Specifically, a new governor could safely reduce Hawai'i's incarcerated population by implementing the existing tiered furlough system. Other promising policy changes could include placing individuals with violent histories who have been granted parole on electronic monitoring; returning all community custody individuals who have completed their programming to Hawai'i; and mandating that technical parole violators cannot be returned to prison.

With the state budget in a crisis, and with crime rates dropping, a new Governor could and should safely implement all these modest changes without any new legislation. The vast sums of money now being paid out to private incarcerators could then be shifted to far more productive and pro-social uses, like restoring funding to public education (both lower and higher) and strengthening the very tattered social service safety net.

SOCIAL SERVICES

SUSAN M. CHANDLER

I broke my finger playing softball in Canada one summer and went to an emergency room. As a visitor from Hawai'i, I was concerned that I would need cash to get my finger set, so I kept waving around my wallet and frequently repeated, "I can pay." The consistent response I received from the hospital staff was "Go get an x-ray. Go to the exam room. Don't worry about paying." As a teacher of public policy for over thirty years, I often begin my lectures with a discussion of why this wouldn't happen in Hawai'i (or in any other state), since the U.S. does not have universal health insurance, or a universal, comprehensive delivery system providing social services. Politicians in Hawai'i believe it is "just not possible" to solve the problem of the uninsured, or to consistently and generously help the needy. It took seventy-five years after the passage of the Social Security Act, and four decades after the passage of Medicare and Medicaid (the federal laws that subsidize health insurance for elderly, poor and disabled persons), for the United States to finally pass a comprehensive health insurance reform package.

It wasn't easy. There was unanimous Republican opposition, and shouts that the government is taking over our healthcare . . . and our rights. Hawai'i in 1973 passed its own progressive and innovative Pre-paid Health Care Act, mandating that all employers provide health insurance to those employees who work over 19.5 hours a week. While a good first step, 10 percent of Hawai'i's residents remain uninsured. Now things are getting worse. Hawai'i is cutting deeply into its public and private sector social services programs, and the cuts have been severe and broad-based. Hawai'i is withdrawing its historical commitment to provide an adequate safety net of health and social services. What happened?

CAUSES: INDIVIDUALISM AND INSECURITY

Social services can be described as the organized programs and efforts—public and private—designed to advance human welfare. They include such programs and benefits as housing, income supports, job training, healthcare, childcare, violence protection, and supportive interventions provided directly by government or funded through private organizations to improve the lives of individuals and families, and to strengthen communities. Most social services target needy children, persons with disabilities, the elderly, and poor people. In many communities, charitable and faith-based organizations provide supportive services, but they can not be depended upon to provide the range of services needed in all geographic communities. They do not have the funds or capacity to provide consistently high quality or sufficient services, and they cannot be held responsible to insure services and rights guaranteed by law.

Social services in Hawai'i have become a fragmented array of underfunded programs. They are residual, meaning that they are designed to be a last resort and provided only sparingly . . . and only when private market forces fail. Individuals are expected to work hard, earn sufficient income to provide for themselves and their families, and not expect the government to support them. America's social welfare philosophy is structured to help as few people as possible for the shortest amount of time possible. It is based on a philosophy of *rugged individualism*—those stories of wealthy and successful people who succeeded through hard work and individual entrepreneurialism, without government help or interference. This ignores such unreported and unacknowledged benefits as public education, clean air and water, tax breaks, inheritance polices, etc. In America, individuals in trouble are often blamed for their own poverty, illnesses, and unemployment. Yet while taxpayers quickly rescue banks, and bail out industries that get in trouble, there is a much slower and weaker response when individuals can't afford their mortgages because of predatory lenders, or when a child gets sick and the family cannot afford the medical expenses. These problems are viewed as *mistakes* of individuals who didn't plan well enough or didn't work hard enough. There is not much collective will to help prevent or solve social problems. The popular belief is that the market will fix all things. "Try wait."

In Hawai'i, we are hearing the mantra that we cannot afford to pay for sufficient social services any longer, nor can we increase taxes to deal with our staggering budget deficits. President Reagan often said that the most terrifying words in the English language were "I'm from the government and I'm here to help." Maybe our local politicians agree, since many are now running on pledges to cut taxes and shrink government. Yet, when Katrina hit, or when a tsunami evacuation is ordered, or an oil rig explodes in the Gulf of Mexico, or a man violates a TRO and murders his wife, then people want the government to *hele on* and intervene. "Where's the government's response?" "Why didn't the government prevent that?" "Hey, we need help!" We can't have it both ways.

WHAT'S HAPPENING NOW?

Hawai'i is currently experiencing a serious economic downturn, and expenses are outstripping revenues. As the State budget shrinks, the needs of our most vulnerable citizens increase and become more devastating. This is a terrible equation. In 1999, to re-affirm support for the disadvantaged and vulnerable, the Hawai'i Legislature passed an Emergency and Budget Reserve (Rainy Day) Fund. This fund promised to protect and maintain essential public health, safety, welfare, and education programs against severe revenue fluctuations. Since the State Constitution prohibits a budget deficit, and since 62 percent of the State budget is spent on education, health, and human services, when money got tight, the Rainy Day funds got threatened. The money was almost used to reduce the deficit, or pay for things considered "more essential" than human services.

The poor and vulnerable are politically weak, and often can not be strong advocates for their own needs. They rarely know about the inner workings of the legislature; they rarely attend legislative hearings, buy tickets to fundraisers, or wave signs for political candidates. As a group, they are not well positioned to defend against cuts to their programs and services, and thus watch them fade away.

FLEXIBILITY AND INSECURITY

In 1996, the national and state landscape changed for social services. A new federal law abolished the country's major entitlement program for the poor, called Aid to Families with Dependent Children. The entire federal support system for poor families became time-limited to five years, regardless of the needs or circumstances of individuals, families, or the state. Ready or not . . . cash assistance stops. Even the name of this new program, *Temporary* Assistance to Needy Families, documented the shift away from supporting poor children and families towards *time-limited* cash supports, albeit with some job training and childcare. The formal title of the new law was "The Personal Responsibility and Work Opportunity Reconciliation Act." People already on welfare as well as new applicants without jobs were expected to find a job, and more importantly, get off welfare. It worked relatively well in a booming economy, and most states creamed the crop of their welfare recipients who were able to work. There were also large monetary incentives for the states that did well—defined as reducing the number of people on welfare. States competed for millions of federal dollars in bonuses to reduce their welfare rolls. Those that didn't lost federal dollars.

The new law provided each state with broad discretion about how to design its own welfare programs, to set eligibility and determine benefit levels. Each state received a federal block grant based on its percentage of people living beneath the federal poverty line. This allocation worked well when/if case loads went down. Then states could use the excess to build bridges, provide tax incentives to businesses, fund new programs . . . whatever its legislature liked. In the mid 90s, the economy was producing jobs, so no one seemed too concerned about what would happen when that changed. And no one ever seemed concerned about the fact that the majority of the people receiving welfare benefits—women and their children—were already living in extremely difficult and sometimes dangerous situations. Joining the work force is hard to do for a single parent whose child gets ill, and who has no reliable childcare or transportation, or has a substance addiction, a mental health challenge, a physical disability, low educational achievement, and/or a poor work history. Even if a job can be found, taking kids to pre-school and then going to work by bus, when you live in Wai'anae but the job is in Kalihi, is challenging and precarious. If you are late a few times, you lose the job. However, the real intent of this new law was *not* to reduce poverty, or even help people earn a livable wage. It was primarily to reduce the welfare rolls . . . and it did just that. Now there are many working poor who work hard, earn low wages, and lose their benefits.

Huge federal and state contracts went to for-profit companies who promised to get people off the welfare rolls. One study conducted by the Urban Institute reported that one in five former welfare recipients lack cash, disability benefits, a job, or a working spouse.[1] And since most welfare recipients cannot be found after they leave the system, and are not likely to respond to such surveys, this number is probably significantly underestimated. The lucky ones who find work often make just enough income to bounce them and their children out of eligibility for a variety of social service programs. So they work for low wages, have no health insurance, and in many places cannot afford a place to live. Is this welfare *reform?*

DEVOLUTION: The state-by-state variability of welfare and social service programs resulted in some states providing work supports such as tax credits for low-income earners, but Hawai'i did not. Hawai'i did design several innovative programs such as providing childcare stipends for low-income working parents, and implemented an innovative program called The Bridge to Hope that helped welfare recipients go back to school and find good paying jobs. It also creatively used State funds to support immigrants living in Hawai'i who, due to the new federal law, had become ineligible for federal benefits. To its credit, Hawai'i designed programs that kept benefit levels relatively high until recently. Now however, as the number of unemployed hits a three-decade high, more people are applying for welfare and Food Stamps, but these programs are being cut and the benefit levels are being reduced. It is hard for a family of three to live on $570 a month. The need is going up, but the services are going down. We really don't have accurate data on the impact of these service reductions on the community, but it can't be good.

Federal money started flowing into the states, dramatically increasing the federal deficit and expanding social service programs . . . for a while. Of course, no state wants to turn down federal dollars, but Hawai'i became so dependent upon them that as those funds began to disappear, it began abdicating its previously strong commitment and responsibility to its poor, homeless, and hungry. Hawai'i is not stepping up to fund these needed social services with State funds.

THE "BUSINESS" OF HELPING: Republican Governor Linda Lingle, inaugurated in December 2002, had run on a Reagan-type platform pledging to reduce the size of government and to implement more efficient and effective governmental services at lower costs. Her strategy was to reduce the number of State workers and encourage competition among private businesses and organizations interested in contracting with the State to provide social services. She bought high-paid consultants, who came into the State with innovations and cost saving ideas. Privatizing (i.e., contracting out previously State-run services) just about any and all public services seemed to be the goal. Rather than invest in the public sector, the administration contracted with corporations like Lockheed-Martin, Maximus, Evercare, and America Works to provide health and human services in Hawai'i. Has this worked?

These for-profit corporations, new to the social service industry, came and went, frequently disrupting previously proven best practices in Hawai'i and disrupting long-held relationships between nonprofit service providers, government, and clients. The nonprofit sector that had partnered successfully with many State agencies, and had previously demonstrated efficient, effective, and flexible service delivery, was now being replaced by mainland, for-profit companies that seemed to have little or no commitment to or understanding of the local communities. And when the going got tough, they left, leaving behind big holes in the shredding safety net and a shrunken capacity of the existing agencies and providers to fill in the gaps.

Now, we are seeing increasing social problems all around us. The homeless have moved from wherever they used to hide into much more public places—into neighborhoods and parks all over the islands. Shelters are full. The community food banks are experiencing big increases in demand even while the Food Stamp rolls are growing at an alarming rate—18 percent in the last two years. Unemployment is high, family violence is increasing, the number of families without health insurance is increasing, and Medicaid is going broke. Over the last two years, none of Hawai'i's social or quality of life indicators have been moving in a positive direction.

POINTS OF DEPARTURE

THE PUBLIC-PRIVATE BALANCE: While the public sector must be ultimately responsible for the provision of essential services to people in need, nonprofit agencies are often better positioned to respond quickly and react to new needs. New organizational networks made up of public and private agencies, community organizations, and volunteers are being created to solve complex social problems that one organization cannot solve alone. While the funding and ultimate responsibility for services remains with the government, others add talent, resources, and innovations. This type of collaboration is much too rare in Hawai'i.

Policies are choices. Governor Lingle is choosing to restrict money appropriated by the Legislature for social services, and use it to balance the State budget. Debbie Shimizu, the Executive Director of the National Association of Social Workers in Hawai'i (NASWHI), complied a list of the impacts of some of these recent restrictions to the community.[2] A few examples make the point.

Mental health case managers who normally saw clients thirty hours a month, and were successfully keeping them on their medications and out of the State hospital or ER rooms, were cut to three hours a month. Two million dollars was cut from community and family respite programs for individuals with developmental disabilities. Childcare subsidies for the working poor were cut drastically, while the case load increased by 22 percent. Healthy Start, a nationally recognized program to prevent child abuse, was cut from a high of $18 million to $1.2 million. Huge cuts were taken from domestic violence programs and essential shelter programs. Over 600 positions were cut from the State's health and human services agencies, and more than 200 more are planned. Even in the face of these looming fiscal challenges and assaults on the safety net, legislators cannot muster a 2/3-majority vote to override the Governor's announced plan to veto anything that looks like a tax hike.

WHAT NEEDS TO CHANGE?

MANAGE THE CUTS: The first thing that must be done is to stop the cuts to social services. It certainly should be obvious that if you decimate a program like Healthy Start, which has been empirically proven to reduce child abuse and protect children from re-abuse, then bad outcomes will occur. The Lingle Administration takes credit for reducing the number of children entering the child protection system and living in foster homes, which is an excellent accomplishment, but then cuts to the bone the very program that it had contracted with to do just that. Investing in service programs that prevent social problems and promote human welfare is vital to the quality of life in Hawai'i. The restructuring and limiting of government responsibility has profoundly influenced and negatively altered the availability of social services. All levels of government must play a role in developing policies and programs that expand opportunities, address social and economic justice, and improve the quality of life for Hawai'i's people.

CHALLENGES

COLLABORATIVE DECISION-MAKING: Hawai'i has experienced budget problems before. After 9/11 the State needed to cut back its expenditures. It did, but with community-based, criteria-driven strategies. State agencies, legislators, community groups, churches, social services providers, foundations, businesses, and other community leaders came together to find solutions that reduced expenditures. They asked questions such as "Which programs and services are most essential? What cuts just cannot be made because the result will be too severe? Could such needed services be provided in another way?" These discussions helped Hawai'i move through the bad times without seeing bad outcomes.

The State needs to continue its investment in people and programs that reduce poverty, prevent family violence, support public education, and reduce homelessness by assisting families to find affordable shelter. We know how to do these things by providing effective social services. Becoming dependent on federal dollars is only a temporary fix. Even the infusion of federal stimulus funds is time-limited. Then what? Oddly, those high-paid consultants who have now left, do not seem to have answers for that . . . no matter what we paid for their advice.

A GOOD IDEA: The State has recently passed the Hawai'i 2050 Sustainability Plan. This plan defines sustainability as "a Hawai'i that respects the culture, character, beauty and history of the state's island communities; strikes a balance between economic, social and environmental priorities and meets

the needs of the present without compromising the ability of future generations to meet their own needs."[3] This statement of goals directs Hawai'i to
look ahead towards a more comprehensive way of insuring a high quality of
life across our communities. Supporting and adequately funding effective social services and the policies that support them advances human welfare. We
know how to this in Hawai'i. We can. We must.

HOMELESSNESS

TRISHA KEHAULANI WATSON

If civilization is to survive, we must cultivate the science of human rela-
tionships—the ability of all peoples, of all kinds, to live together, in the
same world at peace.
                                                            —Franklin D. Roosevelt

RESTORING OUR HOME: HOPE, HOMELESSNESS, AND HUMANITY

Our land was our home.

In pre-contact times, Hawaiians enjoyed community living, where individuals shared sleeping spaces and living spaces as families. With a lack of
motorized transportation, most travel required people to sleep out beneath
the sky. We made do in nature's many elements. Our intimate relationship
with our Earth Mother, Papahānaumoku, and Sky Father, Wākea, granted
us exemplary knowledge about navigating the land and utilizing it to survive.
To sleep out on the land was to sleep in the bosom of our Mother, and since
the dawn of time, humans have known no greater or more comforting rest
than when lying against their Mother's heart.

The land was not only our home, it was our refuge, inscribed in one of
the greatest and best known laws of the Hawaiian Kingdom, Māmalahoe
Kānāwai (Law of the Splintered Paddle):

E nā kānaka,	O my people,
E mālama ʻoukou i ke akua	Honor thy god;
A e mālama hoʻi ke kanaka nui a me kanaka iki;	Respect the rights of all men great and humble;
E hele ka ʻelemakule, ka luahine, a me ke kama	See to it that our elderly, our women, and our children
A moe i ke ala	Lie down to sleep by the roadside
ʻAʻohe mea nāna e hoʻopilikia.	Without fear of harm.
Hewa nō, make.	Disobey, and die.
—Kamehameha I[1]	

The need for people to seek such refuge has not changed. Our society has changed. Our relationship to the land has changed. Our relationships with each other have changed. If we are to heal our world, we must learn to restore the ways we related to each other as members of a community, as members of a larger social family who share this home. We should be ashamed of how we allow our brothers and sisters to live. We should be utterly ashamed of how we are allowing kūpuna to live. Homelessness in Hawai'i is a community's failing, not the failing of individuals. I refuse to believe that any individual ever needs to be, or should be, homeless. The answers are to be found in people, not policies. We must be better. We must renew our commitment to stewardship of one another. We must restore Hawai'i as a home for all people—a place where we are inclusive, not exclusive.

A HAWAIIAN SENSE OF COMMUNITY

Like many non-Western peoples, Kānaka Maoli viewed community differently. Their entire society depended upon the function of the community. As civil rights activist Howard Thurman explains,

> The working definition of community is the experience of wholeness, of completeness, of inner togetherness, of integration, and wherever this is experienced, at whatever level of life, at that particular level there is community. . . . [T]he individual human being experiences in his organism this definition of community. As if the organism, all the parts, had committed to the memory a sense of the whole, a social sense which is the overtone of the biological inner-continuity. Now this is the heritage.[2]

Over the last 250 years, foreigners systemically dismantled this sense of wholeness within the Hawaiian Islands. The result is the fragmented community we find ourselves amongst today.

Keeping families together was of the utmost importance to Hawaiians—and not only the immediate family in Western terms, but an extended family more consistent with the kauhale living system of pre-contact Hawai'i. Handy and Pukui have written about this system: "Kinship in Hawai'i extends far beyond the immediate biological family. The terminology of kinship must be thought of against the background of the whole community of kith and kin, including in-law, and adoptive categories."[3] This system allowed for greater social and community support for all individuals, as the family parcelled out responsibilities in ways that allowed everyone to use their time and resources well.

The kauhale system received a devastating blow when foreign diseases began to ravage the islands as early as the late eighteenth century. The kauhale system depended on a healthy population that could reproduce itself. When foreign diseases led to rampant death and infertility, the system began to crumble within a single generation. By the time missionaries arrived in 1820, the health of the Hawaiian population was already severely compromised, making the social structure vulnerable to external influences, however detrimental they might be to the long-term well-being of the community.

The impact of foreign disease on the Hawaiian population cannot be understated, with a cumulative effect on the extended family and family systems in Hawai'i. Ahupua'a land maintenance relied upon large extended family units for support and labor—the idea behind the kauhale system. When foreign disease cut into the numbers of family members available to maintain the land and family community, the entire kauhale structure began to erode. When a living system depends upon the health of the extended family, any illness, physical or social, will harm the entire community.

Because of these circumstances, Hawaiians out of necessity left their kauhale living systems, and moved into the growing urban environments developed to suit the needs of missionaries and western businessmen. The mimicry of western living in Hawai'i's growing urban sectors reflected the foreigners' desire to model life in Hawai'i after their places of origin. But with western living came western problems.

A HISTORY OF WESTERN HOMELESSNESS

It's unclear what homelessness in the continental United States would have looked like prior to the industrial revolution. Without large cities and urban dwellings from which people could be segregated and excluded, it is difficult to recognize homelessness, at least as we know it today.

Much like Hawai'i prior to western contact, rural America lived off the land's natural resources. United States expansion westward during the nineteenth century required the roaming of otherwise "homeless" individuals, and a continental community that accepted and assisted them. It was the enforcement of exclusionary principles—this is mine, not yours—built up during the long periods of conflict with Native Americans and of slavery that served as the basis for the uncompromising individualism and social fragmentation that led to homelessness in the United States.

American histories of homelessness are extremely ethnocentric, looking almost exclusively at the living conditions of white Americans. But after western arrival, Native Americans were displaced and excluded from land claimed by western settlers, and African-Americans, denied the property privileges of Anglo-Americans, had to find other means of surviving.

Yet, by the end of the nineteenth century, white Americans were also facing issues related to homelessness. As early as the Civil War, individuals, primarily men, were using the railroad system to wander from city to city. But this population garnered little attention in its day. Far more disturbing were the problems developing in the urban settlements, but it was the publication of Jacob Riis's *How the Other Half Lives: Studies among the Tenements of New York* in 1890 that forced people to realize the horrid living conditions of people in settlements.

Here, the history of homelessness in Hawai'i and the continental United States intersect. As slums were developing in the inner cores of American cities, parallel living conditions were arising in Hawai'i's growing urban core. But while Riis's book brought about some reprieve on the continent, little improvement would be seen here.

If anything, the situation only worsened during the Territorial Era. Homelessness across the United States, including Hawai'i, increased during national economic stressors like the Depression, but it wasn't until the 1960s that federal policies set the stage for epidemic levels of homelessness. In 1963, the federal government passed the Community Mental Health Act, which resulted in large numbers of mental health facilities deinstitutionalizing their residents. Without a suitable support system of services, many former patients were forced onto the streets with little or no means of obtaining resources. Generations of urbanization left people without the survival skills that had served others prior to individualization, and notions of family unity and obligations had also changed, leaving Americans with much less sense of responsibility to their extended family or less-fortunate family members. This not only contributed to rising homelessness throughout the country, but was a precursor for the neglect and alienation of the elderly.

Hawai'i's geographic isolation provided protection from an otherwise growing American problem. But homeless Americans began to find their way to Hawai'i, with its tropical weather and liberal public benefits laws. In 2008, a study by the University of Hawai'i showed that nearly half the homeless receiving services in Hawai'i were not lifetime residents, with over 60 percent of those individuals having lived in Hawai'i less than ten years.[4] Many of the homeless in Hawai'i, however, have not just come from the continent: 22 percent have come from other islands in the Pacific. Studies have shown that 20,000 migrants from Micronesia have come to Hawai'i in search of medical and other services that were not made available to them in their home countries, despite agreements with the U.S. that they would be provided in consideration for the United States's use of the islands for nuclear testing in the twentieth century.[5] Hawai'i made up for its moderate social policies, however, through its land use conflicts, which forced the homeless to face efforts to criminalize activities associated with not having a permanent residence.

ACT 50: OUTLAWING HOMELESSNESS

In 2004, while public officials spoke of developing transition and low-income housing, they were also moving a bill through the State legislature that would outlaw the way of life many Native homeless families had grown accustomed to. Senate Bill 2294 amended the

> provision relating to criminal trespass in the 2nd degree. Provid[ed] that a person commits the offense of criminal trespass in the 2nd degree if the person enters or remains unlawfully in or upon commercial premises or public property after a reasonable warning or request to leave by the owners or lessee or their authorized agent or a police officer.[6]

Upon passage, the bill became Act 50. Advocacy groups locally and nationally were outraged, but the State quickly began to use the law against the homeless. In April 2005, hundreds of protestors demonstrated at the Capitol in an effort to encourage legislators to repeal the bill. The conflict garnered national attention. As the National Coalition for the Homeless and the National Law Center on Homelessness and Poverty explained in a 2006 report, "A Dream Denied: The Criminalization of the Homeless in U.S. Cities":

> The protestors asked legislators to fund more homeless programs and shelters, and urged them to repeal Act 50, a law aimed at removing squatters from public parks and beaches. Bob Nakata, pastor of the Kahaluʻu United Methodist Church, noted, "Legally there's no place a homeless person can be except in a shelter and the shelters are full." In addition, the ACLU of Hawaiʻi challenged the constitutionality of the law in federal court, arguing the law is too vague and could be used to ban anyone from public property for any reason.

> In addition, Margot Schrine of Partners in Care says sweeps are conducted throughout the island on an ongoing basis, as well as being instigated by neighborhood resident complaints. According to Schrine, these raids make it difficult for outreach workers to serve people living on beaches or in parks.[7]

Despite tremendous abuse of the law by enforcement officers, a bill to change the offense from a felony to a petty misdemeanor ran into difficulties getting through the legislature.[8] The following session, the penalties were reduced through the passage of HB806, which amended Act 50 to create a section of the law that focused solely on the homeless. While advocates still fought the law, noting that police used it to arrest both "squatters" and others caught in public places, the legislature refused to back down.

The ACLU quickly responded with a lawsuit, forming a coalition with the Interfaith Alliance Hawai'i and the Kōkua Council to sue the State over a law it considered to be too vague. But Senate President Robert Bunda refused to back down: "I say let's go on with the lawsuit—let the attorney general go and fight this in court and see where we end up."[9] In the complaint, the ACLU charged that under Act 50, "a person need not engage in any misconduct to be banned from public property. Rather, it is enough that the police officer or authorized person finds the individual to be unsavory or disagrees with the content or message of the individual's speech or activity." The ACLU and other nonprofit organizations found that police officers aggressively used the law to displace houseless residents at parks and beaches, but offered no assistance to improve their situation.

This only worsened conditions for the houseless, because real estate prices were being pushed up by low interest rates, leading to dramatic increases in rental prices throughout the state. Many families were forced out of their rental units. And with nowhere else to go, they ended up on the beaches.

Despite the public outcry, Bunda got other representatives to subscribe to his position, which relentlessly employed stereotypes of the homeless. But politics at the Senate would help to resolve this issue for the State, as State Senator Colleen Hanabusa successfully unseated Bunda as Senate President in 2006, and Act 50 was repealed altogether that session.

While this was an important victory for the homeless, their conflicts with the State would continue. The homeless are constantly subjected to eviction efforts by the State, City, and private property owners. Sometimes known as "sweeps," these disruptions make it difficult to create stable environments for families, or continuity in receiving support services. Until the approach towards addressing homelessness is holistic and based on community and healing, the problems will continue.

OUR LAND, OUR HOME

Homelessness began with the dismantling of communities and the removal of people from their land. Hawaiians have been the most impacted by these trends, but they are not alone. It is critical to relate the separation of people from their land to the separation of Native people from their families and sense of community. They are intimately interrelated. One Wai'anae woman reflects:

> I see a kind of building up of groups of people, small groups of people wanting to go back and work the land, wanting to find out where the "mana" is, the spiritual power that will hold them together. How you separate people is when you begin to take away some of the things that mean very much to

them. . . . Now big corporations come, big-money people come in and say, "Hey, wait a minute, now, you've been hogging this land, and you've been hogging the water. We want some of it; we want you to turn off some and let us have some of that. We're going to build these big condominiums and these big townhouses." I'm not talking about this from hearsay. I've seen these things happen.[10]

The connections between Hawaiians and their land and natural resources are more than just metaphors. They are microcosms of Hawaiian living. They are examples of how a healthy community lives.

Perhaps our greatest embarrassment is that we have allowed more and more kūpuna to live on the streets alone. This is unacceptable. It is shameful. We all must begin to create opportunities which allow for the extended family unit to redevelop and function, or social illness will continue to devastate our entire community. We must all embrace traditional Hawaiian values, especially in respect to the family. Hawaiian concepts of stewardship were not simply about the land. They were about the family, because the land is our family. Our stewardship must not only extend to Hawai'i as our shared place, it must extend to one another.

The extended family and the kauhale system created the foundation of the community in traditional Hawaiian living systems. The extended family unit came first. Only in modern times do we prioritize the individual above the family or community, and believe that the individual must be cured first. But through the healing of the family and the community, individuals will heal. Part of the problem with modern western solutions to social problems is that they try to rehabilitate individuals without understanding that individuals need healthy communities or families to return to. As long as families and communities remain dysfunctional, individuals will not be healthy. Addressing homelessness is not about rehabilitating individuals, it is about rehabilitating our community.

Moving forward, we must adopt an approach to homelessness that honors and values Hawaiian living. It must be preventative and holistic; it must be realistic. The following strategies would be a start:

Offer tax credits for a limited number of years (similar to the Hope or American Opportunity tax credits) for extended family members sharing a residence due to financial or medical hardship;

Offer tax credits for taking care of elderly parents;

Reduce permitting restrictions for families refitting their home to take care of elderly or disabled family members;

Offer tax credits for remodeling done to accommodate elderly or disabled family members;

Provide greater judicial review of power of attorney actions for the elderly;

Treat drug abuse like a disease, not a crime;

Create adequate medical facilities in Micronesia, so residents are not forced to migrate to Hawai'i;

Give greater power and increased federal funding to states to institutionalize the chronically, mentally ill, particularly those with a history of violence;

Create designated "open spaces" where semi-permanent structures can be built by people in possession of long-term, renewable leases that provide security, outreach services, and opportunities for sustainable living (i.e., farming and fishing).

Many shelters are full. Some of those that aren't demand adherence to rules and regulations that prove too much for some people.[11] There need to be alternatives that are safe and healthy, yet maintain a respect for people's freedoms. Homelessness is not a crime, and the homeless should not be treated as criminals. Further, Native Hawaiians make up the largest percentage of homeless in Hawai'i (Hawaiians = 29 percent, Caucasian = 28 percent, Other Pacific Islanders = 22 percent);[12] if families were given more support to take care of their family members, this would free up resources and services for those without family in Hawai'i.

Residents along the beach in Wai'anae often remind me that they are not homeless, but houseless, because Hawai'i is their home. Right now it cannot be much of a home to any of us, because we have dismantled what makes Hawai'i home.

It is time to restore it.

DOMESTIC VIOLENCE

SUSAN HIPPENSTEELE

I moved to Hawai'i as a teenager, and have lived in many different neighborhoods—first in Wai'anae for several years, later 'Aiea, Hawai'i Kai, and Kailua—and now in Honolulu. Each neighborhood I've lived in had its own unique subculture—all have been tight-knit. I knew my neighbors and they knew me. We watched each others' houses and knew each others' kids. If someone moved in or out of the neighborhood, we all noticed immediately. Newcomers were greeted, and information about them circulated through the neighborhood quickly.

I have also worked in many capacities with victims of abuse and violence. As a young adult, I lived on the Wai'anae Coast and worked at an organization that provided education and other services to kids with substance abuse problems. I met kids only a few years younger than me who were struggling to navigate domestic violence and sexual abuse. I was not "local," so my house served as a temporary escape for some of those kids. I helped several file police reports, and drove some into town to try and set them up with advocacy and counseling services that didn't exist yet in Wai'anae. I was young, inexperienced, and naive. I had a difficult time comprehending, on those drives back home, why no one was available to provide the protection and support those kids needed.

My best friend at the time married a man whose entire family lived in Wai'anae. She came to work most Mondays with bruises on her face and body. She told everyone, including me for awhile, that she was accident prone. No one believed her. She eventually explained to me that at first, she called the police when her husband beat her. But several of his relatives were police officers, and her "reports" were never filed. After her husband set their house on fire and drove her around the island at gunpoint for several hours during a drinking binge, she left the island and returned to a family she had not seen for nearly a decade. To the best of my knowledge, her husband was never arrested.

Twenty years later, after working as a victims' advocate on the University of Hawai'i Mānoa campus for several years, I went to law school. I began working as a family law attorney, and again saw victims of violence and abuse who had nowhere to go. But by that time, services for victims of domestic violence had expanded quite a bit. Although most agencies and programs were overextended and struggling to meet community needs, I was usually able to connect my clients with counseling, emergency shelter, and other important services. I could also help them through whatever legal process they wanted to use to try and keep an abuser from further harming them and/or their kids. But I couldn't help them escape for good.

Hawai'i is a unique place to live. Geographically isolated, residents of these islands have ready access to many advantages of big city life—diverse employment and education opportunities, a network of State and city services, art galleries, museums, restaurants and movie theatres, stimulating nightlife, and a chance to meet new and interesting people. We also enjoy many of the benefits associated with living in a small town. We raise our children in tight-knit communities, have ready access to extended family, know our neighbors, run into people we grew up with on a regular basis, and learn to respect others' privacy by minding our own business.

Most people reading this book probably don't think too much about escaping the small-town aspects of living in Hawai'i—we head to neighbor islands to visit friends and family or just "get away," and travel back and forth to Las Vegas and the West Coast with relative ease.

Victims of domestic violence think about escape differently from the rest of us. For them, the small-town aspects of Hawai'i can be a prison. Moving to a new neighborhood or relocating to another island rarely offers the anonymity victims of domestic violence need to feel safe. The small-town atmosphere the rest of us enjoy is a double-edged sword for those who need protection from the very friends, neighbors, and coworkers we greet every day.

SCOPE OF THE PROBLEM

Since 1997 there have been seventy-three domestic violence homicides in the state. In his December 2008 series "Crossing the Line: Abuse in Hawaii Homes," *Honolulu Advertiser* reporter Rob Perez wrote that Hawai'i has consistently had one of the highest per capita rates of domestic violence homicide in the U.S.[1] Perez also noted that data from the State Attorney General show that reports of abuse of family and household members, arrests for domestic violence, and misdemeanor prosecutions for domestic violence have declined dramatically throughout the state since 1996, while calls to hotlines, protective order filings, arrests for violations of protective orders, and shelter demand all increased during this same period. Most recent Hawai'i State Judiciary data show that in 2009, filings for Domestic

Abuse Protective Orders with Hawai'i Family Courts have doubled since 1996—increasing from 2,553 to 5,095.[2] State of Hawai'i data show that in 2006, local domestic service providers received more than 25,000 calls for information and referral services, while 6,707 calls were made to domestic violence hotlines that same year.[3] A University of Hawai'i/Attorney General report suggests that as many as 44,000 local children are exposed to domestic violence annually.[4]

Because many studies of domestic violence rely on data from victim service programs and shelters, some believe the true picture of abuse has yet to emerge. Many domestic violence service providers and advocates suggest that the majority of victims do not report or seek help in addressing abuse. There are many reasons, including shame, fear of reprisal, lack of faith in law enforcement, reliance on the income of an abuser, and concern for the safety and welfare of children. Victims with resources—money for a hotel, family members with enough space for a victim with children, access to private divorce attorneys—will often not be visible to the victim service system as well. Other victims, such as members of some ethnic groups—recent immigrants in particular—may not be familiar with U.S. social service systems, and may not be comfortable contacting law enforcement or service providers for fear of mistreatment or even deportation.

An additional problem for those trying to understand the scope of the domestic violence problem in our communities is that data about perpetrators are often gleaned from arrest and conviction records, which means those data are subject to the same biases that influence public perceptions of substance abuse and other social problems—for instance, that low-income racial minorities experience higher rates than other groups. In Hawai'i, a common perception is that Hawaiians, Pacific Islanders, and Filipinos are most likely to be both victims and perpetrators of domestic violence. To a certain extent, the arrest and conviction data support this perception. However, when we consider that members of these groups are more likely to live in poverty than Caucasians and those from the Asian continent, and that low income people are more likely to be visible to both the victim service system and the courts, conclusions about direct correlations between ethnicity and domestic violence are suspect.

Perhaps the most significant problem, though, is that while most of us "recognize" domestic violence when we see its evidence in bruises, cuts, and broken bones, we often fail to understand the complexity and impact of assertions of power and control by perpetrators. No one stays in a violent or abusive relationship because they want to. They stay, with or without children, because they don't feel they have a choice, or because they want to find a way to end the violence so their relationship can return to "normal."

The power and control perpetrators of domestic violence assert often make intervention and treatment complicated for entire families. All family members, including perpetrators, may need an array of services to be safe, and to heal from physical and/or psychological wounds, whether they remain together as a family or not. Tending to the needs of children who have experienced and/or witnessed domestic violence is especially important to prevent future generations from repeating unhealthy patterns.

COMMUNITY RESPONSE TO DOMESTIC VIOLENCE

We read accounts of intimate partner violence and murder in Hawai'i and immediately ask ourselves several questions. Where did it occur? Who was the perpetrator? Did she file a protective order? Where were the police? What's wrong with the system? Why didn't she leave?

We have many ways of distancing ourselves from the realities of domestic violence in our communities. If it occurs on a military base, it's not our problem. If it happens in a distant neighborhood, it's not our problem. If there was a history of violence and the victim didn't leave, s/he is at fault. If a victim didn't file for a protective order, s/he should have. If s/he did file for a protective order, the police are at fault since they didn't provide adequate protection.

To a certain extent, it is understandable that we distance ourselves from the reality of domestic violence in our communities. Without personal experience of domestic violence, we may have a very difficult time understanding the myriad ways victims and families feel trapped by economic, geographic, familial, and other circumstances. Some of the stories we read in the paper are truly horrific, and emphasize the behavior and actions of victims while minimizing the responsibility of perpetrators. Most of us have no idea what to do if we do learn about, or witness, domestic violence in our families or neighborhoods. Moreover, there have been instances of harm to good Samaritans who have tried to intervene and protect victims from attack that reinforce our inclination not to get involved.

Unfortunately, denial of the scope and complexity of domestic violence has made us insensitive to the dynamics of domestic violence and the needs of families affected by it. We have failed as a community to ensure that there are adequate numbers of trained and competent providers working in domestic violence prevention and response programs. We assume without knowing that the emergency shelter system is adequate, and we generally trust that first responders are adequately trained and responsive to domestic violence when it does occur. The result is a system that is inadequately resourced and has failed to meet the needs of many, if not most, victims.

Moreover, our uniqueness as a geographically isolated state makes efforts to prevent family violence all the more crucial. Families affected by domestic violence who live in rural communities on the continent might experience the same small-town barriers to finding reliable help in their immediate communities, but they have a much easier time relocating than those who live in these islands.

WHO IS ACCOUNTABLE?

The network of services for addressing intimate partner and family violence in Hawai'i evolved in a manner quite similar to that of the continental U.S. At present, we have over twenty agencies and organizations statewide that provide emergency information, shelter services, transitional housing, counseling and support, and legal and other forms of assistance. In recent years, some agencies in Hawai'i have made an effort to expand services to address the unique needs of specific groups of victims, including immigrants. But like most states, we have not provided an adequate level of service, and many victims of family violence who seek help do not receive it.

On September 15, 2009, the National Census of Domestic Violence Services conducted their annual nationwide study of the services provided by participating programs during a single twenty-four hour period. Ninety-four percent of the identified domestic violence programs in Hawai'i participated. The data are sobering: 505 victims serviced in one day, including 333 adults and children who received non-residential assistance in the form of individual counseling, legal advocacy, or children's support groups, and 107 emergency hotline calls answered. Most disturbing, however, were thirty-five unmet requests for services during that single twenty-four hour period. Of the unmet requests, twenty-four were from victims who sought, but could not receive, emergency shelter to escape from violence in their homes.[5]

The National Census reports that 41 percent of the participating domestic violence programs in Hawai'i report both insufficient staffing and funding. Only 35 percent of the programs were able to provide emergency shelter; 12 percent provided transitional housing. And although 76 percent of the programs reported providing individual counseling or advocacy, only 18 percent provided advocacy related to immigration, and even fewer, 12 percent, provided legal advocacy.

The Hawai'i data are alarming and the national picture is not much better. But there are some important differences between domestic violence service provision nationally and in Hawai'i that are worth thinking about. Roughly the same percentage of programs nationally report insufficient

funding for needed programs and services, yet nationally 30 percent reported insufficient staffing compared to 40 percent locally. Nationally, 60 percent of unmet need requests were for emergency shelter or housing, while
in Hawai'i, the figure was 69 percent. And while Hawai'i has a significantly
higher and more diverse immigrant population than most states—roughly
18 percent of the state's overall population and 25 percent of the population
on O'ahu—nationally 11 percent of programs reported limited funding for
translators, bilingual staff, and/or accessible equipment, compared with 18
percent here.

The recent economic downturn has further stretched programs' abilities
to meet the needs of domestic violence victims they serve. Local advocates
report that most programs have seen a 40 percent or greater loss of funding
over the past two years. All services are stretched, with reductions in staffing,
and some services have nearly disappeared, including visitation and drop-off
centers. These centers have provided crucial monitoring during children's
visits with a parent who has a history of violence, and offer a safe environment in which children can be dropped off and picked up by parents. Local
service providers report that most programs have had to redirect most or all
of their resources to emergency intervention, leaving important longer term
support, training, counseling for batterers, and prevention education needs
unmet. One advocate put the current problem succinctly when she said that
right now, the system is "reactive": there are resources available to a victim "if
she falls, but nothing in place to keep her from falling."

It is challenging to try and track actual domestic violence service needs
across the state. Data collection is not uniform, so service programs keep records that do not always line up. Statewide law enforcement first responder
data do not reflect rates of calls involving domestic violence; the only data
available show aggregate figures for all domestic calls that result in a report,
regardless of the relationship between a victim and perpetrator. And while
there is ample critique of law enforcement response to domestic violence, and
anecdotal data on the difficulty victims face if they do file reports, there is a
dearth of specific data and other information that would enable law enforcement to enact meaningful reform.

The cultural diversity of Hawai'i has complicated provision of services to
victims of domestic violence. Most of the agencies and programs in Hawai'i
employ western (U.S.) trained staff familiar with a model of service provision
and legal advocacy that alienates some local people and immigrants. Some
agency directors, staff, and direct service providers live in Hawai'i a very short
time before going to work in these programs. And while the road to domestic
violence prevention and response is certainly paved with good intentions, and

non-local service providers can provide a level of anonymity some victims seek, there is no substitute for direct knowledge and experience with, or explicit training about, the unique cultural and geographic milieu in which domestic violence occurs around the state.

Overall, domestic violence prevention and response is much more sophisticated than it was when I began working with victims almost 25 years ago. First responders receive more training, a wider range of both emergency and tertiary services to families have been created, and programs for batterers have been developed and implemented in many parts of the state. But in some respects, the economic downturn has put us back to where we were two decades ago, as programs have been forced to cut staff, and crucial prevention education, long-term safety, counseling, and other services have been reduced or eliminated in favor of emergency services. The long-term result will be devastating. The domestic violence community learned long ago that emphasis on legal and emergency intervention does not produce the long-term change in attitude and behavior necessary to reduce violence in our communities.

PRESCRIPTION FOR CHANGE

What can we, as a community, do to improve the network of services to prevent and respond to domestic violence?

First, it is crucial that existing programs receive adequate funding. While emergency service provision is crucial, the needs of victims, their families, and batterers extend well beyond an immediate need for intervention after a violent incident has occurred. Batterer services are relatively new, and the current funding environment has resulted in a renewed focus on victims and reduced attention to families and batterers. One result is that batterer accountability is deemphasized, and services that might help prevent recurrence of violence are increasingly rare. Prevention education efforts have also been reduced or eliminated, including some of those that have been developed in our public schools—a loss with long-term implications for service provision needs, and of course, for the well-being of future families.

Second, services for victims and families must be able to address the unique needs of different communities on each island. An effective network of domestic violence services on Hawai'i Island will be different from an effective network of services on Maui or O'ahu. County by county efforts to tailor services to address differences due to geography, population, and culture are being stymied by reductions in funding and loss of staff. In some areas, services are being delivered by networks of volunteers, but this approach is not sustainable in the long-term.

Third, data collection needs to be comprehensive and systematized to ensure accountability among first responders, State agencies, and other programs. Adequate documentation of the scope of the domestic violence problem in our communities will enable lawmakers and service programs to direct resources where they are necessary, and develop effective responses to unmet needs. A periodic system for evaluating the entire domestic violence service network that includes funding pattern impact on law enforcement responses, emergency intervention services, prevention education, long-term victim and family counseling, and batterer services is long overdue.

Fourth, lawmakers must be held accountable for their role in supporting, or failing to support, legislation and funding for domestic violence prevention and response services. Domestic violence laws have been strengthened, and in 2007 the Judiciary expanded some family court services. These changes in law and increased judicial resources for responding to domestic violence are important, but many victims don't want legal services. They want the violence to end so they can keep their families together. That result requires services that may be more complicated and long-term, and at this point in time, unavailable in many communities around the state.

Meeting the needs of families affected by domestic violence requires community support and additional funding. We must ask lawmakers direct questions about their knowledge of domestic violence, and seek proof of their commitment to fund adequately a full range of necessary services. Most will express dismay about the problem, but only those who understand its depths will take the necessary steps, including raising taxes, that will ensure that our communities become safer, and that the entire range of domestic violence services needs, from prevention education in schools, to emergency shelter for families, to counseling for batterers, are met.

HEALTH AND HEALTHCARE

DEANE NEUBAUER

HAWAI'I THE HEALTH STATE

The intense partisan national debate over healthcare has, ironically, tended to obscure some of the history of efforts within the U.S. to provide it. During his first term as president, Richard Nixon, consistent with then-Republican Party ideas that the states rather than the federal government should take the lead in various aspects of social policy, advocated for expansion of healthcare coverage for "the rest" of the population. This movement followed up the creation of Medicaid and Medicare during the Johnson presidency. Alone among the major industrial countries of the world, the U.S. lacked some form of universal healthcare coverage, and action by the states could serve to close the gap between those who did have insurance, primarily but hardly universally through employment, and those served by the somewhat new national programs.

Hawai'i was the only state to pass such legislation: the Prepaid Healthcare Act in 1974, which created an employer mandate to supply healthcare for much of the working population and their families. Despite legal and political challenges to "Prepaid" as it came to be called, the law survived, and by the mid-1980s it had created a distinctive identity for Hawai'i healthcare. On many levels the label of the health state appeared justified. According to many indicators, people in Hawai'i had better health status than mainland counterparts, and enjoyed higher levels of care, especially primary care, at less cost. According to the data, Hawai'i had

The lowest infant mortality (tied with Vermont)

The lowest rates of premature mortality in the nation —
    for heart disease (one-third less than the national average)
    for cancer (one-fourth less than the national average)
    and for lung disease (one-half the national average)

Low rates of hospital use (one-third less than the national average)

Low emergency room use rates[1]

In accounting for these outcomes, John Lewin, Governor Waihee's Director of Health, emphasized that plantation healthcare had effectively extended primary care, and unique among the states, the basic insurance duopoly of HMSA and Kaiser, while restricting competition in the classic sense, did create two relatively low-cost insurance alternatives. Kaiser was widely viewed in the 1980s as a model for health maintenance organizations, which federal decision-makers saw as cost-effective alternatives to traditional stand-alone practitioner models. HMSA for its part could claim that among Blue Cross and Blue Shield organizations in the U.S., it had the lowest administrative costs, thus returning the largest fraction of the healthcare insurance dollar to providers and subscribers.[2]

Hawai'i also had the lowest percentage nationally of persons without healthcare insurance throughout the 1990s and into the first decade of the twenty-first century. On the mainland U.S., such figures ranged between 12 and 15 percent of the population; in Hawai'i, the spread was between 6.5 and 8.5 percent. Other policy features dating from the Nixon Administration, such as the Certificate of Need process, checked the growth of healthcare facilities, which in turn acted as a brake on cost escalation. Finally, at that time Hawai'i, and especially O'ahu, had significant professional resources, notably physicians, and with the opening of the new John A. Burns School of Medicine, the state seemed to be insuring an adequate physician base for the future.

Significant challenges remained, however, especially in the distribution of health outcomes and status. By the mid-1980s, social changes were transforming health and healthcare environments. The rapid decline of the plantation economy, which had served as a bedrock for providing relatively simple but effective primary healthcare, led to a contraction in coverage for this group of workers. (Plantations lost about 50,000 workers over two decades.) The rapidly growing service sector—and tourism above all—tended to be less well paying, and featured higher levels of part-time employment that deliberately fell below the level of the Prepaid mandate for the employer. Mirroring most developed countries, the rapidly aging population increased demands for healthcare services. The relative shortage of long-term care beds, especially for the elderly, had created an endemic problem by the end of the decade. And as the population grew throughout the 1990s, the more than ample supply of healthcare professionals turned into persistent and growing deficits. Noticeable very early on in nursing, as Hawai'i became a major importer of nurses, primarily from the Philippines, the decline in active physicians continued to increase, especially outside Oʻahu.

Steadily growing costs during this period brought the wellness movement to the fore, an effort to promote individual responsibility for health by emphasizing prudence in diet, exercise, and effective monitoring of individual health status. The rationale for such programs is simple and compelling: if individual health improves, sickness and disease in the population are likely to decline, and along with them the burdens on all aspects of the healthcare system. As critics were quick to point out, such measures and behaviors are powerfully affected by social class and economic status, with the poor having far less knowledge and ability to embrace such actions; by social tendencies to "produce" behavioral options that run against such strictures, such as the proliferation of the fast food culture, which is linked throughout the world to increases in obesity and diabetes; and by actions within the professional healthcare system itself to "medicalize" behavior, and thereby contribute to overall healthcare costs through increased interactions.

Throughout the postwar period, any assessment of health status in Hawaiʻi always has been deserving of a caveat that separated out the indigenous population from others. For almost every basic health indicator, Hawaiians and other Polynesians displayed lower levels of health, and a considerably shorter life expectancy. For example, while Hawaiʻi life expectancy overall has increased over the past sixty years by about eleven years, Hawaiians and other Polynesians continue to lag behind by a constant amount of seven to eight years. (In 1950, Hawaiian life expectancy was approximately sixty-two; by 1990 this had increased to seventy-three.) In 2002, Hawaiians also had some of the worst statistics in Hawaiʻi for morbid obesity, substance abuse, depression and other mental illnesses, diabetes, respiratory illnesses, heart disease, and cancer mortality.[3] Efforts to address the health and healthcare needs of Hawaiians led to the passage of the Native Hawaiian Health Improvement Act of 1988, which established Papa Ola Lōkahi and subsequently the Native Hawaiian Health Care Systems program.

INTO THE PRESENT

The explosive growth in healthcare costs, now totaling almost 18 percent of the Gross Domestic Product, has dominated healthcare policy decisions since the 1980s. Explanations for this explosion differ, but most observers agree on some basic and common factors, many of which are now fundamental features of contemporary healthcare. Perhaps foremost has been the increase in the reach and complexity of healthcare technology, which is a driver of costs throughout the world. As scientific and technological knowledge and invention grow, a seemingly inescapable logic increases the complexity of medical interventions—often by leaps and bounds. On the one hand, modern medicine can do things that were unimaginable just a few years ago; on the other, doing these things costs extraordinary amounts of money. Quickly the overall logic of the healthcare *system* gets caught up in questions of who should have access to which of these sophisticated interventions, and under what conditions.

All modern healthcare systems struggle with this issue of the distribution of healthcare and underlying questions of fairness and equity. How they deal with them differs—and significantly—but they underlie all health policy discussions about who shall pay for what. Part of these torturous policy dynamics is the realization that just as all politics is ultimately local, so all healthcare policy is ultimately local in that cost, access, availability, level of appropriate intervention, patient safety, and supply of adequate personnel and facilities all boil down to situations within families and between healthcare providers and insurance plans. At this level, healthcare stops being about policy, and becomes intensely personal. Experience repeatedly demonstrates that in a large, highly decentralized healthcare system such as that in the U.S., what might be viewed as the larger systemic rationality of decisions ceases to exist. The intense personalization of decisions produces difficult situations. When there is "more that can be done" medically, the pressure is to do it, and let costs be sorted out later down the line. The result is that increasing aggregate costs produce even more distributional issues, which then actually intensify some of the irrational aspects of the system.

This dilemma heavily involves the uninsured, who tend to use high-cost emergency room facilities when they become ill. If they cannot pay the resulting costs, the providing facility distributes them across other payers in the system. The alternative, now much discussed in the national debates, is for everyone to have some form of insurance—a policy option which many (violently!) oppose, especially when claimants to such care may lack accepted standing in the community, as in the much celebrated case of illegal immigrants. The various legal provisions and moral considerations that force hospitals to supply such care constitute unfunded mandates for the healthcare system.

Legal migration under the Compact of Free Association and other Pacific Island jurisdictions creates another unfunded federal mandate for Hawai'i, since those migrants tend to rely on public healthcare funding that is not supported by commensurate federal impact funding, as it is in some other Pacific jurisdictions.

The state's capacity to support existing levels of programs has of course been immensely impacted by revenue declines from the recession. Painful cuts need to be made "somewhere" in state budgets, and the hard reality is that most state budgetary expenditures go to healthcare and welfare, public safety (fire, police, and prisons), and basic and secondary education. In Hawai'i, these four categories in 2008 made up 74.81 percent of government expenditures (up from 55.5 percent in 1999).[4] It is an inescapable fact of modern government in times of declining revenues that without raising taxes, the quantity and quality of social services is bound to suffer. And healthcare to especially needy segments of the population, including the mentally ill, is at the forefront.

HEALTHCARE STATUS

Let's briefly compare Hawai'i's healthcare position with the rest of the U.S., from the late 1980s until now.

The picture is mixed.

Current research (by Gerald Russo and colleagues) on insurance coverage estimates that in 2008 the effective rate of the medically uninsured in Hawai'i was 7.51 percent, compared with a country average of 15.15 percent.[5] Good news, yes, but 7.51 percent is equal to roughly 95,000 persons—still a lot of people without insurance. Who are they? Most of the uninsured are between 19 and 64 years of age, male, and at lower income levels. Children and the elderly are relatively well insured—with the emphasis on *relatively*. Roughly 14,000 persons under 19 were uninsured, and roughly 8,000 of them were from families living at 200 percent of the poverty level, or less.

Basically, national reforms will affect Hawai'i in five ways.[6] Tax credits of up to $14,000 will assist small businesses in supplying coverage to workers. Insurance companies (and eventually others) will not be able to deny insurance coverage to children with pre-existing conditions. Medicare premiums will go down for about 120,000 seniors, and benefits will improve for about 190,000. Perhaps most importantly, the insurance market for the 7.5 percent of the population without coverage will expand.

Over time, the argument goes, reducing the number of people without healthcare insurance will provide greater financial resources to the healthcare system by reducing irrational interactions with its high-cost emergency room portals. This argument confronts the reality of how budget crises are forcing states to reduce their social obligations to provide healthcare coverage. In Hawai'i, such actions are currently being debated, with the deepest cuts anticipated for the State's Medicaid program, QUEST, which would involve moving significant numbers of persons to lower benefit programs.

As for Hawai'i's health status compared with the 1980s, the picture is also mixed.[7] For example:

Infant mortality throughout the period 1980 to 2006 remained below the national average, although in 2000 and again in 2003, it spiked above that level.

While the death rate from coronary heart disease was significantly below the national average in 1980 and 2006, the rate of decrease in Hawai'i was slower than for the country as a whole.

The incidence of lung cancer has dropped throughout the U.S. since 1990, but recently Hawai'i has witnessed an upward trend.

Breast cancer rates in Hawai'i have been significantly below the national average since 1980, and indeed below the target incidence rate established by Healthy People 2010 standards. Within Hawai'i, though, the highest rates occur on the neighbor islands.

Hawai'i has the lowest rates of cigarette smoking in the country, with usage having declined significantly among both adults and youths since 1999.

Diabetes, which some declare a national epidemic, has moved from being above the U.S. average in 1990 to equal that average in 2008. That's the good news. The bad news is that throughout the state, the rate of diabetes in the population has increased from 5.2 percent to 8 percent, which is the national average.

Mortality rates for Native Hawaiians remain the highest for all ethnic groups. When compared with the U.S. average, Native Hawaiians have death rates that are

44 percent higher for cadiovascular disease

39 percent higher for cancers

31 percent higher for cerebrovascular incidents/strokes

196 percent higher for type 2 diabetes

While Hawai'i has the third lowest overall obesity rate in the nation (20.6 percent), the rate for the state's Native Hawaiian population is 39 percent—even higher than Mississippi, the most obese state in the nation at 31.4 percent. As for the health labor force and system capacity, Hawai'i continues to be above the national average on many indicators, but has lost much of its edge:

Hawai'i currently has 3.2 physicians per 1,000, versus a national average of 2.8. However, like other healthcare resources, physicians are concentrated on O'ahu, with an average rate of only 2.1 on Hawai'i Island, Kaua'i, and Maui. A current study forecasts a severe physician deficit in the very near future on the neighbor islands, and a growing physician decline and shortage on O'ahu.[8]

The supply of acute care hospital beds has remained relatively constant over two decades, declining slightly between 1990 and 2006, but the state's relative position has declined, as supply has failed to keep pace with population growth. Hawai'i currently ranks 33rd in the country on this indicator of capacity.

Long-term care beds remain an issue for the state. Hawai'i ranks 49th in terms of the percentage of the population in nursing homes, and at 94.8 percent, its long-term bed occupancy rate is the highest in the country.

Recent data reveal that 1/3 of Hawai'i residents travel to receive care they cannot obtain on their home island: 49 percent in Kona; 42 percent in Hilo; 45 percent on Maui; 40 percent on Kaua'i; and 6 percent on O'ahu.

CONCLUSION

What do these factors tell us, what are the critical healthcare issues, and what needs to be done?

First, Hawai'i has lost several advantages it once had in insurance coverage, healthcare provision and capacity, and cost. In many areas of health-related behavior and so-called lifestyle correlates to health, however, Hawai'i continues to be a leader, and a clear beneficiary of its benign climate. Overall, therefore, it has much less to gain from national healthcare reform.

Second, even within a historically relatively beneficial governmental climate, the bottom tier of the population in terms of income continues to struggle, and is seriously threatened by the current radical downturn in State funding. No other issue even begins to compare with the severe and long-term damage that these possible contractions of governmental services will do to providing healthcare and promoting health for this segment of the population. It is critical to emphasize how long-lasting the effects of such cutbacks may be for the community's health. The current ill-advised trade-off is between short-term budget balancing actions that reduce services now, and the price we will pay in the long term for the effects that these reductions will produce. The most obvious answer is a short-term, targeted increase in taxes to ride out the worst part of the recession.

For all the states and the national government, policy choices in such times are stunningly similar. At the national level, the choices are to (a) cut back in various areas and hopefully cut things that are relatively unimportant. At the State level, Hawai'i's constitutionally mandated balanced budgets mean that borrowing the State out of the fiscal crisis is not an option. That leaves option (b) raising revenues. This is happening across the country, often in specific targeted areas (as distasteful as that is to some in the policy process *and* the public), which is perceived as a better choice than undoing the decades-long achievements of a viable healthcare system.

Third, the growing physician shortage on all islands will severely impact access to healthcare. Only concerted public and private cooperation can resolve this situation, and this will include the investment of State resources.

Finally, despite close to three decades of targeted public policy efforts to improve Native Hawaiian health, it continues to lag behind the health of other groups in the population. This is simply an unacceptable situation, and requires further public will and commitment.

ARTS

MARILYN CRISTOFORI

Can we imagine Hawai'i without the arts? We would be living in a nonsensical, internally gray environment, with sounds of cars and jackhammers. Yet we are constantly challenged to make a case for keeping the arts at the core of our society. Yes, we are blessed with an extraordinary natural environment that deserves honor and protection, but the arts are a necessary part of healthy surroundings in our future.

There are many wise kumu and kūpuna who speak eloquently about Hawaiian culture—how it is integral to life in Hawai'i, central to its history, and essential for the survival of this place. Here I will focus on the arts in Hawai'i since statehood: how we have mirrored and moved in parallel with national developments, and how the state has been a recognized arts leader. The arts refer to music, dance, theater, sculpture, painting, literature, film, poetry, and other aesthetic disciplines that spring from our human imagination and creativity. These disciplines emerge from the life forces of movement, sound, smell, sight (observation), insight, and intuition. As humans, we arrange these elements in ways that appeal to our senses and emotions. We have all experienced that some truths can only be communicated through songs, stories, images, and movement.

The arts are born from the cultures of people and their surrounding environment. As many new populations came to Hawai'i for a variety of economic and other reasons, they brought with them arts from their civilizations. These unique arts have been treasured and integrated into our lives so that we enjoy a rich vein of diverse arts, rare within other states. This unusual, well-defined diversity is among the distinctions that make Hawai'i a prime national example.

During the 1950s, there were serious conversations about the establishment of a national arts agency. Many of our state leaders were in close touch with those on the national scene, and in 1965 both the National Endowment for the Arts (NEA) and our own Hawai'i State Foundation on Culture and the Arts (HSFCA) were established. President John F. Kennedy was the inspirational voice who spoke for the creation of the NEA and a national arts center. He often stated that the arts "are a test of the quality of a nation's civilization." After his 1963 assassination, both the John F. Kennedy Center for the Performing Arts and our own Kennedy Theatre at the University of Hawai'i at Mānoa (UHM) were named in his honor.

National policies greatly influence our state, so it is important to note what the NEA's founding language asserts:

> The practice of arts . . . requires constant dedication and devotion. . . . [W]hile no government can call a great artist . . . into existence, it is necessary and appropriate to help create and sustain . . . a climate encouraging freedom of thought . . . imagination, and . . . the material conditions facilitating the release of this creative talent.[1]

A central function of the NEA is the Federal State Partnership, which allocates 40 percent of its funding to the states. HSFCA received one of the first eleven NEA grants. Since initially these funds were distributed equally, Hawai'i received the same amount as other states—in 1968, $39,383 to California, and $39,383 to Hawai'i—remarkable considering Hawai'i's much smaller population.

In 1967, Hawai'i passed the first law in the nation to designate one percent of construction costs of new State buildings for the acquisition of works of art. This Art in Public Places (APP) program has greatly strengthened the HSFCA's influence upon the field of visual arts, and subsequently, many other states have passed similar laws.

The NEA has helped transform the cultural landscape of the nation, with the number of artists tripling over the last four decades. By 2000, there were a total of 1.9 million artists in the nation. Even though most (27 percent) lived in California or New York, Hawai'i still ranked fourth in artists as a share of its workforce behind only Washington, D.C, New York, and California. This is another example of Hawai'i leadership in the arts.

The arts are critical to our economy through public programs and private nonprofits—corporations formed to help meet critical needs that cannot be supported by the commercial marketplace. Nonprofit corporations receive income from public (government) funds as well as private donations. Hawai'i has several hundred nonprofit arts organizations, all depending on public funds that supplement earned income to conduct business, and offering arts services, programs, exhibits, performances, and education. These nonprofits leverage their public support to bring significant out-of-state funds into Hawai'i.

Public and private funds for the arts are not charity, but are investments in our community, with financial returns. An Americans for the Arts report shows that in January 2010, Hawai'i had more than 3,000 arts-related businesses employing well over 13,000 people.[2] In our state, the expenditures of nonprofit arts organizations exceeded $80 million a few years ago, and additional spending by arts audiences in local and surrounding businesses was estimated at $142.8 million.

In 2008, HSFCA awarded 109 grants to 83 arts nonprofits.[3] The State general funds awarded amounted to only $249,000, but the grants leveraged an additional $1,026,000 from non-State funds. Similarly, the $215,000 from State general funds granted to the Artists-in-the-Schools program helped attract $3,070,963 in private and federal funds. Overall, State grantee projects brought more than $12 million into the state's economy—a 12:1 match. This may no longer be possible, since the current economic crisis has severely reduced the HSFCA budget by at least 40 percent. This threatens most of the private nonprofit arts organizations that deliver arts and arts education, and that depend on public funds to attract other monies.

While these numbers can tell us part of the story, we cannot measure the full impact of the arts on our lives without considering arts education. The human mind is our fundamental resource. Arts education creates neural pathways that link our logical left brain with our spatial/imaginative right brain. Research repeatedly shows that all learning improves in arts-enriched environments. A 2009 longitudinal study of 25,000 students found high arts involvement led to academic success in college, and later in their careers.[4]

As well as being a forerunner in public support for the arts, Hawai'i has been a leader in arts education. When grim budget cuts removed DOE arts educators from school classrooms during the mid-to-late 1990s, the Hawai'i State Legislature passed ACT 80/99, naming the Fine Arts as a core subject and calling for an Arts Education Strategic Plan. Hawai'i named the Fine Arts as a core academic subject prior to national legislation doing the same. Two years later ARTS FIRST was created (ACT 306/01), mandating implementation of the Strategic Plan to include all the arts (music, theatre, dance, visual arts). The six critical stakeholders named in the law as Partners are HSFCA, Hawai'i Arts Alliance, Hawai'i Association of Independent Schools, the State Department of Education, the University of Hawai'i at Mānoa College of Arts and Humanities, and UHM College of Education. Two Affiliate Partners are the Honolulu Theatre for Youth and the Maui Arts & Cultural Center. HSFCA is convener of ARTS FIRST and is accountable to the State Legislature. This role reinforces one of the NEA criteria: that the State arts agency support vital arts education programs.

In 2010, ARTS FIRST programs are benefitting 4,000 classroom teachers through professional development; supporting 139 Teaching Artists plus fourteen organizations that provide arts education for the schools; providing pre-service training for future teachers in standards-based arts integrated curricula; and sponsoring Artists-in-the-Schools, which reaches more than 5,800 students. But this still only touches a small percentage of our 184,000 public school students, and arts programs and arts teachers are being eliminated daily due to furloughs, reduced DOE budgets, and the attitude that the arts are a "frill" or extra that can be discarded in tough times. This severe reduction of support for the arts further erodes the delivery of arts education to our children and youth.

At the end of this first decade of the twenty-first century, no state or individual has escaped the economic recession, with its lost jobs, reduced salaries, disappearing businesses and nonprofits, all of which have engendered desperation, depression, and dismay. But even if we trace how public policies and the actions of decision-makers have often unwittingly resulted in our shrinking arts community, we need not blame. Rather, we must work collectively to help shape the future of the arts in Hawai'i and for Hawai'i.

So what are our next steps to reaffirm Hawai'i's arts primacy? The arts are not for sissies! Everyone who has struggled through learning and creating in any discipline knows the extremely hard work and formidable challenges any artist faces before reaching a level of satisfaction or resolution. We must therefore start by boldly proclaiming that the arts are not an extra or a frill that can be diminished or discarded.

Here are three broad recommendations to make Hawai'i once again first as a model for creative communities.

1. Public/private partnerships for the arts are not an *either/or* option. For a vital civilization and a healthy democracy, they must be both/and. It is imperative to balance both public and private resources to support creative opportunities for all. Without public funds, the arts can easily become the private property of an elite ownership, seriously weakening a functioning democratic society. At the same time, private support is essential to prevent government control of creative talent, and to avoid threats to individual expression.

Even when compared with older and larger states, Hawai'i has long been a leader in the arts. We can reaffirm this special place, and accept our unique responsibility to be an example for the nation. In many visits to our public officials and business leaders, I have heard stories about how they choose to devote portions of their lives to creative, artistic pursuits in music, theater, dancing, visual art, film/media, and literature as creators, performers, and/or as audience. These actions demonstrate that our leaders do not personally regard the arts as "extra." With pride and joy, they reveal their quiet commitments, and acknowledge that the arts define us as people and as a civilization.

We can embrace and honor their need to pursue creativity, and use it to support the role that the arts must play in our state. We can appreciate and praise our leaders' personal involvement in the arts to give them the confidence to make decisions to increase support from both public and private sectors. This requires ongoing vigilance and action, as the arts cannot be considered a commodity. The arts represent a creative process that will continually change and evolve. We might learn from our surfing experts that there is no "arrival," there is nothing solid, only the ability to be keenly aware and constantly adapt to balancing on the ever-moving surface.

Arts and cultural tourism is one area that can benefit from expanded public/private support. On any given day, just on O'ahu there are at least thirty arts performances and exhibits—a myriad of rich options that could fascinate our visitors.[5] Other possibilities for the future should include tax credits that benefit arts organizations on a par with businesses, weighted refunds on State tax returns for donations to the arts, and development of a trust to support the basic operations of arts organizations that make positive change in the community.

2. Arts in the schools have suffered for almost a generation. When children are having learning difficulties or failing, the arts often save the day, but now our days are so bleak that we must bring the arts back into the schools, for with them comes energy, spirit, and excitement about all learning.

The recent Dana Consortium Report on Arts and Cognition, *Learning, Arts, and the Brain,* suggests that training in the arts relates to improvements in math and reading skills.[6] In one study, University of Oregon researchers observed the brain activity of children engaged in arts activities, and concluded that the arts train children's attention and focus, which in turn improves cognition. The thinking skills learned in arts programs are rarely addressed elsewhere in the school curriculum. One key skill is "learning to engage and persist." The arts teach students how to learn from mistakes, to press ahead, and to commit to following through. When students find problems that require creativity, they work with them deeply over sustained periods of time.

In the future, ideas will rule. Even now, on a national scale, creative sector workers generate $1.7 trillion annually—as much as the manufacturing and service sectors combined.[7] The top ten in-demand jobs today did not exist six years ago. We must therefore prepare students for jobs that do not yet exist, and to be ready to acquire skills for technology not yet invented. We will need people who can solve problems that we do not yet know are problems. We must prepare our students to become individuals who have learned more than what to think. They must also know how to sustain attention and how to think creatively. Without the arts to build the creative skills and minds needed in our global economy, we sacrifice a complete education for our children, thereby severely limiting our ability to compete globally, and risking everyone's future.

Our educational system is a constant source of frustration begging for change. We cannot ignore the growing data about the necessity of integrating the arts deeply into the curricula to reform all learning. Although ARTS FIRST programs show very positive results, they only reach about 3 to 4 percent of our public school classrooms. We need to integrate the arts into the core learning at *every* school. This effort relates to public/private partnerships, because it involves public officials, the board of education, teachers, parents, students, and artists working together in their own districts and communities to insist that the arts lead to educational improvement. What if 10,000 people are willing to contribute $1 a day to support an initiative to bring arts back into the schools? This would begin to make a difference, with $3,650,000 or $20 per student for arts education.

3. A new role for the arts will contribute to everyone's survival. Here is a way to position the arts more prominently in society, based on familiar behaviors within arts practices. To bring a play, an opera, or a music or dance concert to the stage, or an exhibit to display, or any artwork to others, all involved have to resolve differences and work together while exercising their best individual talents. While such cooperation is fundamental among artists, there is too often an attitude that the arts are separate from the realities of the rest of society. The economic crisis has increased our social and environmental problems beyond management with our current tools, resulting in conflicts over limited resources. We need different approaches. The arts may not have great economic means, but they possess creative skills and cooperative behaviors that can reach more deeply toward those most needy among our people and environments.

The arts can collaborate with the larger community in new, participatory ways. We can learn some things in a passive role, but we learn much more by being active. This suggestion does not ignore the incredible work already being done by arts organizations and artists for social justice in prisons, in poor neighborhoods, in hospitals. It is a wider call to make a formal, clear, public annual commitment to actively serve a need, to give rather than ask.

Artists are often underpaid, and live among the lower levels of economic wealth. Committed to the pursuit of a creative life, they are often willing to make this trade-off to follow their talents and passions. Similarly, arts organizations are always struggling to survive, to fill the gap between earned income and the basic finances needed to provide any service or program. As such, there is a well-established practice of arts fundraising, including annual requests for donations. The recent Giving Study by the Hawai'i Community Foundation found the people of Hawai'i are more generous than the national average.[8] In keeping with this profile, and as a new approach, artists and organizations could formally begin an Annual *ArtsGiving* Campaign.

This idea is offered with full credit to Kanu Hawai'i and its campaign of commitments and pledges to take action toward improving the environment for a more sustainable and resilient Hawai'i.[9] Each artist or arts entity could pledge one gift per year to *ArtsGiving* that would improve the environment, serve poverty, or help sick people or others with deep needs. This means something more than a free event, although these are very valuable and should continue. The gift would involve an actual participatory experience to awaken or engage the creative impulses of those truly in need. It might mean creating a song or a dance together, sharing arts supplies with a bedridden person and painting with them, bringing music to a beach clean-up—all singing while simultaneously cleaning the area.

Many of these activities may already happen, but not necessarily as a *conscious commitment* to making a difference. Sharing experiences is already embedded into the practices of most artists, but as an artistic behavior. If the arts take on a conscious active role as givers, they will not be undervalued as extras that can be eliminated in tough times. People need direct involvement to nurture the creative impulse, and to lead them eventually to develop new attitudes about the arts. The arts must become an essential part of improving lives, communities, and the environment. If Hawai'i were to have a discussion about a new role for the arts as philanthropists of creative experiences, it would allow a release of productive talent and be another first for our state.

Hawai'i without the arts? Hardly! Let us imagine our future by reasserting Hawai'i as a primary arts leader. It's time to reinvigorate two traditional supports: to increase public/private support for all arts, and to bring the arts back into our schools. But it's also time for a mind shift, and a new role for artists and arts organizations—*ArtsGiving*. And it's time for the arts in Hawai'i to once again permeate all levels and arenas of our state's society.

JOURNALISM

IAN LIND

Water, water, everywhere,
Nor any drop to drink.
　　—Samuel Taylor Coleridge, *Rime of the Ancient Mariner* (1798)

There will be quite a bit of something called "news" in the coming years,
but there will not be very much of what we once called journalism. . . . If
we do nothing we are likely to enter a golden age of even more mindless
sensationalism and spin and propaganda masquerading as "news."
　　—Robert W. McChesney (2010)

Hawaiʻi joined the dismal revolution that has been sweeping the nation's news business with this year's sale of the *Honolulu Advertiser,* the state's largest daily newspaper, to its smaller rival, the *Star-Bulletin*, and the planned merger of the two into a single publication. At the time of this writing, the deal is expected to result in the layoffs of several hundred newspaper employees, and a corresponding decline in the amount of original news reporting being delivered to island residents. Honolulu's experience is, unfortunately, not unusual. More than 140 daily and weekly newspapers across the country stopped publishing in 2009 alone, with many observers predicting the disappearance of newspapers as we have known them.

News consumers can be excused for feeling they are being whipsawed by contradictory trends. Like Coleridge's Ancient Mariner, we're awash in a rising flood of news from sources new and old, but more "news" no longer means a better informed public. On the one hand, we're bombarded with information served up by hundreds of available cable channels, innumerable web sites accessible from the desktop, daily newspapers from small towns and large cities across the globe now easily accessible online, and all of the above enveloped by the "Blogosphere," which quickly spins news and events into viewpoints and opinions from all points of the ideological spectrum. On the other hand, many of the basic mainstays of news reporting—newspapers, broadcast stations, and magazines, along with their extensive networks of reporters, regular beats, news bureaus, and professional editors—have already been closed or gone bankrupt, slashed by repeated rounds of cost cutting, or are struggling for financial survival.

Many factors have been linked to their decline, including changing demographics and patterns of work, the loss of free time, changing public tastes, and the shift to television and the internet as primary sources of news for many people. Mainstream media have all been impacted by an exodus of advertisers, but newspapers have been particularly hard hit. Classified ads, real estate and auto listings, along with job ads, once the backbone of newspaper revenue, have mostly moved online, where free networks such as Craigslist now connect sellers and buyers directly. Across the country, once great names in newspaper history, such as Knight Ridder and the Tribune Company, are gone or in bankruptcy; icons like the *New York Times* and *Boston Globe,* have teetered on the edge of survival; major metropolitan newspapers like the *San Francisco Examiner, Seattle Post-Intelligencer, Cincinnati Post, Kentucky Post, Rocky Mountain News,* and the *Tucson Citizen* have been shut down; and thousands of journalists have lost their jobs.

The decline of news in Honolulu has been equally devastating. Just twenty-five years ago, the *Advertiser* and *Star-Bulletin* were seen as cash cows, splitting an estimated $50 million or more in annual profit. But the *Star-Bulletin* reported this year it had lost over $100 million between 2001 and 2010, while its paid circulation fell from 64,000 to just 37,000.[1] These numbers are also reflected in declining membership in the Newspaper Guild, the union representing employees at most of the state's newspapers. Statewide, Guild membership was stable from 2002 to 2006 at 573 or 574, but by September 2009 it had dropped 23.8 percent to 437, according to the union's annual LM-2 reports filed with the U.S. Department of Labor.[2]

One big loser has been routine coverage of the State legislature, county councils, and the various boards and commissions responsible for key policies at the State and County levels. In the mid-1980s, for example, both of Honolulu's daily newspapers maintained newsrooms at the State Capitol during the annual legislative session, each with four or more experienced reporters as well as a couple of interns. Today only a handful of reporters cover the capitol, and an even smaller number do so full time.

Broadcast coverage has similarly declined. In legislative testimony submitted earlier this year, former State Representative Jim Shon observed that the days when there were reporters and cameras providing in-depth coverage of the State capitol "are mostly gone." "For TV news," Shon said, "the number of genuine investigative reports is almost nonexistent. It is far cheaper to dribble out the weather three or four times every half hour, or download live feeds from national networks. Most stories are little more than reading the headlines with cliched lead-ins and cliched tags. The rest is telling the viewers what is coming up after the break."[3]

The collapse of newspapers and the broader decline in civic news has now drawn the attention of federal regulators. Beginning last winter, the Federal Trade Commission has sponsored a series of workshops on the theme "How will journalism survive in the Internet Age?" "Since the beginning of our Republic, journalism has been essential to making democracy work," Federal Trade Commission chairman Jon Leibowitz said in his introduction to a December 2009 program: "By ensuring that citizens are well-informed about civic matters, news journalism helps create the informed electorate that is vital to a well-functioning democracy."[4]

There has been no shortage of soul-searching within the news industry over how to reshape news to fulfill its civic mission, while more effectively capturing the attention of readers and viewers and developing new sources of revenue. But while there is widespread agreement that broad-based, critical reporting on government and public affairs is necessary to sustain a democratic form of government, there is no similar consensus on what can be done to reverse the ongoing loss of news resources. "Finding a new business model for journalism will not be easy," the FTC's Leibowitz observed: "The hard truth is that U.S. citizens have never paid subscription fees that cover all the costs of researching, gathering, analyzing, articulating, editing, and producing the civic news required for the proper functioning of our democracy. Nor do citizens in other democracies, many of which subsidize the news through public funding."

In response to the sale of the *Honolulu Advertiser,* labor and public interest groups were joined by concerned individuals to rally political support to maintain two daily newspapers in Honolulu, as was done successfully in 1999. But there has been surprisingly little discussion of the kinds of public policies that could be pursued at the State and local level to support quality news journalism in a post-newspaper age. The lack of policy discussions may not be surprising given the response to the idea of direct government financial support from most professional journalists, which has ranged from tepid support to angry opposition.

Professor and media critic Robert W. McChesney at the University of Illinois at Urbana-Champaign argues that journalism and the production of news must be seen as a public good rather than a private commodity:

It is like military defense, physical infrastructure, education, public health and basic research in that regard. It is something society requires, and people want, but the market cannot generate in sufficient quantity or quality. It requires government leadership to exist. There may be an important role for the private sector, but with public goods the government plays quarterback or the game never starts.[5]

Schooled in the value of independence, and possessing an innate suspicion of becoming fettered by political controls, professional journalists have not however warmed to the idea of government support, fearing direct public aid will necessarily come with strings attached. A recent study by the Annenberg School for Communication and Journalism traces the history of federal support for journalism, including postal subsidies for magazines and newspapers that trace back to the Postal Act of 1792.[6] Other traditional forms of public support include requirements for the publication of legal notices, targeted tax breaks, and direct subsidies, such as those going to National Public Radio and the Public Broadcasting Service. The Newspaper Preservation Act of 1970 and its predecessor, the Failing Newspaper Act of 1967, which created a federal antitrust exemption for newspapers that allowed rival newspapers to pool their business operations, are further examples of public policies that were intended to sustain the business of journalism. The *Honolulu Advertiser* and *Star-Bulletin* shared business operations through the Hawaii Newspaper Agency from 1962 until March 2001, when HNA and the joint operating agreement were dissolved.

Among policies being considered by the FTC are new antitrust exemptions, as well as the loosening of other restrictions, including current rules against owning a newspaper and broadcast station in the same market. However, antitrust exemptions would favor the largest media companies, already criticized by many for concentrating too much media power in the same hands, while crowding out diverse local voices and viewpoints. For example, Media Council Hawaii (MCH), a nonpartisan organization promoting greater public understanding of the role of the media, is asking the FCC to reject the 2009 operational merger of television stations KHNL, KGMB, and KFVE that consolidated their newsrooms and resulted in an estimated sixty-eight layoffs. The "shared service agreement" between the three stations sidesteps FCC rules that would have blocked a direct merger, and was defended as a way to strengthen the stations' finances. It is the kind of move that might benefit from the loosening of federal controls reportedly being discussed by the FTC. But in a press release announcing the group's petition to the FCC, MCH President Chris Conybeare noted that "Their advertising proclaims: 'More News, More Options, More Voices.' But in reality, the same news is shown on all three stations, limiting news, options, and voices."[7]

Although newspapers aren't going to disappear completely any time soon, few expect them to regain their former preeminence as primary engines for the reporting of news. Internet consultant and analyst Clay Shirky has argued that the economic model behind the success of newspapers was an accident of technology. Printing presses are extremely expensive to set up and operate, and this simple fact created a wide economic moat protecting newspapers from competition. If you had enough money to set up a press and publish a newspaper, you were almost guaranteed to make money because advertisers had few other places to go, and they would pay to be included in the newspaper even though they may have had little interest in the news being reported, especially reporting critical of the status quo.

But this economic model has been undercut by the internet, a shared public resource that now allows anyone with a computer to reach a far larger audience than printed newspapers ever could. The expensive presses that once assured the success of newspapers have now become weighty liabilities unable to compete cost-effectively in this digital age.

"Society doesn't need newspapers," Shirky writes: "What we need is journalism. For a century, the imperatives to strengthen journalism and to strengthen newspapers have been so tightly wound as to be indistinguishable. That's been a fine accident to have, but when that accident stops, as it is stopping before our eyes, we're going to need lots of other ways to strengthen journalism instead."[8]

In the future, it is likely we will have to rely on a combination of news sources, commercial and non-commercial, private and public, professional and community-based, to provide the same broad-based reporting formerly provided by newspapers. State and local governments should be pursuing public policies that will bolster both familiar sources of news as well as new adventures in public media and non-traditional citizen journalism through tax policies, leveraging of public resources, and improved information practices. Here are some preliminary suggestions to start the policy discussion.

TAX POLICY

Tax credits could be offered to encourage private investments in news ventures covering public affairs, whether print, broadcast, or online, similar to the high-technology tax credits promoted by the tech industry.

Individuals could be allowed state tax deductions for the cost of subscribing to local newspapers, magazines, web sites, or news services.

Citizen journalists and bloggers who regularly use their own time and resources to generate original local news and analysis could be allowed to deduct costs associated with their noncommercial efforts.

INFORMATION POLICY

Restoration of funding to the Office of Information Practices, which administers the State's open meeting and public record laws, would indirectly aid news gathering. Budget and staff cutbacks over an extended period of time have reduced OIP's ability to meet one of its key original purposes, which was to provide a timely and inexpensive alternative to litigation when agencies fail to comply with the requirements of open government.

Updating of the State sunshine law to bring it into the computer age is overdue. Current law requires a six-day advance notice of public meetings, but the requirement can be met by mailing notices, although delivery can take several days. The law should be updated to provide timely notice of public meetings and distribution of agency minutes via email when requested, and to explicitly extend the right to record public meetings to include video or digital formats as well as audio recording.

The Fair Information Practices Act should more clearly provide for fee waivers for document requests by nonprofessional citizen journalists not affiliated with commercial mainstream media.

State and county agencies should be required to make additional types of public records readily accessible via the internet, similar to the Obama administration's Data.gov initiative.

Honolulu policies limiting the number of news racks in Waikīkī should be reconsidered to provide access to high-volume locations for a greater range of news publications.

COMMUNITY JOURNALISM

Expand the reach and effectiveness of existing PEG access (public, education, and government) programming currently funded through cable franchise fees and provided through public access organizations in each county. Consider expanding programs to include basic training in journalism techniques and research methods in addition to technical training in video production. Access centers could also provide direct facilitation of larger news projects, enabling volunteer producers and journalists to play a larger role in ongoing news coverage. PEG access centers could also extend their reach by encouraging print journalism, online or on paper, as well as video projects.

PBS Hawaii's Hiki No project, which is building the nation's first statewide student news network involving middle and high school students, should be supported as a model for similar news initiatives. Resources could be provided to encourage the University of Hawai'i, and Hawai'i's private universities and colleges, to pursue similar initiatives.

TERRESTRIAL ECOSYSTEMS

PATRICIA TUMMONS

To save Hawaiʻi's terrestrial ecosystems, save Hawaiʻi's forests.

Of course, it's important to reduce solid waste and recycle, keep pollutants out of our water supplies, develop and carry out sound land use planning, and foster conservation and renewable energy resources. But protecting and expanding Hawaiʻi's forests is of paramount importance. Nothing else matters if we fail in this.

Why?

Forests are, above all, the source of our fresh water. Desalination may provide a trivial amount in limited areas, but it is expensive and energy-intensive. Allowing our mountain slopes to capture water, having it percolate into our precious aquifers, and withdrawing it with the help of gravity makes ever so much more sense. Our aquifers are unlikely to run dry, but if they are no longer recharged, they will become salty, as ocean water intrudes. Once that happens, forget about water for agriculture or even washing your car; start thinking about sponge baths from the rain barrel.

Forests are also home to what remains of native birds and plants, Hawaiʻi's one terrestrial mammal (the bat), and its wondrous and amazing invertebrates. What is truly unique about Hawaiʻi does not lie in our beaches or snorkeling opportunities. It is not found in our snazzy hotels or verdant golf courses. It is the unique plant and animal life, the forbears of which arrived against all odds to these islands and over millennia adapted to fill every conceivable ecological niche in the remotest archipelago on earth.

That these plants and animals are at risk is beyond dispute. News that another Hawaiian plant or animal has been added to the endangered species list has become so much a part of the warp and woof of daily life that members of the public could be forgiven if they greet it with a bored yawn.

Why should they care anyway? One tree is just as good as another for watershed purposes, isn't it? And who really can be expected to mourn the loss of a species of bird that few people today have seen or heard—*or even heard of?* As for the smallest creatures—untold thousands of species of snail, beetle, fly, moth, and spider, whose existence is testament to the amazing ability of life forms to adapt to new circumstances—if native birds get no respect, these animals are literally squished underfoot, appreciated by few apart from the odd entomologist or malacologist.

Such attitudes of indifference and ignorance toward the very qualities that set Hawai'i apart from the rest of the world have contributed to their current precarious status. Nowadays, when people talk of saving Hawai'i's environment, too often what comes first to mind is the idea of recycling paper and cans or cleaning a beach. The notion that saving Hawai'i's environment has to entail a sincere effort to save every remaining part of its ecological systems rarely jumps to mind. But if the species that evolved here, that can truly be said to be native to these islands, can no longer survive, something is fundamentally out of whack in our environment.

The disturbances began as soon as the earliest settlers landed. Many of the plants and animals that once occupied coastal regions disappeared as Hawaiians cleared lands for settlement and farming. When Westerners arrived, the pace of extinction picked up. Cattle, sheep, European swine, and goats were loosed into the mountains, and within decades, watersheds were devastated. The trade in sandalwood in the early nineteenth century augmented the losses. Forests where native birds and plants could thrive shrank at a prodigious rate.

In 1826, a whaler in Lahaina dumped a barrel of water containing mosquito larvae. At once, people living in the area felt the effects. But there were longer-term consequences as well, none more devastating than those suffered by native Hawaiian birds. Decades later, when birds from other lands were introduced, they carried in their blood mosquito-borne parasites that would ravage native birds, which lacked immunity that the interlopers had developed as a result of repeated long exposure. As a consequence, many of the remaining native forest bird populations survive only because they were able to retreat to elevations where mosquitoes do not regularly breed.

By the turn of the twentieth century, damage from fires, logging, and ungulates (pigs, goats, sheep, cattle, horses, and deer) had laid bare vast areas of hillsides above the sugar plantations and in the distant watersheds, whose streams were diverted to fill the elaborate ditch systems built to bring water to their lands. Planters were justifiably worried that this meant the eventual drying up of water sources essential to their ongoing economic success. Working with the government, they began to replant the slopes. Eventually the territorial government, pushed by the planters, established an extensive system of forest reserves, where landowners received tax benefits for fencing off forests and leaving them intact. To expand these reserves on public land, the territorial government, working with the U.S. Department of Agriculture, planted hundreds of thousands of fast-growing trees.

Today, it is difficult to imagine the hills above Mānoa, Makiki, and Nuʻuanu as bare as those along the Waiʻanae Coast are today, but the reports of the Territorial Board of Agriculture and Forestry document how many thousands of trees—right down to the numbers of individual species—were planted in the early years of the twentieth century to reforest those slopes.

The territorial government and the planters also recognized the value of removing hooved animals from the forest reserves. Right up through the 1930s, drives conducted at regular intervals pushed goats from mauka lands right down to the coast, where they were slaughtered by the thousands. Cattle, pigs, and sheep were allowed to be hunted, with the goal of completely eradicating ungulates from the forest reserves.

A fundamental tension existed, however, between the Board of Agriculture and Forestry (later the Department of Agriculture and Conservation), which sought to defend forest lands, and the Commission on Public Lands, which was tasked with generating revenue by putting public lands under lease, with ranchers far and away the largest sector seeking to encumber an ever greater share of vacant lands, including forests. The outcome of their struggles continues to be visible today, in the vast areas of marginal grazing lands that still remain in pastoral leases, where payments to the State are on the order of a few dollars per acre per year.

Statehood brought fundamental changes to the government's management of its lands and wildlife. The new Department of Land and Natural Resources took over responsibility for managing the forest reserves and hunting (formerly the *kuleana* of the Department of Agriculture and Conservation) and for leasing public lands (the task of the Commission on Public Lands).

Even before statehood, however, a subtle change was occurring in the government's view of wild animals—a shift that was barely noticeable at the time, but which had long-range implications for the management of Hawaiʻi's forests. Since its inception, the annual reports of the Bureau of Agriculture and Forestry gave specifics on the "eradication of destructive wild animals" from the forest reserves. By the mid-1950s, the heading over the table listing the same information had morphed into simply "Harvest of Wild Animals."

Unlike the Department of Agriculture and Conservation, the DLNR did not put a high premium on the protection of forests. Instead, as reflected in the makeup of the Board of Land and Natural Resources that governed the department, its priority was to make State lands generate revenue, whether by leasing marginal lands to ranchers or by replanting stands of native trees with ones that were judged to be of greater commercial value. In 1974, the State Animal Species Advisory Committee, established by the Legislature (but largely inactive in recent years), warned that a five-year "forest planting plan" developed by the Division of Forestry "does not seem to have adequately considered the possibility of using native Hawaiian species."[1] The Division of Forestry was hardly slowed by this judgment, and proceeded with such nightmares as a chipping operation that razed the forest above Laupāhoehoe and the disastrous Waiākea timber plantings that to date have been a commercial cipher.

Instead of forest reserves being protected with an aggressive program of ungulate removal and fencing, as they were in territorial times, under the DLNR, fences failed and were not rebuilt. Ranchers routinely allowed cattle to graze (at no cost) in adjoining forest reserves. Other ungulates in the forests were now regarded as game and were no longer to be eradicated, but to be managed with the goal of "sustained yield."

A 1977 DLNR report on recreational opportunities shows just how much the ethic of protecting forests from ungulates had been turned on its head. Statewide, the report noted, "public hunting areas" included 713,092 acres in forest reserves owned by the State and just 85,124 State-owned acres *not* in the forest reserves.[2]

Statehood brought other developments that reinforced the distance between the DLNR and the ethic of conservation of native forests. Funds from a federal tax on the sale of hunting gear helped support game management, but until the mid-1970s, money from this source was unavailable to assist with research and conservation of native birds.

In 1970, recognizing that Hawaiian forests were disappearing quickly, the Legislature established the Natural Area Reserves System, intended to provide more robust protection for the relatively few pristine tracts of State land representing a cross-section of native habitats. Yet time and again, efforts to include high-value and disappearing habitats into the NAR system were frustrated when powerful ranching interests objected. (Puʻu Waʻawaʻa on Hawaiʻi Island, once described as a "botanical bonanza," was early on nominated for designation as a Natural Area Reserve, but by the time the ranch lease expired, the botanical value had disappeared, thanks to fires, grazing pressures by cattle and feral ungulates, and, not least, by the unpermitted "improvements" of the lessee, including an airstrip and landfill on State-leased lands.) Even now, proposals to remove ungulates from Natural Area Reserves are met with fierce resistance from hunters, who at one point, with the blessing of the DLNR's Division of Forestry and Wildlife, actually tore down a recently erected fence in the Pu'u o 'Umi reserve on Hawai'i Island.[3]

One of the most devastating developments in terms of forest protection occurred in 1981. That year, the Legislature transferred management of all land animals to the Division of Forestry, now rechristened the Division of Forestry and Wildlife, and renamed the old Fish and Game division the new Division of Aquatic Resources.

If the DLNR had previously been a house divided against itself, having to manage both hunting (in Fish and Game) and non-game wildlife (in Forestry), it now was even more conflicted. Forestry and Wildlife was now charged with *protecting* forests and native species *and protecting* the very game that was destroying them. This is illustrated with startling clarity in the State's anemic response to the 1979 landmark federal court decision ordering it to remove sheep, and later mouflon, from Mauna Kea as a means of protecting palila habitat. Thirty years after the initial court order, hundreds (if not more) sheep and mouflon continue to roam the mountain slopes. While hunters protest that the occasional State-sponsored helicopter kills deprive them of their sport and take food from the mouths of babes (really!), it is indisputable that hunter pressure on populations of *all* game mammals is so minimal as to be meaningless as a tool in their control. Put simply, in the absence of natural predators, these herbivores reproduce at so rapid a pace, and in such remote areas, that hunters are incapable of keeping their populations from increasing.

According to the DLNR's published records—a good index of effort up until the mid-1990s, when the department just stopped putting out an annual report—the numbers of game mammals taken year after year hover in the range of a few thousand a year. Given the huge amount of money and effort spent by the department in managing game, the losses to forests and watershed resources "sustained yield" hunting entails, the piddling population of hunters (around 10,000) relative to the total population, and their manifest ineffectiveness in controlling populations of game of any kind, be it deer, goats, pigs, sheep, or mouflon, any argument that the State should defer to hunter wishes in the management of natural resources is silly at best and craven at worst.

Invasive plant species pose almost as great a threat to native forests as do ungulates. Strawberry guava, or waiawi, and miconia are among the most serious of these invaders. While few protests have been raised against the eradication of miconia, a tiny but vocal troop of contrarians has come out against waiawi control, and in a testament to the failure of Hawai'i's educational system, they have been able to gain support for their position from several members of the Hawai'i County Council. Their protests, defending waiawi against the "speciesists" who have a bias against anything not native to these islands, have already delayed by years the release of an insect that has undergone years of testing to ensure it targets nothing other than waiawi. With every day that passes without action, the losses of native forest mount.

How can these problems be addressed in a meaningful way?

First, it is unreasonable to expect the DLNR to serve two masters. The hunting program should be turned over to the Department of Agriculture (if hunting is regarded as a means of putting food on the table) or the Department of Business, Economic Development, and Tourism (if hunting is regarded as a sport to attract tourists). Game animals in Hawai'i are not *natural* resources at all, and do not belong in an agency charged with protecting such resources. As a corollary to this, forest reserves must be fenced, and whatever pigs, goats, sheep, cattle, or mouflon remain inside the fence should be removed. Give hunters first crack, but if they are unable to take them all out, other means must be pursued. By giving the headache of dealing with hunters to another agency, the DLNR staff will be free to defend aggressively and uncompromisingly native forests and wildlife.

Second, the DLNR needs to take a look at its pasture leases. As each one expires, the pros and cons of continuing to have the land be grazed need to be weighed. In many cases, the damage to State lands—from erosion and overgrazing, from trampling by cattle, from encroachment by animals into neighboring forest reserves, and from foregone opportunities for more beneficial and lucrative use—far exceeds the risible lease rents paid by ranchers. While the goal of increasing the percentage of island-grown beef may be laudable, it needs to be weighed against the heavy costs this entails.

Third, the department must resume publication of meaningful, substantive reports on its activities. Past annual reports to the governor allowed the public to know who was occupying State land, what they were paying, what activities were to be conducted on those lands, and when leases expired. The numbers of hunting licenses and animals taken by hunters were regularly given, as was the acreage of forested lands, numbers of trees sold by State nurseries, and thousands of other data bits that gave the reader an impression of where the department's priorities lay and how it was working (or not) toward achieving its mission.

Now a bunker mentality exists in the department. Requests for information are met with hostility and bills that rise quickly into the four digits. When the department does not make available information in regular reports, and imposes impossibly high charges for anyone seeking such information, any notion of transparency is thwarted, making it all the more difficult to rally public support for its programs.

Still, it is vitally important that the budget of the Department of Land and Natural Resources not just be restored to levels of support it enjoyed a decade ago, but augmented to enable it to address the dire and imminent threats to native forests. The loss of key staff as a result of recent budget cuts will be difficult to overcome in the best of circumstances, but will be utterly impossible if the State does not fully fund the effort.

Expenditures by the DLNR have accounted for less than one percent of the State's general fund outlays in recent years. And yet no agency has greater responsibility for ensuring the perpetuation and health of the natural environment on which the entire economy and welfare of the state rests.

To be sure, other agencies have a role to play in protecting the state's terrestrial environment:

The Commission on Water Resource Management is all but dysfunctional. Its greatest duty is to approve and implement the State water plan, yet that task is years overdue. It has also made virtually no progress in its charge to protect aquatic resources through the establishment of instream flow standards for streams. The status quo flows, adopted as interim standards when the Water Code was adopted more than two decades ago, remain the norm for nearly every stream in the state.

The Office of Planning, which is charged with reviewing the State Land Use boundary designations every five years, has not even attempted this task since the early 1990s.

The Environmental Council, which plays a vital role in overseeing compliance with the State's environmental policy law, has been virtually disbanded by a lack of support from the administration; it last met in July 2009.

The Department of Agriculture is charged with protecting the state against the arrival of potentially invasive plants and animals, yet the branch responsible for this has been eviscerated.

Restoring these agencies to a level where they can carry out their missions is more than a matter of finding the funds. It is a matter requiring political will, and in the special case of the Department of Land and Natural Resources, the removal of its Achilles' heel, the charge to manage game.

CLIMATE CHANGE

CHIP FLETCHER

Hawai'i's climate is changing in ways that are consistent with the influence of global warming. In Hawai'i

Air temperature has risen

Rainfall and stream flow have decreased

Rain intensity has increased

Sea level and sea surface temperatures have increased

The ocean is acidifying

If these trends continue, scientists anticipate growing impacts to Hawai'i's water resources and forests, coastal communities, and marine ecology. As a result, there is a compelling need for sustained and enhanced climate monitoring and assessment activities, and for focused research to produce models of future climate changes and impacts in Hawai'i.

Should they continue, these trends point in certain directions and raise questions. Water, already a scarce resource in places on the islands, may grow scarcer. Will we continue building subdivisions in recharge areas? When will privately controlled water return to the public? Flash flooding, presently managed with aquatic-ecosystem-killing channelized waterways, may increase in intensity. How will we manage this threat yet continue attempts to restore native watersheds? Sea-level rise is likely to accelerate, threatening beaches and coastal communities. Who will lead the process to develop a shared vision of what is at risk and what qualities to protect? Rising sea surface temperature and ocean acidification threaten coastal and marine ecosystems. Removing water-shed stressors may improve reef sustainability. What management options lessen the impacts of acidification? Declining stream flow and rising sea level threaten coastal plain agriculture. What options do taro farmers have?

While researchers work to improve understanding of likely future changes to Hawai'i's climate, we need also to begin the process of managing climate risk. Do we love future generations as much as we love ourselves? If the answer is "yes," then the community discussion of how we manage climate risk in Hawai'i needs to begin soon.

SURFACE AIR TEMPERATURE

Hawai'i is getting warmer (Figure 1). Data[1] show a rapid rise in air temperature in the past thirty years, averaging 0.3°F per decade—a little less than the global average rate of about 0.36°F per decade. There is stronger warming at high elevations (above 2,600 feet; about 0.48°F per decade) than at low elevations (about 0.16°F per decade). Most of the warming is related to a larger increase in minimum temperatures compared to the maximum—a net warming about three times as large—causing a reduction of the daily temperature range.

This response to global warming is consistent with similar trends observed in North America.[2] Despite recent years where the rate of global warming was low,[3] surface temperatures in Hawai'i have remained high. Rapid warming at high elevations threatens water resources and may have significant ecological impacts, such as the spread of avian disease, decreased rainfall and cloud water, and threats to native forests.[4]

FIGURE 1. AIR TEMPERATURE IN HAWAI'I.

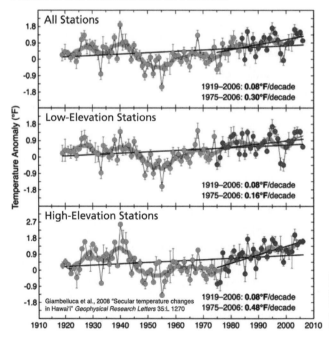

Air temperature is rising in Hawai'i, and has accelerated since the 1970s. High elevation temperature stations record greater warming than those at low elevations.

RAINFALL AND STREAM DISCHARGE

Perhaps nothing is as critical to life in the islands as rain, and in Hawai'i there are two principal sources: trade winds and Kona storms. Cloud formation by trade winds (Figure 2) is the most reliable and abundant source of water to the aquifers we rely upon. Although atmospheric circulation in the tropical Pacific has decreased, and global warming is identified as the cause,[5] it is not yet clear how the trade winds will respond to global warming. It also remains unclear how future rainfall will respond to global warming. The results of modeling studies have been equivocal,[6] although to some extent they indicate that we should anticipate decreased rainfall. Studies of rainfall records corroborate this. Rainfall in Hawai'i has steadily declined about 15 percent over the past twenty years.[7]

FIGURE 2. CLOUD FORMATION BY TRADE WINDS.

Figure 2. In the Hawaiian language, waiwai signifies an abundance of fresh water, and embodies the meaning of wealth. Though blessed with annual rainfalls much greater than many parts of the world, Hawai'i nonetheless experiences localized water shortage problems. How will climate change affect the trade winds and the production of cloud water? (photo by C. Fletcher).

Streams are one beneficiary of rain. Rainfall feeds streams in two ways: storm flow and base flow. Storm flow responds very quickly to rainfall, and causes stream levels to rise during and immediately after rainfall. Base flow, on the other hand, is supplied by groundwater, and maintains stream flow during periods between rainfall events. Base flow also responds to changes in rainfall over time, but much more slowly than storm flow. Beginning in the early 1940s, base flow has declined around the state,[8] and the cause is likely related to decreased rainfall. In Hawai'i, rainfall combines with steep geographic features to produce unique ecosystems that support diverse plants and animals. This pattern is threatened by rising air temperatures and decreased rainfall and stream discharge. Taro farming, a form of wetland agriculture common on low-lying coastal plains, is also tied to stream flow, but vulnerable to sea level rise. Between intruding salt water and declining stream flow, some farmers may be experiencing the impacts of global warming.

RAIN INTENSITY

Between 1958 and 2007, the amount of rain falling in the very heaviest down-pours (defined as the heaviest 1 percent of all events) has increased approximately 12 percent in Hawai'i.[9] Heavy rainfall means more than simply getting wet; it is a major challenge for civil defense agencies and emergency responders. Intense rains trigger a domino effect of other impacts, including flash flooding, mudslides and debris flows, road and business closures, infrastructure damage, and loss of public services to isolated communities. It was heavy rain that caused over $80 million dollars of damage in Mānoa Valley, O'ahu; isolated Hāna, Maui for weeks; flooded homes in Lā'ie, O'ahu; and swept houses off their foundations in Hilo, Hawai'i. When intense rains struck on New Year's Eve 1987, forty thousand people in Hawai'i Kai, Waimānalo, 'Aina Haina, and other east Honolulu communities went without power, emergency aid, communication, and road access for up to twenty-four hours. While these events cannot be directly tied to global warming, they are consistent with expectations in a warmer world, and they illustrate the severe impacts associated with intense rains.

Ironically, global warming appears to be taking Hawai'i into a time of declining fresh water resources and more intense rainstorms.

OTHER POTENTIAL WATER CYCLE IMPACTS

Look to the mountains, and see the nearly perpetual band of clouds on their slopes. Scientists infer that rising temperatures could result in a shallower cloud zone because of a possible rise in the lifting condensation level, which controls the bottom of the cloud, and a decline in the height of the trade wind inversion, which controls the top of the cloud. Where clouds intercept the land, forming fog, they deposit water droplets directly on the vegetation and soil. This process is a significant source of water for the mountain ecosystems of Hawai'i, and especially at windward exposures. With a smaller cloud zone, less cloud water would be available to these important forests.

Another concern is changes in the process of evapotranspiration. While rainfall and cloud water are the sources of water to the ecosystem, evaporation and transpiration (the emission of water vapor through the leaves of plants) return water to the atmosphere, thus reducing the amount going into streams and groundwater. Effects of warming on evapotranspiration are as yet unknown, but changes could further impact water resources already being affected by reduced rainfall.

Because surface air temperature, cloudiness, and rainfall depend on the trade winds, forecasting Hawai'i's climate depends on accurately modeling trade wind changes. Intergovernmental Panel on Climate Change[10] models do not agree on these aspects of climate for the region around Hawai'i. Other modeling[11] has shown that wind and rainfall responses to warming around the Pacific are not uniform, and depend strongly on the climate model being used. Skillful projections[12] of island climate must take into account the interaction of trade winds with island topography, and will rely on continued and enhanced monitoring of key climate variables.

SEA LEVEL

Sea level has risen in Hawai'i at approximately 0.6 inches per decade over the past century.[13] This may not seem like a substantial rate; however, long-term sea-level rise can lead to chronic coastal erosion, coastal flooding, and drainage problems, all of which are experienced in Hawai'i. This long-term trend also increases the impact of short-term fluctuations due to extreme tides,[14] leading to episodic flooding and erosion along the coast.

Although coastal erosion is not uniquely tied to global warming, it is a significant factor in managing the problem of high sea levels. Sea-level rise accelerates and expands erosion, potentially impacting beaches that were previously stable. Chronic erosion in front of developed lands has historically led to seawall construction, resulting in beach narrowing and loss.[15] Approximately 25 percent of beaches on O'ahu have narrowed or been lost to seawall construction. Losses are similar on other islands, where the average long-term rate of eroding coasts is about 1 foot per year.[16] On Kaua'i, 72 percent of beaches are chronically eroding, and 24 percent of them at an accelerating rate.

Although the rate of global mean sea-level rise has approximately doubled since 1990,[17] sea level not only did not rise everywhere, but actually declined in some large areas. The pattern of global sea level change is complex,[18] due to the fact that winds and ocean currents affect sea level, and those are changing also. In Hawai'i, improving our understanding of sea-level impacts requires attention to local variability, with careful monitoring and improved modeling efforts.

Because of global warming, sea-level rise is expected to continue, and to accelerate, for several centuries. By the end of the twenty-first century, sea level may exceed three feet above the 1990 level.[19] Continued sea-level rise will increase marine inundation of coastal roads and communities. Salt intrusion will intensify in coastal wetlands and groundwater systems, taro lo'i, estuaries, and elsewhere. Extreme tides already cause drainage problems in developed areas.

Sea-level rise threatens Hawai'i beaches (Figure 3), tourism, our quality of life, and our infrastructure. Hawaiian communities located at the intersection of intensifying storm runoff and rising ocean waters will endure increased flooding.

FIGURE 3. SEA-LEVEL RISE.

Sea-level rise threatens beaches and water-front development. The groundwater table in the coastal plain moves with sea level; hence, drainage problems will grow into a major problem among coastal communities (photo by C. Conger, reproduced by permission of C. Fletcher).

SEA SURFACE TEMPERATURE AND OCEAN ACIDIFICATION

At Station ALOHA (62 miles north of Kahuku Point, O'ahu), marine researchers at the University of Hawai'i and cooperating institutions have measured an increase of sea surface temperature of 0.22°F per decade, a result that is consistent with other estimates[20] for the latitudes of Hawai'i in the eastern North Pacific. Because of global warming this rate is likely to rise, potentially exposing coral reefs and other marine ecosystems to negative impacts related to temperature increases, including coral bleaching.[21] Bleaching results when corals lose the symbiotic algae that provide them with their principal source of food. Hawai'i is located in the cooler subtropical waters of the North Pacific. Although bleaching has become a major ecosystem catastrophe for many reefs around the world, Hawaiian reefs have largely escaped major, widespread bleaching events (Figure 4). However, continued warming of Hawaiian surface waters may eventually lead to bleaching.

FIGURE 4. LOCAL ECOSYSTEM DAMAGE.

In general, Hawai'i reefs have escaped global impacts. But overfishing and watershed practices[22] have produced significant local ecosystem damage (photo by K. Stender, reproduced by permission of C. Fletcher).

As rising carbon dioxide in the atmosphere mixes with seawater, the ocean acidifies. Measurements[23] at Station ALOHA over two decades document that the surface ocean around Hawai'i has grown more acidic at exactly the rate expected from chemical equilibration with the atmosphere. Continued acidification may have a host of negative impacts on marine life, and has the potential to alter the rates of ocean biogeochemical processes.

When carbon dioxide reacts with seawater it reduces the availability of dissolved carbonate. Carbonate (CO_3) is vital to shell and skeleton formation in corals, marine plankton, some algae, and shellfish. In coming decades, ocean acidification could have profound impacts on some of the most fundamental biological and geochemical processes of the sea. Plankton is a critical food source that supports the entire marine food chain. Declining coral reefs will impact coastal communities, tourism, fisheries, and overall marine biodiversity. Abundance of commercially important shellfish species may decline, and negative impacts on finfish may occur. This rapidly emerging scientific issue, and its potential ecological impacts, have raised concerns across the scientific and fisheries communities.

CLIMATE RISK MANAGEMENT

Like other science-based planning challenges, managing climate risk involves complex assessment based on the best available information originating, in part, with scientific research. Effective progress on the problem is facilitated by a strong partnership between scientists and planners; but how to proceed? The roadmap must come from an informed and involved community working to leave a resource-rich Hawaii to future generations.

Hawai'i's *risk* of damage from climate change is increasing because humankind refuses to take meaningful steps to counteract global warming. However, our *vulnerability* is increasing because Hawai'i leaders have not recognized the problem as worth planning for. If we are vulnerable to climate impacts, it is our fault. The danger is evident in all sectors. Water is key to agriculture, and efforts to advance local agriculture will be set back by declining rainfall, base flow, and stream discharge. Sea-level rise threatens much more than beaches. Intense rainfall events will have nowhere to drain when high ocean waters have flooded the storm drain system, and damaging marine events such as storm surge, tsunami, and high waves will penetrate further landward with each year. Acidification and sea surface temperature increases threaten our marine economy and tourism.

A place-based planning framework is needed that provides a strategy for moving forward. Appropriate steps will require substantial research and scenario-based decision-making (best, worst, and moderate cases).

SCENARIO-BASED DECISION-MAKING

Define the problem on a place-based scale

Explore the issues of climate change with the community

Develop a shared vision of what is at risk and what qualities to protect

Form a steering committee of stakeholders

Gather data, information, and tools

Develop models and monitoring of climate hazards

Make maps of the problem on time scales of concern

Identify and value the assets at risk

Identify and explore alternative strategies

Identify strategies for dealing with scenarios

Develop guidance/policies

Stage strategies on appropriate time scale

Build and sustain capacity and support

Align existing programs

Build the institutional capacity and political will to execute strategies

Institutionalize climate risk management programs and keep them current

CONCLUSIONS

The effects of global warming are evident in Hawai'i: air temperature is rising, rainfall and stream flow have decreased, rain intensity has increased, sea level and sea surface temperatures have increased, and the ocean is acidifying. Because these trends are likely to continue, scientists anticipate growing impacts to Hawai'i's water resources and forests, coastal communities and environments, and marine ecology. Now is the time to increase climate monitoring and assessment activities, and to produce skillful models of future climate changes and impacts. Climate change education and public awareness of the problem should expand in order to open a community discussion and implement place-based strategic planning.

ENERGY

HENRY CURTIS

In the late nineteenth century, Hawai'i energy and electricity systems were based on locally available resources, including biomass, bagasse (sugar waste), and hydropower. The twentieth century was the fossil fuel era, both in the U.S. and in Hawai'i. Reliance on petroleum, coal, and natural gas became the backbone of the economy. That changed in 1973, during the fourth Arab-Israeli war, when the Organization of Petroleum Exporting Countries (OPEC) launched the Arab Oil Embargo. The oil price shocks propelled energy issues onto the front burner around the world. Visionaries, exploring new heights, laid out bold new initiatives based on energy conservation, energy self-sufficiency, and alternatives to fossil fuels. Nowhere was the vision stronger than in Hawai'i, where advocates suggested that we become the international model for sustainability. The Hawai'i State Constitution was amended in 1978 with an energy self-sufficiency clause.

Shortly thereafter, the backlash of status quo forces regained the upper hand. President Reagan ripped out the recently installed solar panels at the White House. Hawai'i sought to diversify away from oil by turning to coal, which is now Hawai'i's number two fuel source. In 1988–89, AES Corporation built a 180 megawatt coal plant in Campbell Industrial Park, which currently supplies 20 percent of O'ahu's electricity. The Hawaiian Commercial and Sugar Company (HC&S) Pu'unēnē power plant on Maui consumes 60,000 tons of coal per year. Gay and Robinson (Kaua'i) proposed using coal and biomass to produce ethanol. Coal was also used at the Hilo Coast Power Company (1985–2004). Hawai'i's other major fuel sources are now wind, garbage-to-energy, and geothermal. In 2008 the price of oil rose to $140/barrel, affecting rates for electricity and transportation. For the U.S., oil accounts for only 2 percent of electricity, but in Hawai'i it accounts for 75 percent. Thus we were hit twice. We now export about 10 percent of the State Gross Product to buy foreign fossil fuels: petroleum and coal.

We must change our economic paradigm. Similar to the way a rock dropped in a pond creates waves rippling across the surface, each dollar spent

in Hawai'i generates $3–4 of local economic activity. Keeping the $6 billion
in Hawai'i would add $20 billion to the state economy.

KEY CONCEPTS

All energy options in the world are derived from three sources: the sun, the
moon, and the earth. Solar power includes photovoltaic panels, wind power,
biomass, biofuels, ocean thermal, coal, hydroelectric, oil, ocean wave energy,
and natural gas; lunar power includes tides; and earth power includes geothermal and nuclear (uranium deposits).

Firm power, also called baseload power, is power that is always available,
and includes coal, oil, gas, nuclear, geothermal, and ocean thermal energy
conversion (OTEC). Intermittent or variable sources are those that are available part of the time but not all of the time: wind, solar, and ocean wave energy. Most of the power on a grid must be baseload.

PATHS FORWARD

Seven paths lead forward: the macro, biofuel, ocean, battery, micro, high
tech, and energy efficiency paths. Each path can, but does not necessarily,
lead Hawai'i towards energy independence. They each have unique benefits,
costs, winners, losers, and intended and unintended impacts. There is an opportunity cost associated with each path: spending billions of dollars to promote one path precludes spending billions of dollars on each of the other
paths. Hawai'i can choose a path, or wait until someone else suggests a path.
The process can be planned or haphazard.

The Macro Path relies on an interisland grid interconnecting the grids
of Hawai'i Island, Maui, and O'ahu, and utilizing wind and geothermal to
power the grid. This path was conceived in the 1980s, when geothermal was
intended to power the State.

The Biofuel Path converts existing fossil fuel generators to biofuels. Locally grown vegetation allegedly can provide all of the electricity and transportation fuel that the state needs. Achim Steiner, Executive Director of the
United Nations Environment Programme, said in October 2009: "Biofuels
are a subject that has triggered sharply polarized views among policy-makers
and the public. They are characterized by some as a panacea representing a
central technology in the fight against climate change. Others criticise them
as a diversion from the tough climate mitigation actions needed . . . simplistic
approaches are unlikely to deliver a sustainable biofuels industry."[1] To understand biofuel impacts one must look at the whole system, rather than emis-
sions from smokestacks and pipes. Agriculture uses fossil fuels at every step,

from powering farm tractors, to making fertilizers and pesticides, to harvesting crops and converting them to a usable form. Farm runoff carries pesticides into the ocean, where there are now large dead zones. Slash and burn techniques are used to grow palm oil in Indonesian/Malaysian rainforests, while soybeans are displacing the Amazon rainforest.

In Hawai'i, it is unclear which crop grown in which area and under what conditions will be the solution. Large landowners are therefore unwilling to commit their land to bioenergy crops. Furthermore, the refineries needed to convert the crops to biofuels do not exist. The infrastructure is not in place, and water and labor issues have not been resolved. A serious issue that must also be addressed is Indirect Land Use Changes (ILUC). This refers to shifting production from food to bioenergy crops in one area of the world, and using virgin land in another area to make up for the lost food crop. For example, U.S. subsidies to convert corn into ethanol will encourage some American soybean growers to convert from soybeans to corn, which may lead to some Brazilian companies to destroy rainforests to grow those soybeans. Sometimes multinational agricultural businesses are responsible for both actions. The environmental impact is often far greater in the less developed country seeking to replace the world food stocks. American farmers have blocked the Environmental Protection Agency (EPA) from analyzing the net climate impact due to ILUC.

Another controversy surrounds carbon. Plants absorb carbon dioxide by photosynthesis. About half of the carbon is returned to the atmosphere via respiration by organisms. The rest is returned to the Earth via soil microorganisms. This partially decomposed organic matter becomes soil. Many industry studies allege that substituting biofuels for petroleum is carbon neutral. That is, when bioenergy crops grow, they absorb carbon from the atmosphere, and when they are burned they release this carbon back into the atmosphere. These two processes cancel each other, proponents assert; thus biofuels are better than other fossil fuels. This is a very naive approach based on spin, not reality. Besides the amount of fossil fuel used in farming, most of the carbon is left out of the analysis.

Most carbon in the world is found in marine sediment and rocks, and most of the rest is in the oceans. Carbon is also in fossil fuel, the soil, the atmosphere, and vegetation, in that order. Most industry studies examine only the last two sources: the atmosphere-vegetation interaction. Combined, these two sources account for less than 1 percent of the Earth's carbon. An analysis must also include changes to the amount and type of carbon found in the soil.

Finally, it takes about 1,000 tons of water to produce one ton of grain. Agricultural interests use over 70 percent of the world's fresh water supply. In the U.S. and in California it is over 80 percent. The rest of the water is used by industry, government, and residents.

The Ocean Path relies on Sea Water Air Conditioning, Ocean Thermal Energy Conversion (OTEC), and Blow-Hole Wave Energy Conversion Systems to replace all land-based generators. Sea Water Air Conditioning involves heat exchange between freshwater pipes pulling heat from buildings, and cold seawater pipes transferring the heat to the ocean. Cornell University built a 6-mile intake pipe from a cold lake in upstate New York. A thorough multiyear environmental analysis of the impacts found them to be minimal. The total heat added to the lake over the course of a year is equivalent to the heat that the lake absorbs from one hour of summer sunshine. The Cornell and Toronto systems were installed by Makai Ocean Engineering, a Hawai'i firm. O'ahu could handle six or seven systems, including two for Waikīkī, displacing 40 percent of the energy load in urban areas.

The Electric Power Research Institute (EPRI) is a national utility think tank. Its members represent over 90 percent of the electricity generated by shareholder-owned utilities in the United States. In 2004, EPRI examined wave power, and more specifically, looked in detail at Hawai'i's potential wave power. EPRI found that each island could meet its electricity needs through wave energy. Wave Energy Systems do not involve waves crashing down along reefs and the coastline, but rather ocean swells which provide predictable power.

The Blow-Hole Wave Energy System consists of a compartment with water at the bottom and air on top. When a swell arrives, the water level rises and air is forced out of the blowhole. When the wave recedes, the air is sucked back into the blowhole. A two-way air turbine spins in the same direction as the air goes in and out, generating electricity. Having the spinning device rotating in the same direction regardless of which way the air is moving significantly increases the efficiency of the generator. There is only one moving part in Oscillating Water Column systems, and unlike most other wave energy systems, it is above water, with the physical structure rising about thirty feet above sea level. After accounting for the power to run the system, blowhole energy systems can produce net power with a six inch ocean swell. An Oceanlinx system is being deployed off Maui.

OTEC systems create usable energy through the differential in temperature between two different ocean layers. OTEC can only work in warm water areas without continental shelves. Warm surface water brings sufficient heat to vaporize a working fluid such as ammonia, and send it through a turbine. Another pipe containing deep cold ocean water turns the ammonia back into a liquid. The ammonia is self-contained in a looped pipe. The pipes are constructed to minimize harming sea life, which can be trapped on the intake valve, sucked through the system, or affected by the water discharge. These three impacts are called entrainment (the traveling of biota through the system), impingement (the hitting and trapping of biota against the screen on the intake pipes), and secondary entrainment (caused by biota interacting with the turbulent discharge water).

The Battery Path focuses on converting all vehicles from internal combustion engines to electric vehicles, allowing electricity to flow both ways from the grid and the vehicle batteries. Batteries can store night-time wind energy for use during the day. Ten 100-watt light bulbs that are lit for one hour use one kilowatt-hour of energy. That same amount of energy will move an electric car about four miles down the road. There is no reduction in greenhouse gases emitted by using an electric vehicle on the mainland, because half of the electricity there is generated from coal. However, in Hawai'i there is often night-time wind power available that is normally wasted but that could be used to power vehicles. Tawhiri, the wind farm at South Point on Hawai'i Island, is able to produce night-time power that is not being used by the Hawaii Electric Light Company (HELCO). In 2007, twelve million kilowatt-hours of wind energy was wasted. By 2008, the amount reached eighteen million kilowatt-hours. Electric vehicles could easily tap into the power grid at night, absorbing the excess energy produced from wind power.

Better Place, a California-based company, has recently proposed a model for electric vehicle infrastructure. Electric charging stations would be built throughout a region, and existing gas stations would be replaced with a network of fully-automated battery exchange stations. These stations could process vehicles made by many different manufacturers. Vehicles would be powered by lithium ion batteries, which are currently in widespread use in laptops, cell phones, and power tools. Rechargeable lithium ion batteries can reliably deliver driving distances of over 100 miles on a single charge. The batteries can be recharged in the same amount of time that they were used for driving. Since the average vehicle is driven less than 100 miles per day, they could be recharged easily during the night. Car batteries can be automatically plugged into a recharging station about the size of a parking meter. The voltage of the recharging station is similar to a wall socket in a house.

The Micro Path is based on small grids powered by rooftop wind and solar, and by reusing vegetable oil to make biodiesel. Each day more solar energy falls to the Earth than the total amount of energy the planet's 6 billion inhabitants consume in twenty-seven years. The entire U.S. electricity demand could be met by covering 9 percent of Arizona with photovoltaic panels. Traditional solar panels are flat and convert sunlight into electricity. Concentrated Solar

Power (CSP) systems use a parabolic mirror to focus sunlight onto a pipe containing mineral oil. The oil transfers its heat to an adjacent water pipe through a heat exchanger. The water is thus converted to steam which drives a turbine which in turn generates electricity.

In Hawai'i, unlike California, the peak energy use occurs after sunset. The hot mineral oil can be stored for a few hours with minimal heat loss. Thus CSP offers a way of capturing the heat of the sun and using it during the evening peak.

Small wind systems could be installed on thousands of rooftops in Hawai'i. The advantage of wind is that it is the cheapest renewable energy source of electricity in Hawai'i and much of the world. Rooftops could be used for multiple systems: solar water heaters, photovoltaic panels or concentrated solar power, and micro-wind. The Department of Urban and Regional Planning (DURP) at the University of Hawai'i at Mānoa is housed in Saunders Hall, where the roof has a solar panel and a micro-wind system. Pacific Biodiesel is making biodiesel from used vegetable oil.

The High Tech Path merges the internet, computers, and electricity, allowing the utility to know the moment-to-moment energy use of every energy user. This approach uses "smart" meters and "smart" grids that can send and receive data in real time from the utility's grid management system. Discounted electricity rates can be offered to those who will allow the utility to turn off energy loads when demand exceeds supply. Net Metering allows a ratepayer to transfer electricity to the grid during the day, remove electricity from the grid in the evening, and pay only for the net used from the grid. Under federal law, ratepayers may not receive payments from the utility if they give more electricity than they get. Feed-In Tariffs get around this problem. Ratepayers have two meters. One is the traditional meter that records the electricity the ratepayer buys at the regular rate from the utility. The other meter sells electricity to the grid at a rate set by the Hawai'i Public Utilities Commission (PUC), so that the average system owner can recover costs and make a small profit. In addition, transparent contracts can allow for customers' systems to connect quickly and efficiently to the grid. Feed-In Tariffs in Germany and Spain have led to a rapid growth in renewable energy systems.

The Energy Efficiency Path relies on reducing the demand for grid-based electricity. Solar water heating relies on solar power to provide hot water. Solar heating systems are generally composed of solar thermal collectors and a fluid system to move the heat from the collector to its point of usage. The system may use electricity for pumping the fluid, and have a reservoir or tank for heat storage and subsequent use.

Light shelves placed below windows can reflect sunlight upward to ceilings to create general illumination. Rooftop Solar Tubes capture sunlight from a number of directions, and through reflective material and/or mirrors within the tube, transfer that light to where it is needed within buildings. Skylight windows or domes placed on building roofs provide natural sunlight.

Often electronic devices use almost the same amount of electricity whether they are on or off. This is a "consumer" convenience allowing quick starts. These phantom loads can be measured in real time by installing small meters between the appliance cord and the wall socket. Consumers can readily turn off systems that use a lot of phantom power.

Toy ovens are often powered by an incandescent light bulb; it cooks food because practically all of the energy emerging from traditional bulbs is heat, not light. In buildings, this light bulb heat must be removed from rooms by using air conditioning. Compact fluorescent light bulbs provide the same lighting but without the heat.

The energy efficiency path results in unintended side effects. Lord Jevons pointed out in 1865 that reducing the cost of products via energy efficiency lowers the price and increases demand, which raises the total energy used. Businesses may switch to lower cost energy efficient air conditioners, which will drive down their cost of business. This may reduce the price of the goods they sell to undercut competition, thus increasing their sales. The amount of electricity in each of the goods they sell drops; however, they need more electricity because they are producing more goods. Residents who replace their existing air conditioner with a new, more efficient air conditioner find that their energy bill drops, allowing them to spend more money on other things. Residents who rely on opening windows may see all the advertisements for efficient air conditioners and decide to buy one. This increases their energy bill. The net effect of these positive and negative impacts is unknown. There is a lack of current peer reviewed studies to know which impact dominates. When energy efficiency and renewable energy systems are installed together, the former lowers economic costs and the latter decreases dependence on foreign fossil fuel. Thus they have a positive synergistic effect.

CONCLUSION

Hawai'i is at a crossroads. Climate change, peak oil, oil spikes, and an economy which exports 10 percent of its value to purchase foreign fuel all threaten Hawai'i's self reliance. This is not sustainable.

Our host culture sees everything as interconnected—the web of life. Self-reliance exists at the local level, and should increase to move us to total energy self-reliance as soon as possible. Hawai'i must develop a decentralized, distributed, community supported approach to sustainability. Energy is the cornerstone of sustainability. Hawai'i has every natural resource to create our own energy, and an abundance of human resources and technological know-how to design innovative systems. Hawai'i can be the petri dish for renewable energy systems. With the political will, we can become the world's laboratory for energy innovation.

Solutions should include utilizing building rooftops to provide solar and wind energy; encouraging electric cars that take from and give power to the electric grid; beautifying communities with tree-lined streets, bike lanes, and jogging and walking paths; promoting mālama 'āina; and building healthy and safe communities by investing in social capital. Hawai'i can create a peaceful, just, and shared future where everyone's voice matters, where communities are interdependent, and where schools build the leaders of tomorrow.

WATER

D. KAPUA'ALA SPROAT

AIA I HEA KA WAI A KĀNE?

E ui aku ana au iā 'oe,   One question I put to you:
Aia i hea ka Wai a Kāne?   Where is the water of Kāne?
Aia i ke kuahiwi,   Yonder on mountain peak,
I ke kualono,   on the ridges steep,
I ke awāwa,   in the valleys deep,
I ke kahawai;   where the rivers sweep;
Aia i laila ka Wai a Kāne.   There is the water of Kāne.

E ui aku ana au iā 'oe,   This question I ask of you:
Aia i hea ka Wai a Kāne?   Where, pray, is the water of Kāne?
Aia i kai, i ka moana,   Yonder, at sea, on the ocean,
I ke kualau, i ke 'ānuenue   In the driving rain, in the heavenly bow,
I ka pūnohu, i ka ua koko   In the piled-up mist wraith, in the blood-red rainfall
I ka 'ālewalewa;   In the ghost-pale cloud form;
Aia i laila ka Wai a Kāne.   There is the water of Kāne.

—from "He Mele nō Kāne"[1]

IN SEARCH OF HAWAI'I'S LIFE-GIVING WATERS

The mounting challenges facing Hawai'i's natural and cultural resources provide a perfect opportunity to ponder a timeless question: "Aia i hea ka Wai a Kāne?" Where are the waters of Kāne, the waters of life? "He Mele Nō Kāne," an ancient song from the island of Kaua'i, explains in poetic detail that fresh water permeates all aspects of life in Hawai'i. These waters rim the horizon from where the sun rises in the East to where it sets in the West. They are found on mountain peaks and in river bottoms, at sea and on land in the forms of rain, clouds, and rainbows, and hidden deep within the earth as aquifers or bubbling up as springs. "He wai e mana, he wai e ola, e ola no 'eā"[3]—It is fresh water that empowers and provides life.

As this ancient wisdom demonstrates, Native Hawaiians possess a keen understanding of the hydrologic cycle that reflects both the interconnection between Hawai'i's water resources and the relationship between human beings and our environment. In contemporary times, however, the same wisdom that enabled Native Hawaiians to thrive in these islands for countless generations no longer drives water management practices. Hawai'i's water resources and communities have suffered as a result. The waters of life are no longer as abundant as "He Mele Nō Kāne" proclaimed. Most of Hawai'i's streams no longer flow continuously from mauka to makai (from the mountains down into the ocean). Where they still flow, stream and marine ecosystems are often polluted or choked with invasive species as opposed to native species. They no longer thrive. Meanwhile, ground water supplies that feed nearshore marine ecosystems and provide drinking water for most of Hawai'i's communities have also declined in quality and quantity. Native Hawaiian traditional and customary practices, and other local activities dependent on abundant fresh water supplies, including fishing and gathering in streams and in the ocean, as well as traditional agriculture and aquaculture, are no longer conducted to the extent that they once were.

Where is the water of Kāne today? What happened to the waters of life that nourished our communities physically and spiritually? Most critically, what must be done *now* to ensure that Hawai'i's water resources, people, and practices can endure into the future? This essay explores the current troubled state of Hawai'i's water reserves—how we got to this point, and what we must do in response.

HOW DID WE GET HERE?

As "He Mele Nō Kāne" illustrates, Native Hawaiians understood the interconnection between Hawai'i's water resources and people. We recognized that lush forests and healthy watersheds gathered abundant rains that fed streams and seeped deep into the earth to recharge drinking water supplies. We knew that fresh water flowing down streams and bubbling up as springs, especially in coastal areas, was vital to feed an estuary system where freshwater and marine life could thrive. We understood that the cultivation of kalo (taro, or *Colocasia esculenta*) required an abundant supply of fresh water to flow through irrigated terraces and back into streams, and that this was necessary to sustain the larger community. "He wai e mana, he wai e ola, e ola no 'eā." Water truly empowered and provided life for ecosystems and the human communities that depended on them. These fundamental truths were cultivated through years and generations of living close to the land and learning from past mistakes and successes.

As island people who rely on fresh water to survive, Native Hawaiians developed an intimate relationship with our resources. In addition to providing a foundation for indigenous society, fresh water was also deified as a kinolau or physical embodiment of Kāne, one of the four principal akua or gods of the Hawaiian pantheon. As Handy, Handy, and Pukui explain, "Kāne—the word means 'male' and 'husband'—was the embodiment of male procreative energy in fresh water, flowing on or under the earth in springs, in streams and rivers, and falling as rain (and also as sunshine), which gives life to plants. . . . Regardless of all such distinctions, life-giving waters were sacred."[3] Given the physical and spiritual nature of Native Hawaiians' relationship to fresh water, these resources were held in trust for present and future generations.

Laws and customs both prior to Western contact and during Hawaiʻi's independent kingdom reflected these important principles, recognizing that water could not be "owned" in any sense, but instead must be proactively managed as a resource for generations to come.[4] For instance, the Kingdom of Hawaiʻi's first Western-style constitution in 1840 included strong public trust principles, declaring that the land, along with its resources, "was not [the King's] private property. It belonged to the Chiefs and the people in common, of whom [the King] was the head and had the management of the landed property."[5]

The arrival of Western foreigners to Hawaiian shores beginning in about 1778 and the subsequent decimation of the indigenous population by introduced diseases affected everything in the islands, including the management of water resources. This transformation resulted from numerous trends, including the institution of private property via the Māhele (between approximately 1845 and 1855), the subsequent consolidation of land ownership by foreign (largely American) interests, and the growing recognition that Hawaiʻi's climate and year-round growing season made plantation agriculture, and especially sugar cane, a lucrative business.

To establish and expand plantations, massive irrigation systems were constructed to transport and use water in ways and locations that nature never intended. Instead of utilizing water within watersheds, and allowing geology and hydrology to decide where and how water should flow, plantations began to redirect natural systems radically. To satisfy their thirsty crops, sugar planters constructed ditches that diverted streams from wet, Windward, predominantly Native Hawaiian communities, to the drier Central and Leeward plains where sugar was cultivated, and wells siphoned ground water. This was often done with no consideration of or consultation with affected communities.

Water was simply taken and streams and springs dried up. The affected communities—both natural and human—were left to live or die with the consequences. This rapid change altered the natural environment, and also inflicted significant physical and cultural harms on Native Hawaiians, many of which remain unaddressed to this day. Within a short period, plantations and their irrigation systems took root on the major Hawaiian Islands, fundamentally changing how and where water was used for over a century.

Sugar's rise to dominance rewrote the social contract. Plantations used public trust resources for private commercial purposes, but in turn, the plantations supported entire towns, communities, and even whole islands. Plantations *were* the economy. This economic dominance pervaded the government as well. Management practices and even court decisions in the Hawaiian Kingdom and Territory reflected increasingly Western notions of private property. Instead of continuing to respect water as a physical embodiment of Akua Kāne, and a fundamental requirement for a balanced and healthy environment, water was commodified and available to the highest bidder.

Not surprisingly, conflicts over water ensued—first, between plantation interests and Native Hawaiians, and later, between competing sugar plantations. A Commission of Private Ways and Water Rights was created in 1860 to address controversies over water. Initially, a board of three commissioners (two Native Hawaiians and one foreigner) was appointed from each election district within the Kingdom to resolve water disputes. Although both the boards and courts were directed "to declare and to protect these rights as they existed, under the ancient Hawaiian customs and regulations," the ability to respond to individual cases and reapportion water was constrained, as decisions and practices reflected increasingly Western notions of ownership as opposed to management.[6] Amendments over the years substituted a single commissioner for the boards and changed the appeals process; eventually, the boards' duties were transferred to circuit court judges in 1907 to maintain the new status quo.

After about a century of plantation rule, a movement emerged in the 1960s and 1970s to reaffirm public management and control over water resources. One critical stimulus to this movement was that after statehood in 1959, Hawai'i judges were appointed in Hawai'i, as opposed to being selected in Washington D.C., as they had been during the Territory. This proved crucial, because locally appointed judges better understood Hawai'i laws and issues, including Hawaiian custom and tradition, which provides an important legal foundation.[7]

The case of *McBryde Sugar Company v. Robinson* on the Island of Kaua'i brought the tensions regarding water as public resource or private property to a head.[8] Two sugar companies were embroiled in litigation over their respective rights to take water from the Hanapēpē river. The Hawai'i Supreme Court, led by Chief Justice William S. Richardson (who was also Native Hawaiian), took the occasion in 1973 to settle both the bickering between the sugar companies and the larger issue of water management in Hawai'i. The court clarified that although the parties in that case had rights to use water, they had *no ownership* interest in the water itself.[9] Those rights were never included when fee simple title was instituted in Hawai`i. Instead, the court ruled that the sovereign—currently, the State of Hawai'i—holds all water in trust for the benefit of the larger community. The sugar companies disagreed and filed multiple appeals in both federal and state court. Ultimately, those appeals were resolved in favor of the State.

Around the same time that the *McBryde* litigation was taking place, sugar plantations began to close and lost their dominant economic role to tourism and the military. Communities seized this opportunity to reexamine the current legal framework, and to manage more proactively Hawai'i's water resources for the benefit of the larger community, and not just for the profit of a handful of private interests. The 1978 Constitutional Convention passed amendments that were later ratified by Hawai'i's voters to enshrine resource protection as a constitutional mandate. Article XI, section 1 of Hawai'i's constitution now declares that "[f]or the benefit of present and future generations, the State and its political subdivisions shall conserve and protect Hawai'i's natural beauty and all natural resources, including land, water, air, minerals and energy sources, and shall promote the development and utilization of these resources in a manner consistent with their conservation and in furtherance of the self-sufficiency of the State." And Article XI, section 7 mandates that "[t]he State has an obligation to protect, control and regulate the use of Hawai'i's water resources for the benefit of its people." In 1987, the Legislature enacted Hawai'i's Water Code, Hawai'i Revised Statutes chapter 174C, which established a new framework for water resource management that balanced resource protection with reasonable and beneficial use.

WHERE ARE WE TODAY?

At the date of this publication, Hawai'i's water resources continue to decline.[10] Changing weather patterns influenced by global warming have led to long-term decreases in rainfall, which have contributed to declines in ground water recharge. With less water returning to nature's underground storage facilities, water levels in Hawai'i's aquifers and flow in our streams have waned. Over one hundred years of plantation stream diversions have also prevented waters from flowing along natural courses and recharging ground water supplies in appropriate areas. This lack of mauka to makai stream flow has compounded the impacts of already decreasing ground water levels, negatively impacting instream uses (including native stream life, aesthetics, and public recreation), while also decreasing the amount of water available to feed coastal waters and support marine life in those areas.

Despite declining water levels, ground water withdrawals are on the rise, due to increasing urbanization. Growing use at a time of shrinking supplies has reduced water quality, which on Maui, for example, has threatened the resource to the point that specific wells can no longer be used.[11] To make matters worse, the impacts of global warming will continue to complicate issues in ways that currently are not fully understood.

Given the fragile state of our resources, proactive management is needed now more than ever, but the Hawai'i Water Commission—the primary agency responsible for managing water resources—is facing a budgetary and staffing crisis. Over one third of the agencies' positions are vacant, and it is unclear whether they will be filled. Despite laws on the books, large companies—former plantations included—continue to take advantage of this situation, and treat public water resources as their private property. Our management system has been reduced to might makes right, fueling even more litigation.

And more change lurks on the horizon. All but one sugar plantation in Hawai'i has closed. In the absence of proactive management, communities on O'ahu, Hawai'i Island, and Maui are employing the Water Code's legal tools to take back waters from plantation agriculture and to restore mauka to makai stream flows to support community and other uses, such as small family farming and traditional and customary Native Hawaiian practices. For example, in the battle over the water diverted by the Waiāhole Ditch on O'ahu, a struggle which began in the mid-1990s, the Water Commission balanced competing needs.[12] It ordered the partial restoration of Windward streams for small family farming and other public uses, but also allocated water to Leeward commercial interests. Some have argued that the Commission backed away from fully implementing the public trust, and instead gave the former plantation interests everything they wanted. For example, corporate giants like Del Monte and the Estate of James Campbell received just about every drop of water they sought by declaring their commitment to agriculture, and their need for Waiāhole stream water in particular. But since getting the permits, Del Monte has closed its operations, and Campbell Estate has sold off farmlands for urban development.

The same pattern is now playing out on Maui. The Water Commission's lack of resources and political will to enforce the law vigorously has left management priorities to be set by litigation. Only one sugar plantation remains on Maui, and communities in both Nā Wai 'Ehā (Central Maui) and East Maui are using the Water Code's legal tools to restore mauka to makai flow to diverted streams to support the myriad community uses dependent upon them. But Hawaiian Commercial and Sugar Company (HC&S) now puppets what Del Monte and Campbell Estate argued in the *Waiāhole* case on Oʻahu. Claiming it wants to stay in agriculture forever, HC&S says it needs every drop of water it has now, regardless of what the law requires. The truth of the matter is that in Nā Wai ʻEhā, for example, HC&S historically split diverted stream water with the former Wailuku Sugar plantation, using only one third. With Wailuku Sugar's closure and sale of about 5,400 acres, HC&S is now using the lion's share of the water taken from Nā Wai ʻEhā communities on a fraction of the original plantation-irrigated acreage. In the meantime, HC&S and others, especially the Hawaiʻi Farm Bureau, are maneuvering politically to amend the Water Code to ensure that their monopoly over public trust resources continues. HC&S has also sought federal taxpayer subsidies to pursue biofuel research, even though portions of their over 35,000-acre plantation have already been slated for development, and pending legal actions make it unclear how much water HC&S will be entitled to keep taking in the future.

WHAT DO WE NEED TO CHANGE?

Despite Hawaiʻi's long struggle to manage water resources appropriately, there is hope for the future. Years of private appropriation of public resources inspired and informed Hawaiʻi's Water Code, which actually balances protection with beneficial use, and seeks to restore long-neglected resources. This law can work efficiently if the Water Commission receives the resources necessary to do its job. Without more positions and funding, however, litigation as opposed to departmental planning will continue to establish public priorities.

   The time is now to invest in Hawaiʻi's resources, by supporting the Water Commission and others engaged in resource management and data collection, and by looking beyond the law to ensure that we—all of Hawaiʻi's people—are doing what is needed to protect these resources into the future. Funding for scientific monitoring and research at the county, state, and federal levels has declined along with the resources themselves. For instance, the Water Commission's entire data collection branch was eliminated in 2009. In addition, the gauging network operated by the Pacific Islands Water Science Center of the United States Geological Survey (USGS), a federal agency dedicated to collecting, analyzing, and disseminating hydrologic data, has been forced to cut its stream gauging every year for the last several years. This reduction is not because management agencies have all the information they need; at this time of increasing pressure on declining resources, we need more information, not less. As a community, we must demand and provide support for a better scientific understanding of these complex issues to inform management decisions. This will require more funding for data collection and research, especially by USGS. We cannot continue to dole out water without a more complete understanding of how to manage these resources with at least one eye towards the future.

Given the fiscal reality of the current budget crisis, we need creative solutions to get this work done. Although government agencies have played an important role, and must continue to do so, we cannot rely solely on those agencies to do all the work for us. As communities we need to take the initiative to educate ourselves and kōkua; for example, by supporting watershed partnerships, or by getting actively involved in management ourselves. Much of this can be accomplished by learning more about the water resources in our own communities. Where does our water come from when we turn on a faucet, and where does it go when we flush a toilet? What laws protect our water resources, and what can we do to help enforce them?[13]

Finally, and most importantly, both individuals and government agencies must dig deep to find the political will to do the right thing and move forward from the plantation past. To sustain Hawai'i into the future, fresh water must be actively managed as a public trust, not as the private property of any business or individual. To accomplish this, some redistribution of resources is necessary. Streams must be restored so that they can flow continuously into the ocean for ecological and human benefit, including recharging underground supplies and providing drinking water for our communities into the future. Using alternative sources must be required, especially reclaimed and brackish water sources, both of which are largely underutilized and wasted. Existing water users, whether individual homeowners or large sugar plantations, must invest in making their uses more efficient. Gone are the days when people or companies got away with wasting one of life's most precious resources because no one could be bothered to line a reservoir or install low-flow fixtures. We have both the technological capacity and the social responsibility to do more with less, so that our natural systems will be protected and water supplies will be available into the future.

As we ponder what has happened to the waters of life, we must take decisive action now to protect these precious resources. If we leave that to future generations, it may be too late. After all, "he wai e mana, he wai e ola, e ola no, 'eā!" It is water that empowers and water that provides life!

SOVEREIGN GROUND

DANA NAONE HALL

RETHINKING THE WAY FORWARD: OLA NĀ IWI

Protests erupted over the excavation of an ancient Hawaiian burial site at Honokahua, Maui in October 1988; by December of that year, Governor John Waihee halted the digging. Honokahua was the first time that massive desecration and destruction of a burial site had been stopped. The disturbed remains of 1,100 individuals, which archaeologists estimated represented about half the number of those buried there, were reinterred at the site, and out of that sacrifice, Hawai'i's burial protection law was born.

Honokahua was not the first large-scale disturbance of a sand dune burial site, given the penchant for building hotels on Hawai'i's shorelines. Stories still abound about the earlier development of Kā'anapali, several miles south of Kapalua, and one can only imagine the displacement of thousands of ancient graves in Waikīkī. However, the point of this reflection is not to mourn what is gone, but to move forward with the understanding that it is possible to renew our connection to the past and rethink the future.

Hawai'i's post-Contact history is filled with episodes of Native Hawaiians' alienation from the land to the point where many of our people are homeless today—both those forced to live on beaches or under freeways and those unable to afford the price of a house and consigned to rent other people's houses for the rest of their lives. The alienation of land through its acquisition and development by others (in the case of hotel development by out-of-state and, frequently, international entities) compels a deeper understanding of the past.

Since Honokahua, I have encountered hundreds of ancestral burials and the funerary objects that sometimes accompany them. Some of the burials are a thousand years old and more, while others date from the fifteenth to the nineteenth centuries. Our State burial law declares that all burial sites are significant, and this statute is weighted toward preservation in place of these sites. Each site, whether found alone or among a concentration of burials, is unique.

No one owns a burial site except perhaps the individual whose remains are interred at that site. Importantly, not even a landowner owns the burials that may be present on property he or she owns. This fundamental fact gives the burial places of our Hawaiian ancestors an inherent sovereignty.

Wherever our Hawaiian ancestors are buried, an island of sovereignty exists. Each time a decision is made to disinter Hawaiian iwi from their place of burial, their home for numberless years, our right to exist is affected. On the other hand, every decision to preserve in place a native Hawaiian burial site strengthens us as a people.

In recent years, the State Historic Preservation Division (SHPD) has allowed politics and economic demands to trump laws and administrative rules designed to protect and preserve significant cultural and historic sites for future generations. One high-profile case involved the redevelopment of the Ward Villages property in Kaka'ako. More than sixty burials were identified during the course of subsurface excavations, and many of these burials were disturbed or completely disinterred during initial phases of the project.

A number of the burials were found in a sandy matrix that comprised the original sand dune system. I was amazed that beneath urban fill the iwi had slept undisturbed in the dunes until now. For me, this was history at its most intimate. But just as we were rediscovering these ancient vestiges, they were being destroyed.

The poignancy of this situation was underscored by another bit of history. The land once belonged to Victoria Ward (born in 1846) and her family. Victoria Ward was a great supporter of the Hawaiian monarchy, and remained a loyal friend to Queen Lili'uokalani after the overthrow. As an expression of her sentiments, she slept under a Hawaiian flag attached to the canopy of her bed.

While I believe that serious mistakes were made in the Ward Villages case, and that SHPD was derelict in its duties, nevertheless, Honokahua, as its name indicates, has given us the opportunity to make our foundation stronger. As living descendants, we honor those who placed the iwi in their resting places with the intent that they remain undisturbed throughout time. Fulfilling this responsibility, we reaffirm who we are as a people—that we too have a place here, and it comes from the bones of our ancestors.

THE PRICE OF PARADISE REDUX

Hawai'i ranks first in state tourism spending among the fifty states. As the fourth smallest state in area, it might be said that more money is spent per acre to market Hawai'i than any other state. Hawai'i also spends more per visitor. In 2009, Hawai'i spent $60 million to draw 6.5 million tourists. California, the third largest state, expended $50 million to capture 28 million visitors. Florida, twenty-second largest, paid $13.5 million and attracted 94.7 million visitors.

Even though tourism revenue accounts for nearly 30 percent of Hawai'i's gross state product, the comparative figures given above argue for a rethinking of the commitment of so much public money for this industry. Most political candidates dutifully recite the need to diversify our economy without any real follow-up. If we are serious, a community-wide public discussion must be undertaken and priorities for State spending must be shifted. Otherwise, Hawai'i will continue to be buffeted by economic winds and global events beyond its control.

THE EDUCATION OF HAWAIIAN CHILDREN

Everyone has a stake in the education of Hawai'i's children. Kamehameha Schools has a particular stake in the education of children of Hawaiian ancestry. In the years that I attended Kamehameha, there was only the Kapālama campus on the island of O'ahu.

Soon after decisions were made to construct new schools on Maui and the island of Hawai'i, the Bishop Estate Trustees, charged with implementing the will of Bernice Pauahi Bishop, became engulfed in controversy. One of the trustees was a former District Superintendent of public schools on Maui; she was known as the "education" trustee. Education was her fiefdom, and she ruled with an autocratic hand.

I felt, at that time, that if new schools were to be built on neighbor islands that the emphasis should be on educating orphans and the indigent, as Princess Bernice, or Ke Alii Pauahi as she is now referred to, intended. I have always hoped that after Kapālama, the trust's resources would be directed toward educating the least advantaged of our children.

With the majority of the state's population residing on O'ahu, gathering approximately 3,000 academically gifted Hawaiian students at the Kapālama campus (including students from outer islands who boarded at the school) did not impoverish other schools, whether public or private, of academically successful native Hawaiian student role models. This is not the case on Hawai'i Island and Maui. There is a much more insular quality to these campuses, and while I do not begrudge these fine students the opportunities presented to them, I cannot help but feel that as the "best and brightest" they were likely to be successful at whatever school they chose to attend, and in the public school context, they would have added to the vitality of these schools.

The more difficult decision would have been to educate the underserved. It may not be as attractive to take on the task of addressing learning disabilities and learning delays, but surely it can be just as rewarding. We have one bright shining academy on a hill. Did we really need two more?

I know and appreciate that Kamehameha Schools offers a number of important outreach programs, but what I am advocating is not the provision of limited, intermittent services, but a comprehensive and sustained effort to serve those for whom a meaningful education, and its attendant opportunities, is out of reach.

LIVING IN A SOVEREIGN LAND

In 1990, the sale of Molokai Ranch to a Hong Kong firm was completed. I wished, at the time, that the purchase of one-third of the island's land (55,680 acres or 87 square miles) had been accomplished by the Office of Hawaiian Affairs—the price seemed reasonable enough to be within OHA's reach.

The sovereignty debate had long been raging, and I thought that what was needed was a land base where sovereignty could actually be practiced. Moloka'i seemed suited to this endeavor because traditional and customary subsistence practices are largely intact there. Since full Hawaiian sovereignty has been suspended for more than a hundred years, we need to familiarize ourselves with its outlines in practical ways. What would the skin of sovereignty feel like? How would we organize and regulate our sovereign world?

To date, the manifold discussions on sovereignty have tended to divide rather than unite us. It would help to see a living example of sovereignty in action. We could practice, correct mistakes, change direction. I am concerned that without some experience of self-governance on a discrete land base that when sovereignty arrives we will be unprepared. The return of political power, while sought after, can also be a dangerous genie.

Different models of sovereignty can be established on different islands. Integrating ancestral knowledge with the dictates of modern life is a challenge we are ready for. As native people we could soon find ourselves once again living in a sovereign land.

CITIZEN PARTICIPATION

Eight years under the anvil of Governor Linda Lingle's administration is a lesson in the wisdom of term limits. As students and parents of students learned after conducting an eight day protest during the 2010 legislative session against school furloughs, the governor was not interested in hearing what they had to say. Instead of using the occasion as a teaching moment, the governor was inhospitable and intractable, chiding the protestors for being underfoot in her front office, never once engaging them in dialogue.

Governor Lingle prides herself on never compromising except on her own terms. This refusal to engage openly with constituents over vexing issues has led to pitched battles and deep divisions. Perhaps the most striking feature of her tenure has been a willingness to ignore the law.

Chapter 92, Hawai'i's law on public agency meetings and records popularly known as the Sunshine Law, contains stirring language that "the people are vested with the ultimate decision-making power" in a democracy, and that "[o]pening up the governmental processes to public scrutiny and participation is the only viable and reasonable method of protecting the public's interest."[1] Those who found their way to the governor's office were attempting to influence decision-making politely and directly for the sake of Hawai'i's students. Unhampered by the animosity between the governor and the Hawai'i State Teachers Association, they offered another plan for ending the stalemate. Many were first-time participants in government decision-making, and one parent spokeswoman told a local newspaper that everyone involved from the protestors' side "learned a lot about how government works and how to be a part of the process."[2]

It could easily be said that governmental processes work only when they are open. Such a perspective would involve not just impartiality and fairness on the part of government decision-makers but also what I would call a certain disinterestedness, meaning that the decision-maker is guided more by applicable laws and administrative rules than by loyalty to one party or another. Too often decisions appear to be foregone especially when it comes to development projects or virtually any decision involving the economy. The opposite of a disinterested posture is exemplified by the dismissive response of Ted Liu, director of the Department of Business Economic Development and Tourism, to a reporter's question about the irregularities found in an audit of DBEDT: "I serve at the pleasure of Governor Linda Lingle," he said.[3]

Hawai'i has a number of laws established to require a weighing of economic interests in concert with other equally valuable considerations. Economic interests are undisputedly important, but are not meant to dominate decision-making.

These include the statute governing our coastal zone areas and Hawai'i's environmental protection law. Often these two laws work together to protect vulnerable and important coastal resources. In recent years, when the State has sought to duck environmental review, citizens have been forced to seek relief in the courts, at times with spectacular success—a notable example is the Hawai'i Superferry case.

The laws discussed in this section along with Hawai'i's historic preservation law are all worthy models for a Native Hawaiian entity to consider. No matter how large the land base of the eventual Hawaiian nation, it is not likely to incorporate all the land in Hawai'i. We must remember that any modern division, mahele, of lands will not include all culturally significant properties. Therefore our responsibility to advocate for and negotiate on behalf of these lands will continue. Endeavors of this nature will require us to work in common cause with other citizen allies who also love Hawai'i.

HISTORIC PRESERVATION

SARA L. COLLINS

One small State agency—the State Historic Preservation Division—is at the nexus of historic preservation and development, both large and small. By statute, SHPD is responsible for providing "leadership in preserving, restoring, and maintaining historic and cultural property," standards that are squarely in the public interest. The SHPD fulfills two mandates in historic preservation—State and federal—and though many of their requirements are parallel and even overlap, State law contains additional responsibilities.

The division's mandates, however, bring it into direct conflict with development forces—both public and private—that view historic preservation as a hindrance, and the office as nothing but an obstacle to getting permits. These interests have essentially prevailed. Today, SHPD has ineffectual leaders and a greatly diminished professional staff. It is a crippled program. How did this office, once a major force for historic preservation in Hawai'i, turn into a constantly undermined, unstable, and weakened government agency? Over a century and a half of government leadership in historic preservation seems to have withered away. What can be done to restore this important regulatory and advisory office, and the public's confidence in the state's historic preservation program?

WHAT DOES SHPD DO?

Among the most visible and contentious of SHPD's duties under both State and federal law is the review of actions that may harm historic sites—everything from building a hotel, to repairing a sewer main, to replacing window frames on a historic house. When done well, the review and compliance program can identify historic sites before ground-disturbing work damages or destroys them, or can recommend ways to avoid or minimize harm. At its best, the review process also promotes the preservation of significant historic sites or landscapes, and ensures that the sites, and/or the scientific and cultural information from them, are accessible to the public.

Identifying historic sites is also at the heart of both the federal and State historic preservation mandates, because it is primarily through review and compliance work that new historic sites are found. In a recent year, the office conducted over 3,400 reviews. In all cases, the SHPD must work with landowners, the agencies that issue permits for their actions, and with the consultants landowners hire to advise them. All of this is done on strict, short timelines. When valued sites are not preserved, or when a development is delayed for months or years to complete historic preservation requirements, SHPD is rightly or wrongly blamed.

As comprehensive as SHPD's review mandates may seem, they are still limited—something the public does not always understand. The division's reviews of private sector applications are only recommendations to the County or State agency that actually issues the permit. While the permitting agency may include SHPD's recommendation as a permit condition, subsequent enforcement often falls between government offices, with too little being done too late about damage or destruction of historic sites.

My time at SHPD as a regulatory archaeologist was a dual exercise in satisfaction and frustration. Satisfaction came from working with historic preservation professionals and landowners to preserve historic sites, or a cultural landscape that gave a glimpse of past times. Frustration came from failing to save historic sites from damage or destruction, and from having to deal with scofflaw developers, or with government agencies that excused themselves from compliance. Small wonder that one of the agency's nicknames is the "historic mitigation division."

SHPD's regulatory and advisory role has never been an easy one, but it has become much harder. Over the last eight to ten years, the SHPD has deteriorated alarmingly. It can no longer do much of its basic work. Management problems have persisted despite efforts to address them. Those who have worked for or with the agency over the years say that its current state has been a long time coming, and that the combination of the recession and poor management has only aggravated serious problems left unsolved from one administration to the next. Most recently, the National Park Service, which provided about 40 percent of SHPD's funding for 2010, put the agency on "high risk grantee" status because of its lack of compliance with grant requirements. The SHPD has been given two years to address shortcomings, or face losing federal support altogether—something neither the office nor our state can afford.

A BRIEF ACCOUNT OF HISTORIC PRESERVATION IN HAWAI'I

From the founding of the Hawaii National Museum in 1872 by Kamehameha V, Hawai'i's citizens and their government have always valued the tangible vestiges of the past. In the 1880s, King Kalākaua expanded the Museum's holdings, and revived and promoted Hawaiian culture through establishment of the Hale Nauā Society. In 1889, Bishop Museum was founded to honor the memory of Princess Bernice Pauahi Bishop, and to house priceless heirlooms of the Kamehameha dynasty. The Territory of Hawai'i created the Historical Sites Commission and empowered it to locate important historic sites, record them on tax maps, and conduct limited reviews of government construction projects, to be sure that sites weren't damaged or destroyed.

At Statehood, the Territorial commission became a government agency, and the Historic Sites Section was placed within the State Parks Division of the Department of Land and Natural Resources (DLNR). Several years later, the Historic Sites Section took on the duties of the State Historic Preservation Office under the National Historic Preservation Act of 1966, which established a national program and authorized the creation of individual state programs, allotting funding to Hawai'i for this purpose.

In 1976, the Hawai'i Legislature enacted the law now designated as Chapter 6E, Hawai'i Revised Statutes, which established a historic preservation program to be carried out by the State, in addition to participating in the national program. Though Chapter 6E parallels the National Historic Preservation Act, it is actually somewhat stronger. Among other things, the new statute included a strong review mandate for State and County projects, and required that the State Historic Preservation Officer be a historic preservation professional.

Over the years, important amendments to Chapter 6E expanded the State's role in protecting historic and cultural sites. In 1988, the Legislature added a provision that required giving historic properties due consideration in the review of private sector projects needing State or County permits. In 1990, following public outcry over the exhumation of nearly 1,000 Native Hawaiian burials at Honokahua, Maui, the statute was amended to include sections about the care and treatment of prehistoric and historic burials. Additional amendments have strengthened the penalty provisions for damaging or destroying historic sites, and clarified the definition of historic properties.

In 1990, historic preservation became a separate division—the SHPD—within DLNR, and during the next decade it grew to meet its regulatory responsibilities. By 2000, SHPD had sufficient archaeological, architectural, and cultural staff to conduct reviews of private, State, and federal actions, and provide technical assistance to the public. Neighbor island offices were established on Hawai'i, Maui, and Kaua'i. The History and Culture staff managed the Burial Sites Program, which included the island burial councils. Clerical and administrative personnel handled correspondence generated by professional staff, the island burial councils, and the Hawai'i Historic Places Review Board.

One archaeologist managed the Geographic Information System (GIS), an electronic mapping program used by most government agencies. The SHPD's system contained data on the tens of thousands of historic properties recorded throughout the state, with the sites' descriptions linked to their locations on maps. Federal, State, and County agencies relied on the GIS data when carrying out their own planning.

The division had problems during this time period. Nearly a quarter of the staff was laid off in 1995, and in 1998 more layoffs were threatened. At the same time, the main agency operations were moved to Kapolei, with a smaller office still maintained in Honolulu. The move itself caused temporary difficulties, but the split office made existing management and operational problems worse. More recently, the problems that led the Park Service to place SHPD on "high risk status" have come to threaten its very existence. It has lost most of its experienced staff from its middle supervisory level, and is plagued by high turnover when vacancies are filled. Subsequent budget cuts and the "freezing" of positions by the Executive Branch have made these problems worse, and the loss of knowledge and corporate memory has affected the office's most basic functions. The resulting turmoil has made it very difficult to attract qualified and experienced professionals to work at the division.

SOLUTIONS

How can the years of neglect and damage be reversed? If SHPD is to regain its former potential and move ahead, changes to core functions and structure in three areas are essential: (1) improving the quality of information the agency works with, and how it is gathered; (2) strengthening the staff; and (3) increasing public participation through greater transparency and more opportunities for involvement.

I. GOALS FOR INFORMATION GATHERING

The statewide inventory of historic places—a master list of all historic and cultural properties recorded over the past forty years or more—must be restored and updated. This information is crucial for many of SHPD's statutory duties, and the inventory should include such basic data as brief site descriptions, the Tax Map Key, and links to relevant correspondence, reports, or other documents. Once updated, the inventory must be made available, ideally online, with supervised access so that sensitive data are not released. A registration system would provide oversight, while permitting access to information for those who need it.

The GIS is a vital tool for SHPD, for professionals working with the agency, for other government offices, and for the public. It is unconscionable that the current administration has allowed SHPD's GIS to fall into disuse. Restoring the GIS will require updating the software, incorporating current data on historic sites and studies, providing the necessary hardware for all SHPD offices to have access, and developing a means of safe public access.

The SHPD also maintains the most comprehensive library of historic preservation reports and plans in the state. Historic preservation professionals, government agencies, private companies, and the public all use the library. In recent years, though, the library has become highly disorganized. Reports have gone missing, and the online library databases are only current to 2004 or 2005. Putting the library into order and updating the existing databases should be another high priority in restoring SHPD; these updated library databases should then be made available on the division's website.

The administrative rules for the historic preservation project review process need to be revised. Since their adoption in 2002, these rules have provided standards for both SHPD's project reviews, and for the work of historic preservation professionals, such as archaeological inventory surveys. Revision should take place in consultation with the relevant stakeholder groups to ensure that acceptable professional standards for archaeological, architectural, and ethnographic work are clearly presented for both the professional and public.

II. Goals for Improvements in Personnel and Staffing

The core SHPD professional staff should be qualified historic preservation professionals who meet the Secretary of Interior's Standards for such staff in one of the four defined disciplines—architecture, history, historical architecture, or archaeology—or in a closely related field, such as Hawaiian Studies or Geography. These individuals should have considerable experience in historic preservation work in Hawai'i before coming to SHPD. Much of the work in review and compliance requires professional judgment that only comes through sufficient training and experience. Without this background, staff members are more likely to produce inadequate reviews, and are more vulnerable to outside pressure—especially when they lack a firm grounding in historic preservation. Currently, the division is woefully understaffed, and lacks enough qualified, experienced individuals to guide more junior colleagues.

The majority of professional positions at SHPD are classed as "exempt," meaning "exempt from civil service." It is high time that these positions be converted to civil service status. The Legislature required in 2000 that all exempt positions be reviewed, and either eliminated if unnecessary, or converted to civil service. Even though they have existed since the program's founding in 1976, SHPD's exempt positions have never been seriously evaluated. Converting these positions to civil service—hardly a matter of rocket science—will result in greater fiscal responsibility, improved budget planning, and protection of these regulatory staff from inappropriate pressure and treatment. Civil service conversion will also require producing position descriptions that define qualified applicants. An established process for conversion is in place; there is no good reason for further delay.

Since Hawai'i's historic preservation program began in the 1960s, the Director of DLNR has been the titular State Historic Preservation Officer. When the Legislature passed 6E-5 in 1976, they wisely included professional qualifications for this position. Nevertheless, the SHPO has never been a qualified historic preservation professional. Attorneys, business executives, and an engineer have served as the State's lead historic preservation official. Even if all of these individuals had managed DLNR well—which they haven't—historic preservation has received short shrift time and again, and especially when State and federal historic preservation law ran counter to DLNR's other interests. We would never accept a non-attorney being appointed as the State's Attorney General. Why then do we allow an attorney without any historic preservation experience to be appointed as State Historic Preservation Officer? It's time to separate these functions, and make the SHPO a stand-alone position with direct and sole oversight of the historic preservation program. The SHPO should not have divided loyalties, but instead carry out his or her duties without a conflict of interest.

The SHPD administrator should also be a qualified historic preservation professional with considerable experience *in Hawai'i.* Elsewhere in DLNR, qualified professionals serve as administrators in Engineering and Forestry and Wildlife. Historic preservation is not a hobby, but a profession, requiring training and experience. If we want the best for Hawai'i's historic and cultural heritage, we should demand that only a qualified and experienced individual should serve as the SHPD administrator.

III. Bring Transparency and Sunshine to SHPD's Operations

SHPD could make much better use of its web presence. At a time when agency funds and staff are being severely cut, SHPD should conduct a significant part of its business online, whether it be posting required documents, or providing public information.

According to its own regulations, SHPD must provide weekly postings of all reports and plans it has received for review, and a list of its determinations. The public has thirty days to review these materials and provide comments or objections to SHPD. Since 2005, the online postings have been absent for months or years at a time. The weekly postings have resumed recently, but they are minimal, lack lists of incoming materials, and are very difficult for the public to interpret. SHPD needs to include all the required materials, and create an online list that clearly shows all relevant information.

SHPD has the technical ability to make electronic copies of entire reports and plans upon receipt; this should be done as part of reinstating the required weekly postings. In addition, the agency should post all review correspondence as it is sent out, including correspondence to agencies and to professional firms, such as archaeological contractors. Posting this correspondence would not only increase the transparency of the agency's activities, but would also allow the public to gauge the relative performance of archaeological contractors and other historic preservation professionals by seeing the letters that evaluate their work.

SHPD provides administrative support to the island burial councils and the Hawai'i Historic Places Review Board, which are important and autonomous public commissions. The timely posting of agendas and minutes—required by law to be available no more than thirty days after the commissions' meetings—is important for members of the public who want to participate in the commissions' work. SHPD now posts these documents online, but their appearance is very sporadic and unpredictable. It should be an SHPD priority to have these postings meet the law's standards for timeliness. What's more, the public should not have to guess when minutes might appear, or endlessly check SHPD's website for new additions. A Really Simple Syndication (RSS) feed on the SHPD website can alert subscribers to any changes to SHPD's website, such as new burial council minutes, or an updated weekly posting of reviews and incoming documents. At present, few if any executive agencies in Hawai'i State government use RSS feeds, but the Legislature has made great use of this simple web tool, to the public's benefit. The Executive Branch—including SHPD—should do the same.

Many state historic preservation offices post an annual report on their websites, which provide clear and concise summaries of accomplishments, such as grants-in-aid, historic sites listed on the state's register, or the number of compliance reviews done. SHPD's activities used to be included in DLNR's annual reports, published from 1960 to 1994, but since then, neither DLNR nor SHPD has provided regular updates of its work. To increase transparency, and as a form of public outreach, the SHPD should publish yearly reports on its website. The reports could also include the basic data that SHPD provides to the National Park Service for its required annual grant report for federal funding. These reports need not be elaborate or time-consuming; summary statements with supporting statistics would be helpful to the public, and would increase accountability.

The State's historic preservation statute, Chapter 6E, should be amended to link to Chapter 343, the environmental law, to allow for public comment on historic and cultural resources during the environmental review process, when applicable. This would improve the public's ability to assess the potential effects of a project on historic sites, and increase the opportunity to participate in the review. If historic sites issues require changes to a development, the problems could be addressed earlier and for far less trouble and expense than if historic preservation concerns are raised separately from the environmental review process.

The preceding goals may seem to have little to do with heiau or burial sites, but if achieved, they would go far towards righting what is now so wrong at SHPD. If we can restore the division's ability to conduct the comprehensive reviews that federal and State historic preservation law call for, if we can protect SHPD from shortsighted and deliberately destructive attacks by large business and development forces outside and inside State government, we may again be able to have an SHPD that leads in "preserving, restoring, and maintaining historic and cultural property."

HAWAIIAN SUSTAINABILITY

DAVIANNA PŌMAIKA'I MCGREGOR

E mau ka hana pono o ka 'āina.
I mau ka ea o ka 'āina i ka pono.

Let's strive to preserve the good of the islands
So that righteousness may continue to be with us.
—"E Mau," 1941, Alvin Kalelani Isaacs, Sr.

CULTURAL KĪPUKA AND THEIR SIGNIFICANCE

Even as Pele claims and recreates the forest, she leaves intact whole sections or large oases of the forest, with tall old-growth 'ōhi'a, tree ferns, creeping vines, and mosses. These oases are called kīpuka. The beauty of these natural kīpuka is not only their ability to resist and withstand destructive forces of change, but also to regenerate life on the barren lava which surrounds them. From these kīpuka come the seeds and spores carried by birds and blown by the wind to sprout upon and regenerate the forest on the new lava, sparking a new dynamic cycle of coming into and passing out of life.

Kīpuka serve as natural reminders of the origins of our islands and the delicate native species and natural beauty which make our island home unique and special. They also serve as a model of our potential as an island society to sustain our way of life, despite global economic and social trends.

Cultural kīpuka are rural communities that have been bypassed by major historic forces of economic, political, and social change in Hawai'i. Like the dynamic life forces in a natural kīpuka, cultural kīpuka are communities from which Kānaka 'Ōiwi culture can be regenerated and revitalized in the contemporary settings of Hawai'i. Moreover, by examining the lives of the kua'āina, those families who have lived in these cultural kīpuka for generations, a profile emerges of the strongest and most resilient aspects of the Kānaka 'Ōiwi culture and way of life. Such an examination provides insight into how the Kānaka 'Ōiwi culture survived dynamic forces of political and economic change throughout the twentieth century. Protection of the natural resources and the subsistence livelihoods of the kua'āina in the cultural kīpuka is essential to the perpetuation of Kānaka 'Ōiwi culture as a whole for future generations. What is at stake in planning for the future of these cultural kīpuka is not just the perpetuation of a rural lifestyle, but of the Kānaka 'Ōiwi way of life itself.

Cultural kīpuka also indicate the direction that we need to take together to keep the Hawai'i that we know and love strong, resilient, and valued by future generations. In this light, cultural kīpuka are not nostalgic reminders of days gone by, or isolated and anachronistic lifestyles, but rather, sources of inspiration and direction for those of us who want to address today's problems and the challenges of the future. By holding fast to Hawaiian values and practices, the kua'āina of these kīpuka have provided an indigenous wisdom for innovation and action for a sustainable future that we have already witnessed—the island of Kanaloa Kaho'olawe, Kawainui Marsh in Kailua, Ka'ala Farm in Wai'anae, Loko I'a o He'eia, Mo'omomi Moloka'i, Kīpahulu, Maui, and even Ka Papa Lo'i o Kānewai at the University of Hawai'i Mānoa campus.

VALUES OF CULTURAL KĪPUKA

A sense of community and the sharing of resources and responsibilities for childrearing and kūpuna care are parts of the lifestyle valued by longtime residents of cultural kīpuka. Abundant natural resources and the ability to provide for families through subsistence fishing, hunting, and cultivation are also part of this valued way of life. Historically, non-Hawaiians in these predominantly Hawaiian communities adopted Kānaka 'Ōiwi life ways as their own, and were thus accepted as part of the "local" community. An expression of these shared values appears in the following excerpt from the Moloka'i Enterprise Community, Ke Aupuni Lōkahi Vision Statement:

> Moloka'i is the last Hawaiian island. We who live here choose not to be strangers in our own land. The values of aloha 'āina and mālama 'āina (love and care for the land) guide our stewardship of Moloka'i's natural resources, which nourish our families both physically and spiritually. . . . We honor our island's Hawaiian cultural heritage, no matter what our ethnicity, and that culture is practiced in our everyday lives. Our true wealth is measured by the extent of our generosity.[1]

The Lāna'i community has recently engaged in a facilitated 'Ohana Dialogue process in which over one hundred Lāna'i families shared their stories.

A summary of the emergent themes reflects the same important values discussed above:

> Families indicated that they chose Lānaʻi as a place to live, work, and raise their children because of Lānaʻi's lifestyle and strong sense of community. They described the following elements as key to this lifestyle and sense of community: [a] sense of ʻohana—people share, sacrifice for each other, and take care of and look out for each other; [b] rural lifestyle—the pace of life on Lānaʻi; easy access to open areas; ability to hunt, fish and grow your own food; [c] resiliency of families—sharing and sacrifice, creative problem solving and actions, and subsistence activities help Lānaʻi families to help each other survive and thrive even in the hardest of times.[2]

In my own experience with family histories shared by students, and in numerous oral histories I have conducted, I have found that these core values are not only limited to cultural kīpuka, but are also shared by Kānaka ʻŌiwi and "local" families throughout our islands. These are integral to what we value about Hawaiʻi.

THREATS TO KĪPUKA

In our twenty-first century island society, our cultural kīpuka and highly valued customs and life ways are threatened with ruin by dynamic forces of change.

The phasing out of agribusiness in the late twentieth century created unemployment in rural communities and left large tracts of land open for development. While diversified agriculture developed in some of these areas, resorts and subdivisions attracted more investment and higher profits. This led to the development of resorts featuring hotels, time-share units, luxury homes, mini shopping malls, and golf courses along pristine shorelines for celebrity and multimillionaire landowners from outside of Hawaiʻi.

Such development transformed the way of life for nearby longtime families. Traditional subsistence gathering and fishing grounds were ruined, and access to these areas was limited or blocked altogether. These developments increased property values and taxes, not only for the properties themselves, but also for the properties of surrounding neighbors. Exorbitant property values and taxes made it difficult for Kānaka ʻŌiwi families to hold on to their ancestral lands. Individual families or extended ʻohana who inherited valuable properties were driven to sell the property rather than keep it or share it among numerous heirs and pay excessive taxes. The high price of land and housing makes it difficult for young families to start out on their own in these rural communities.

The jobs lost when large-scale agribusiness phased out of our rural communities have never really been replaced, even by the tourist resorts that developed in their place. Most rural residents lack the skills, capital, and capacity for self-employment and the development of small businesses and enterprises. The lack of affordable housing, combined with limited or low paying job opportunities, drive most rural youth to urban Oʻahu or the U.S. continent for their careers and to start their families. This has resulted in a culture drain, as wealthy newcomers, mostly from North America, are replacing longtime kamaʻāina families. The traditional sense of community has been altered by gates and walls enclosing multimillion dollar luxury homes, and by disagreements over rights of access to subsistence fishing and gathering resources.

Nor have our isolated cultural kīpuka been immune to the "ice" epidemic that has ruined the lives of so many of our youth, and devastated our families. The closeness of families in rural communities has facilitated organizing efforts to identify sources of the problem and seek solutions. Nevertheless, drugs have taken a severe toll on the lives and well-being of rural and urban communities alike.

Long-term care for our kūpuna or elders and those stricken with chronic conditions is too expensive to sustain in rural communities, and thus unavailable. Sadly, our kūpuna and chronically ill are separated from their homes, families, and the community they love to receive the long-term care they need, when they most need the support of loved ones. The proposed phasing out of Department of Human Services offices in rural communities would have a devastating impact on families in need. Most families cannot afford and do not have access to computers, the Internet, or even telephone service. Closing direct service offices will effectively cut them off from essential services.

KULEANA: RESPONSIBILITY OF STEWARDSHIP

Those who live in and enjoy our islands need to work together to re-connect with and care for the land and water resources of our individual islands, beginning with our own ahupuaʻa and moku (district and region). I believe that living on the lands of Hawaiʻi engages us in a relationship of stewardship that connects us to those who lived on the land before us. This involves a respect for the indigenous spiritual knowledge of the land, and for the Kānaka ʻŌiwi ancestors who provided stewardship for the land. Each part of our islands has its own unique history, reflected in the place names, oli (chants), and moʻolelo (traditions) of the ʻāina. Each part of our islands requires stewardship unique to its natural resources and cultural history. We need to embrace a sustainable approach to our lives and livelihoods to offset and reverse the dramatic transformations of the natural and cultural landscapes of urbanized Oʻahu.

Living in our islands also places us in a relationship of community with our neighbors who live on and care for the land today. We need to pay attention to what's going on in our neighborhoods, and look after the well-being of our community. We need to support the kua'āina of our cultural kīpuka to engage in livelihoods that can sustain their families and the families of their children, and at the same time sustain their communities and way of life.

The recently published book *Kailua* is an excellent model of an O'ahu community working together to document the natural and cultural history of their ahupua'a as a step toward assuming collective stewardship of their district.[3] There are several Kailua organizations working together to restore the cultural and natural resources of their ahupua'a, including the Kawainui Heritage Foundation, the Kailua Hawaiian Civic Clubs, the Kailua Historical Society, and Ahahui Mālama i Ka Lōkahi. Together they are working to restore Kawainui and Hāmākua wetlands, Ulupō Heiau, Nā Pōhaku o Hauwahine, and the Maunawili Valley watershed.

*   *   *   *   *

Given the above trends and my experience and perspective, I have the following measures to suggest. They are not comprehensive, and can of course benefit from broader review and discussion.

RESPECT PLACE NAMES

Our ancestors carefully observed the landscape over time. And then, just as they named their own children, they named the various features of the landscape for their character, nature, formations, and resources. Even the winds and the rains of each district are named for their manner of traveling across the landscape, the scent that they carry, or how they feel when they caress our bodies. We should respect these names and use them, as they provide us with valuable insights as we seek to make sustainable use of our resources.

MAPPING OF RESOURCES

Communities should engage in the mapping of the natural and cultural resources of their ahupua'a. This will enable the community to protect these precious resources from the negative impacts of development. In addition, the State Historic Preservation Division should be fully funded to update the GIS mapping of the cultural and historic sites inventory. The State Survey Office should be funded to digitize the historic maps which document cultural and natural resources of each island.

CULTURAL AREA RESERVES

Just as the State of Hawai'i has recognized the importance of designated Natural Area Reserves for special stewardship and selected uses, significant cultural areas also need to be recognized and designated for protection and culturally appropriate uses.

COMMUNITY VISIONING AND PLANNING INITIATIVES

Communities should be encouraged to engage in visioning and planning initiatives. In 1998, several rural and urban communities participated in such efforts to qualify for federal empowerment zone designations and funding. None of the communities received this funding, but Moloka'i received funding as an enterprise community. Nevertheless, all of the communities who engaged in the effort benefitted from the collective process, and developed a common vision for the future of their communities, and goals, objectives, and strategies to achieve that vision.

COMMUNITY-BASED ECONOMIC DEVELOPMENT

Expand the Department of Business, Economic Development and Tourism funding of the Community-Based Economic Development Program. The mission of the program states that "Successful community-based economic development integrates viable economic projects to promote a community's vision for its future health and quality of life. The CBED program provides training and capacity building opportunities to promote, support, and invest in community-based development projects that result in measurable economic impact."[4] The Hawai'i Alliance for Community-Based Economic Development was established in 1992 to encourage increased investments in sustainable and community-based approaches to economic development. This Alliance provides communities with a systematic approach for developing common goals, objectives, and strategies for sustainable economic development in their communities.

COMMUNITY-BASED SUBSISTENCE FISHING MANAGEMENT AREAS

The concept of establishing community-based subsistence fishing management areas was developed by Mac Poepoe for the northwest coast of Moloka'i from 'Īlio Point in the west and going east to Nihoa Flats. To preserve inshore subsistence fishing and marine resources, a no-commercial-take zone would be established from the beach to the edge of the reef, or out one-quarter of a mile where there is no reef. Within this zone, only subsistence harvesting by local families would be allowed. Harvesting of resources would be monitored. Kapu would be established as necessary. A successful pilot project at Moʻomomi Molokaʻi was not permanently established, but communities at Hāʻena and Miloliʻi have established such management areas. The expansion of these management areas can empower communities and help restore and sustain marine resources for subsistence harvesting.

PLAN AROUND THE SUSTAINABLE YIELD OF WATER RESOURCES

Fresh water is the most essential and vital natural resource in our islands. Indicative of its singular importance to Kānaka ʻŌiwi is that the Hawaiian word for water, wai, was the base word for wealth, waiwai. The U.S. Geological Survey has the capacity to estimate the sustainable yield of water resources for each island. This information should be used to plan the management of water resources on each island, and to set limits on development. The distribution and allocation of water resources should be the centerpiece of general plans for each island.

CULTURAL ASSESSMENTS

Cultural assessment and impact statements need to rely upon longtime kamaʻāina families who are familiar with the affected area to assess changes in condition, integrity, use, access to, boundaries of, ownership of, and quality of experience with natural and cultural resources.

FULL FUNDING OF THE STATE HISTORIC PRESERVATION DIVISION

The State Historic Preservation Division provides the primary scrutiny of proposed projects to determine potential negative impacts on valued cultural resources. This office needs to be fully funded. In particular, positions for principal archaeologists for each island need to be funded and filled.

FULL FUNDING OF THE HAWAIʻI LEGACY LAND CONSERVATION PROGRAM

One of the best laws passed in 2005 provides for the transfer of 10 percent of the land conveyance taxes to the Land Conservation Fund. From this fund, the State of Hawaiʻi Legacy Lands Program and its counterparts at the counties have provided critical funding to establish permanent protection for private lands with important cultural and natural resources. Full funding of the program is essential for the future protection of valuable resources for our future generations.

ENERGY SELF-SUFFICIENCY

Electricity rates on Lāna'i and Moloka'i are excessive. While these islands have the capacity to generate electricity from solar and wind power, plans for windmills on these islands are to transmit power to O'ahu through an undersea cable that will cost a billion dollars and increase utility rates. None of the electrical power generated from the proposed windmill project will serve the homes on these two islands. Each island, and especially O'ahu, should develop its own sources of energy for electricity and transportation, and become truly energy self-sufficient.

RURAL HUMAN SERVICES

Rural communities need to have direct service offices. It is unrealistic to expect families who cannot afford and do not have access to computers, the internet, or even telephone service to obtain assistance utilizing such technology.

LONG-TERM CARE

Establish long-term care services on the islands of Moloka'i and Lāna'i to enable kūpuna and the chronically ill to have the support of their families and friends, and to live out their time on their home islands.

SUPPORT THE ALI'I TRUSTS, OHA, AND DHHL

Kānaka 'Ōiwi ali'i endowed their people and their descendants with a legacy of landed wealth. Mō'ī Lunalilo established a home to provide nursing care for kūpuna. Mō'īwahine Emma established the Queen's Hospital with her husband during her lifetime, and in her will left her estate for the support of the hospital. Ali'i Bernice Pauahi Bishop established the Kamehameha Schools for the education of Kānaka 'Ōiwi. Mō'īwahine Lili'uokalani established the Queen Lili'uokalani Children's Center to provide social services for orphaned and indigent Kānaka 'Ōiwi children. These ali'i trusts, together with the Office of Hawaiian Affairs and the Department of Hawaiian Homelands, provide essential services that complement those provided by the State and federal governments. These entities deserve the support of the broader Hawai'i community, especially as their mission, purpose, and chosen beneficiaries are being challenged with racial litigation.

Ha'ina 'ia mai ana ka puana, e mau ka hana pono o ka 'āina. So ends my story, where it began. Let's strive to preserve the good of the islands. Aloha . . . Aloha 'Āina!

HĀʻENA

CARLOS ANDRADE

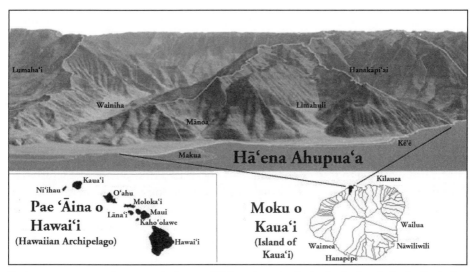

Contemporary computer-generated map of Hāʻena (map by Carlos Andrade; photos by the Indigenous Communities Mapping Initiative Hāʻena Team: Chipper and Hauʻoli Wichman and Carlos Andrade).

Hāʻena, an ahupuaʻa—a traditional land division, often extending from mountains to sea, and central to the system of ordering these islands—on the island of Kauaʻi, is a land richly endowed by Native sensitivities. Its attributes have been chronicled from antiquity. Today, its sheer physical beauty has attracted many newcomers who now occupy most of it, greatly outnumbering the aboriginal people and longtime residents, the descendants of immigrants from earlier historical times. All who come to Hāʻena see and experience it through the cultural lens of their own experiences, the history of their homelands, and the unique sense of values they bring with them. These they drape over the ʻāina somewhat like early missionaries put clothes upon the naturally naked natives to hide what was unfamiliar especially to those from frostier climes, dispositions, and standards. Permeating these diverse offerings, the foundational elemental measure of value rode in like those soldiers in the Trojan Horse. This devastating army manifested itself as the measuring of value according to money!

The following mele and accompanying narrative chronicle the 'āina as seen through the eyes of the Native people. The 'āina—our ancestor, elder sibling, and source of our identity—is celebrated by recounting some of the many treasures there that represent the value of Hā'ena in non-monetary terms. The changes brought about by more recent developments are also commented upon. The mele also tells the younger generations to be maka'ala (alert and vigilant), lest more of what is really valuable be lost forever.

"Aloha Hā'ena" is composed in a style that reflects the poetry of Hawaiian people that celebrates places they have inhabited for more than two thousand years. This song is also a map, containing references to real places and natural phenomena, and allusions to spiritual elements, present in the landscape, part of Native consciousness. Places mentioned in the song appear in the order they would be encountered if one walked through Hā'ena today.

The mele is composed in the 'ōlelo makuahine (mother tongue) of the Hawaiian people, one of the highly valued treasures of the 'āina. The Hawaiian language was outlawed when our independence as a country was wrested away and we were annexed by the United States, despite the strenuous protests of our kūpuna (elders, ancestors). It was not until the mid 1980s that activism by groups working to restore the language succeeded in reversing the legislation banning it. But governmental policies of assimilation are still the norm, and so those who cherish the language continually struggle to keep it alive in their homes, in the school system, and wherever possible in the community at large.

Mo'olelo (histories), ka'ao (stories), 'oli (chants), and mele (songs) transferred information about places and people's relationships to them from person to person, from generation to generation. Our kūpuna continue to encourage us to maintain our familial relationship with 'āina (all in the universe that nourishes mind, spirit, and body), and to continue composing mele about the times in which we live. This is only one such mele.

Aloha Hā'ena

Beloved Hā'ena

In stories of our origins as a people, the land/sea continuum is both ancestor and elder sibling. The result of the mating of Papahānaumoku (the firmament) and Wākea (the expansive breadth of sky and space) was the birth of the islands. Next in order of birth was the kalo (taro plant), followed by kānaka (humans). The term for those who live upon the land is hoa'āina (companion/ friend of the land). The bond to our island home is expressed as aloha. Though that word has been appropriated in many hundreds of inappropriate ways, it is still the word that describes best the attachment of our people to the 'āina. Aloha is a bond of affection, of family, of reciprocity—one that presupposes a responsibility to care for and pay heed to the 'āina appropriately to maintain a state of pono (balance and harmony).

Aloha nō 'o Hā'ena i ka 'ehukai
Me nā 'ale e holu 'ana i ke Kai o Hiala'a.

Hā'ena loves indeed the spray of the sea
with the deep ocean waves swelling and undulating on the sea of Hiala'a.

Some stories of our origins say our kūpuna have always been here. Other stories chronicle that some of our ancestors first approached these islands from the sea, as does this mele. Hā'ena is the northwestern point of Kaua'i. As such, it is affected profoundly by the prevailing Northeasterly Trade wind (Ka Moa'e). As it bends around the island, a Venturi effect is caused by the stream of air compressing itself against the cliffs that stand in close proximity to the narrow coastal plain. The wind accelerates considerably, and sea spray coats houses, cars, windows, and plants alike with a film of salt. Formal names were given to the seas fronting most ahupua'a in the islands, since each ahupua'a extended out to include the waters sheltered by the fringing reef, and if there was none, the sea reaching out a mile from the beaches.

For centuries these waters were the responsibility of the people of Hā'ena. It was their "icebox," medicine cabinet, and main source of seafood. It sustained a thriving population who cared for it and regulated its use for more than a thousand years. Today, pleasure seekers from faraway lands trample through, scaring fish and degrading the coral gardens, mostly out of ignorance. Struggling with State government, licensed and unlicensed companies catering to the tourist snorkel and water sports trade, a multitude of surfers, jet ski enthusiasts, and literally thousands of day trippers, the remnant Native community is trying to institute a community-managed fishery to maintain some semblance of protection for the ocean resources that have traditionally sustained them.

Ua la'a ka pu'u o Makana e hea mai ana
I ka po'e 'ōiwi, e ho'omalu i ka 'āina.

Sacred is the mountain Makana calling
the Native people to protect the land.

The peak Makana (gift), a centerpiece of the Hā'ena skyline, would have been very important in traditional times as a signpost for travelers making landfall here. A line from a traditional song about Kaua'i says: "Hea mai o Makana me he ipo ala, 'ike i ke ahi lele, 'ike i ke ahi lele, hoohihi na ka malihini" (see the leaping fire, know the leaping fire, entrancing to the newcomers). The leaping fire alludes to a ceremony performed at Makana during which flaming firebrands were cast off the tops of the peak to commemorate graduation from training for those aspiring to become experts in the performing arts of dance, chant, and song.

ʻŌiwi, one of our words describing a Native person, contains the word iwi (bone), alluding to the many ancestors whose bones lay sleeping in our sand dunes and caves, now extremely vulnerable and threatened by increasing development impacting coastal and other lands. One of the last Native-speaking kūpuna of Hāʻena suggested the name Hui Hoʻomalu i ka ʻĀina (Alliance to Protect/Shelter the ʻāina) for a group who began organizing resistance to elements increasingly threatening the pono of Hāʻena. A major point of contention that continues today is the unearthing of the bones of the ancestors to make room for building what usually are second homes and/or vacation rentals. One State agency even went so far as to install a leach field for a public toilet right in the middle of a burial site, unearthing bones in the process. There the leach field remains, befouling the resting place of kūpuna.

The second line in this verse echoes the calling of kūpuna for people to continue the work of being vigilant, sheltering Hāʻena's places from the onslaught, striving to preserve and restore the treasures of the ʻāina in the face of increasing settlement on the land, the changing of names of the ʻāina, and the growing population, who more and more impose their values on the ʻāina.

Hoʻolaʻi i ka poli o Makua one hānau o nā kūpuna
Kiaʻi! mālama! ʻonipaʻa! he kuleana ko nā Mamo.

Shelter in the bosom of Makua, birth sands of our ancestors
Stand guard! care for! stand fast! this is the responsibility of our generation.

Makua (parent) is the name of a sheltered bay formed by a reef protruding several hundred yards into the sea beyond the furthest point of land near the eastern border of Hāʻena. The coral reef reaches seaward, bending westward and forming a sheltered, natural harbor. This was a haven in traditional times for canoes traveling the coast. In recent years, it has become a great tourist attraction for the snorkeling and scuba set. The reef has and still does provide fishing grounds for feeding the few remaining Native families who have managed to hold on to their land.

Coastal dunes form the landward side of this picturesque lagoon. These are the traditional burial grounds of our people, but this valuable 'āina on the sunny coastal dunes continues to be transformed into an area of beach-side mansions. Today, celebrities, rock stars, and beneficiaries of the dot.com revolution excavate the dunes for foundations of lavish houses, disturbing the bones of our ancestors, and exposing them to the sun. At this writing, one wealthy investor from the continent is putting the finishing touches on a home built over more than thirty identified graves, despite protests from Native Hawaiians and rulings by the local Burial Council.

Kilohi aku iā Mānoa me ka wailele ona
He Pilipali ka makani, he Moani ko Maniniholo.

Look upward to Mānoa with its falling water.
Pilipali is the wind, Moani is that of Maniniholo.

Mānoa is the valley just inland of Makua that housed a large part of the population in pre-Euro/American times. Sacred sites and many stone walls still exist, delineating the pond field lo'i that sustained the taro once intensely cultivated there. Now overgrown with alien plants and trees, and increasingly being encroached upon by house building, the stone-faced terraces are a tangible legacy of a population who once sustained themselves with the fruits of their own labor on the 'āina. Today, the words "sustainable" and "self-sufficient" are bandied about while most of these once productive lands lie buried in anonymity, locked up by invasive species, or bulldozed to cater to an aesthetic based on dollars per square foot and total dependence on food imported from foreign lands.

References to wind are often allusions to spirit, one of the alternative meanings for makani, the Hawaiian word for wind. Wind names are given for every place on the island in a chant attributed to Pele (Goddess of Fire and Volcanoes) recorded in Hawaiian language newspapers of the eighteen hundreds. Pilipali (clinging to the cliffs) is the name for the wind of Mānoa. Moani (gentle breeze usually associated with fragrance) is the wind of Maniniholo, a cave and beach area adjacent to Mānoa. A county park across the government road from the cave has become a gathering place for tourists, peddlers, lunch wagon crowds, and transient campers. However, when the great mango trees overshadowing the valley are in season, the fragrance of fallen fruit rides on the mountain wind out of the mouth of Mānoa and drifts past the edge of Maniniholo cave, out across the narrow coastal plain there and over the sea. These winds, names, and allusions to Akua are the intangible treasures nourishing our identity as a people, as well as documenting the character of the 'āina itself.

Holo aku i ka Hale Pōhaku, kahi o Pōhakuloa.
Nānā i uka iā Pōhaku Kāne, nānā i kai iā Hauwā.

Travel on to Hale Pōhaku, to the place of Pōhakuloa.
Look inland to Pōhaku Kāne, look seaward to Hauwā.

Past Maniniholo stands a small hill once used as a ceremonial site. Today, fishermen ascend it to spot fish on the nearby reef, and surfers use it as a vantage point to check the waves breaking on both sides of the bay. Further along, adjacent to the government road, lies an immense rock (pōhaku) called Pōhakuloa (long stone). Spoken of in the ancient stories, he is one of three siblings who arrived from Tahiti many generations ago. Hauwā, his sister, another pōhaku, lies submerged in the sea a few hundred yards below the spot where her brother lies. High along a ridge running inland is the third sibling, brother Pōhaku o Kāne, a large geosymbol representing the intervention of Kāne, one of the main deities of the Hawaiian pantheon of akua (gods). After arriving in Hā'ena, Pōhaku o Kāne persisted in attempts to climb up onto the steep ridge, despite many falls onto the beach below. Kāne, feeling compassion and appreciation for his efforts, reached down and placed him where he stands today. The story of Pōhaku o Kāne continues to be retold from generation to generation, celebrating the value of persistence and faith. Stories attached to elements of Hawaiian landscapes present patterns for appropriate behavior, and preserve values, traits, points of view, and aspects of humor treasured by those who have been long on the land.

Ne'e aku i ke awāwā 'o Limahuli, inu i ka wai aloha.
'Au'au i ka waipuna hu'ihu'i, ho'opili i ka Mea Aloha.

Move on to the valley of Limahuli, drink the water of aloha.
swim and bathe in the cool water, close to one beloved.

Westward, beyond the family of stones, is the valley of Limahuli, the second of two major valleys in Hā'ena. The valley's attendant alluvial plain and fringing reefs supported a great number of people in traditional times, as shown by the extensive network of stone-faced terraces and aqueducts now covered with alien brush and forest. Only one or two Hawaiian families retain small parcels of land there, due in large part to incredibly high real property taxes resulting from the high prices paid for adjoining land by wealthy haole (foreigners), and in turn imposed on the neighboring families.

Along the highway, a spring emerges from the cliffs. Named Ka Wai Aloha (Love Water), water from this spring is still sought after by those who prefer to drink water that hasn't been chemically altered by government providers. A stream runs through Limahuli, and a pool known today as the "Cold Pond" is constantly replenished by frigid waters from the nearby mountains. It has become a community swimming hole enjoyed by residents and visitors alike. In the aftermath of the last hurricane, when public water service was disrupted, this pool became indispensable for community water needs.

Places in Hawaiʻi great and small were named by the people who inhabited them. One Native Hawaiian family still retaining family lands in Limahuli are heirs to an ancestor simply known as Kamealoha (the beloved). The family land referred to in this verse is located just behind sand dunes framing the mouth of the Limahuli stream, which empties into the sea there. All of the oceanfront land there had to be sold as land prices skyrocketed, and the family could no longer pay the escalating real property tax. Real property taxes continue to rise everywhere in Hawaiʻi, with seemingly no end in sight. The most recent sale in this location was for fifteen million dollars, to a movie star. How many more families will fall victim to the economic pressure brought by those who move onto the ʻāina armed with substantially greater economic and other resources than the local and Native people?

Māʻalo i ka wai o Kanaloa, akahele i ka pali o Keʻē
Hihia paʻa ʻo Lohiʻau iā Pele, hōʻola ʻia e Hiʻiaka.

Passing by the water of Kanaloa, be cautious of the cliffs at Keʻē
Lohiʻau was ensnared by Pele, revived by Hiʻiaka.

Caution is called for from those who traverse the land of Hā'ena, especially at Ke'ē, the setting for stories of interactions between kānaka (people) and other beings. Here, mo'o (dragon) women battle healing akua, water sprites lure handsome young warriors to their demise, and mysterious mountain dwellers populate the nearby hanging valleys with their works.

In one of the more famous of these stories passed down from antiquity, Lohi'au, a young ali'i (chief) captivated by the beauty and wiles of Pele, fiery akua of the volcanoes, is overcome by a love affair so passionate that he died after three days of lovemaking. The long saga of their affair is set against a background spanning the entire Hawaiian archipelago. Places and beings are celebrated as Hi'iaka, sister of the fiery one, is sent from Hawai'i island to Hā'ena, Kaua'i to retrieve Lohi'au. In the process she does battle with many mo'o, bringing Lohi'au back from the dead as she plays out her role as healer and patroness of the hula. Ke'ē in traditional times was the site of a center for teaching hula, and is still visited by its adepts on yearly pilgrimages.

These stories document Hawaiian character and spirit, and continue to inform those who extend the traditional and customary practices of the ancestors. The 'āina, however, is now being draped with the geography of newcomers, who call the sacred mountain Makana, Bali Hai—a reference to a musical composition created in a big city on the far shores of the eastern continent about a fictitious land existing only in the minds of the hordes that now subscribe to this new nomenclature. What identity is exemplified or rooted in these new names on the 'āina, such as "the blue room," "reefers," "tunnels," and "the end of the road"?

> Ha'ina 'ia mai ka puana o kēia mele o nā wahi pana.
> Aloha 'ia nō 'o Hā'ena e ka Hui Maka'āinana,
> Hui Maka'āinana o Makana.
>
> Let the refrain of this song of the storied places be told.
> Beloved is Hā'ena by the people of the land,
> the people of the land of Makana.

The final verse of the song is framed in terms found in many traditional songs composed over the last hundred years. It urges that the stories be told: of wahi pana, the treasured and storied places of the land; of the hoa'āina, the companions and guardians of the 'āina; and of all those aspects of 'āina, all that nourishes the physical, mental, and spiritual life of the people. The Hui Maka'āinana o Makana are those people who have banded together to preserve, restore, and guard that which encompasses the valued treasures of the 'āina.

The value of Hawai'i lies much deeper than merely the surface beauty, benevolent climate, and potential for it being a fun park for the rest of the world.

The 'āina contains the soul and spirit of an oceanic people whose experience permeates the stories found on the land and in the sea, soars on the winds, falls with the rains, and glimmers down from the stars. Their ways of being in the world may not only enrich our lives in ways not measured by money if we learn about, care for, and perpetuate them. The value of Hawai'i as recorded in the repository of 'āina and practiced by generations of hoa'āina may even contain practical principles that will ensure our survival on this island of rapidly shrinking resources, earth.

Aloha Hā'ena

Aloha nō 'o Hā'ena i ka 'ehukai
Me nā 'ale e holu 'ana i ke Kai o Hiala'a.

Ua la'a ka pu'u o Makana e hea mai ana
I ka po'e 'ōiwi, e ho'omalu i ka 'āina.

Ho'ola'i i ka poli o Makua one hānau o nā kūpuna
Kia'i, mālama, 'onipa'a, he kuleana ko nā Mamo.

Kilohi aku iā Mānoa me ka wailele ona
He Pilipali ka makani, he Moani ko Maniniholo.

Holo aku i ka Hale Pōhaku, kahi o Pōhakuloa.
Nānā i uka iā Pōhaku Kāne, nānā i kai iā Hauwā.

Ne'e aku i ke awāwā 'o Limahuli, inu i ka wai aloha.
'Au'au i ka waipuna hu'ihu'i, ho'opili i ka Mea Aloha.

Mā'alo i ka wai o Kanaloa, akahele i ka pali o Ke'ē
Hihia pa'a 'o Lohiau iā Pele, hō'ola 'ia e Hi'iaka.

Ha'ina 'ia mai ka puana o kēia mele o nā wahi pana.
Aloha 'ia nō o Hā'ena e ka Hui Maka'āinana,
Hui Maka'āinana o Makana.

NOTES AND FURTHER READINGS

CRAIG HOWES, INTRODUCTION

1. Randall W. Roth, ed., *The Price of Paradise: Lucky We Live Hawaii?* (Honolulu: Mutual, 1992): 4.
2. Roth 3
3. Roth 3.
4. Roth 3–4.

RECOMMENDED READING

Randall W. Roth, ed., *The Price of Paradise: Lucky We Live Hawaii?* Vol. 2 (Honolulu: Mutual, 1993).

TOM COFFMAN, REINVENTING HAWAI'I

1. Alexander MacDonald, *Revolt in Paradise: The Social Revolution in Hawaii after Pearl Harbor* (New York: Stephen Daye, 1944): 155.
3. See State of Hawai'i, Department of Business, Economic Development, and Tourism, "Historical Visitor Statistics, May 5, 2010 <http://hawaii.gov/dbedt/info/visitor-stats>.
3. John Dominis Holt, *On Being Hawaiian* (Honolulu: Star-Bulletin, 1964).
4. Davianna Pōmaika'i McGregor, *Nā Kua'āina: Living Hawaiian Culture* (Honolulu: U of Hawai'i P, 2007).

RECOMMENDED READING

Lawrence Fuchs, *Hawaii Pono: A Social History* (New York: Harcourt, Brace, and World 1961).

JONATHAN KAY KAMAKAWIWO'OLE OSORIO, HAWAIIAN ISSUES

These readings have informed my chapter.

THE HAWAIIAN SOVEREIGNTY MOVEMENT

Jon Kamakawiwo'ole Osorio, "Kū'ē and Kū'oko'a: Law, History and Other Faiths," *Law and Empire in the Pacific: Fiji and Hawai'i,* ed. Sally Engle Merry and Donald Brenneis (Sante Fe: School of American Research, 2003): 213–37.

———. "Sovereignty in Hawai'i," *Sovereign Stories,* Pacific Islanders in Communication, Honolulu, 2004 <http://www.sovereignstories.org>.

———. "What Kine Hawaiian are You?," *Contemporary Pacific* 13.2 (Fall 2001): 359–79.

Haunani-Kay Trask, *From a Native Daughter* (Honolulu: U of Hawai'i P, 2000).

Kanalu Young, "Kuleana: Toward a Historiography of Hawaiian National Consciousness, 1780–2001," *Hawaiian Journal of Law and Politics* 2 (2006): 1–33.

Economy, Politics, and Law

George Cooper and Gavan Daws, *Land and Power in Hawai'i, the Democratic Years* (Honolulu: U of Hawai'i P, 1990).

J. Kēhaulani Kauanui, *Hawaiian Blood: Colonialism and the Politics of Sovereignty and Indigeneity* (Durham: Duke UP, 2009).

Noel J. Kent, *Hawai'i: Islands Under the Influence* (New York: Monthly Review, 1983).

Jonathan Kay Kamakawiwo'ole Osorio, *Dismembering Lāhui: A History of the Hawaiian Nation to 1887* (Honolulu: U of Hawai'i P, 2002).

Hawaiian History and Culture

Carlos Andrade, *Hā'ena: Through the Eyes of the Ancestors* (Honolulu: U of Hawai'i P, 2008).

Lilikalā Kame'eleihiwa, *Native Land and Foreign Desires: Pehea Lā e Pono Ai?* (Honolulu: Bishop Museum, 1992).

Noenoe Silva, *Aloha Betrayed: Native Hawaiian Resistance to American Colonialism* (Durham: Duke UP, 2004).

Kanalu G. Terry Young, *Rethinking the Native Hawaiian Past* (New York: Garland, 1998).

SUMNER LA CROIX, THE ECONOMY

Sources

George R., Ariyoshi, John Waihee, and Ben Cayetano, "Hawai'i's Children First," Jan. 31, 2010 <http://www.hawaiichildrenfirst.org/hawai'i's-children-first>.

Hawaii gross domestic product (GDP) data: Bureau of Economic Analysis, U.S. Dept. of Commerce <http://www.bea.gov/regional/gsp/action.cfm>. See also Robert C. Schmidt, *Historical Statistics of Hawaii* (Honolulu: UP of Hawai'i, 1977): Table 6.1.

Honolulu Consumer Price (CPI): Bureau of Labor Statistics, U.S. Dept. of Labor <http://data.bls.gov/cgi-bin/srgate>; see also Schmidt, *Historical Statistics,* Table 5.2.

Andrew Kato, Sumner La Croix, and James Mak, "Small State, Giant Tax Credits: Hawaii's Leap into High Technology Development," *State Tax Notes,* Nov. 30, 2009: 641–52.

State of Hawai'i, Tax Review Commission, Report of the 2005–2007 Tax Review Commission (Honolulu: State of Hawai'i, 2006).

Recommended Reading

David L. Callies, *Preserving Paradise: Why Regulation Won't Work* (Honolulu: U of Hawai'i P, 1994).

Edward L. Glaeser, "Housing Supply," National Bureau of Economic Research, *NBER Reporter* (Spring 2004): 12–14 <http://www.nber.org/reporter/spring04/glaeser.html>.

Christopher Grandy, *Hawaii Becalmed: Economic Lessons of the 1990s* (Honolulu: U of Hawai'i P, 2002).

James Mak, *Developing a Dream Destination: Tourism and Tourism Policy Planning in Hawai'i* (Honolulu: U of Hawai'i P, 2008).

———, *Tourism and the Economy: Understanding the Economics of Tourism* (Honolulu: U of Hawai'i P, 2004).

Maja-Leah Revago, James Roumasset, and Kimberly Burnett, *Resource Management for Sustainable Development of Island Economies,* Dept. of Economics, U of Hawai'i Working Paper No. 08–04, Oct. 2008.

RAMSAY REMIGIUS MAHEALANI TAUM

1. World Tourism Organization, "About UNWTO—Why Tourism?" Apr. 30, 2010 <http://www.unwto.org/aboutwto/why/en/why.php?op=1>; see also "Weathering the Storm of Global Recession: The Challenge for Destination Management," 5th UN-WTO Conference on "Destination Management and Marketing," Hangzhou, Sept. 21–22, 2009.

2. Hawai'i Tourism Authority, "Annual Report to the State Legislature," Oct. 31, 2009, Apr. 30, 2010 <http:// www.hawaiitourismauthority.org/documents_upload_path/reports/HTA09_AR_FINAL.pdf>; see also Hawai'i Tourism Authority, "Tourism Research Visitor Statistics," Apr. 30, 2010 <http://hawaiitourismauthority.org/index.cfm?page=tourism_research&level=tourism_research&pageid=1000#>.

3. "Hawai'i Tourism Strategic Plan 2005–2015," Hawai'i Tourism Authority, Honolulu, 2005, Apr. 30, 2010 <http://www.hawaiitourismauthority.org/pdf/tsp2005_2015_final.pdf>.

4. "Hawai'i Tourism Strategic Plan 2005–2015": 25.

5. Pasifika Foundation Hawaii, *A Model for a Community-Based Host-Visitor Program in Hawaii: Maoli Values and Perspective; Pasifik Talanoa* (2007): 6.

6. Gerry Park, "HTA hones marketing strategy," *Honolulu Star-Bulletin,* Mar. 18, 2010, Apr. 30, 2010 <http://www.starbulletin.com/business/20100318_hta_hones_marketing_strategy.html>.

7. For more on sense of place, see "Words of Wisdom: What Does Sense of Place Mean to You," *Hawai'i Magazine,* Mar.-Apr. 2006, Apr. 30, 2010 <http://www.moolelo.com/Sense-of-Place.pdf>.

RECOMMENDED READING

State of Hawai'i, Dept. of Business, Economic Development and Tourism, "Planning for sustainable tourism, Honolulu, 2005," Apr. 30, 2010 <http://hawaii.gov/dbedt/info/visitor-stats/sustainable-tourism-project/drafts/Sustainable-Tourism-Study-Group-Report.pdf/view?searchterm=tourism report>.

State of Hawai'i, Dept. of Business, Economic Development and Tourism, "Annual Visitor Research Report," Apr. 30, 2010 <http://hawaii.gov/dbedt/info/visitor-stats/visitor-research>.

CHARLES REPPUN, AGRICULTURE

AUTHOR'S NOTE: this essay relies on an unpublished article written with Bob Tam.

RECOMMENDED READING

For the National Agricultural Statistics Service data, see <http://www.nass.usda.gov>.

Michael Pollan, *The Omnivore's Dilemma: A Natural History of Four Meals* (New York: Penguin, 2006); see also *The Omnivore's Dilemma for Kids: The Secrets Behind What You Eat* (New York: Penguin, 2009), and *In Defense of Food: An Eater's Manifesto* (New York: Penguin, 2008).

Paul Roberts, *The End of Food* (New York: Houghton Mifflin, 2008).

KATHY E. FERGUSON AND PHYLLIS TURNBULL, THE MILITARY

1. William Aila, Personal interview, Mar. 22, 2010.
2. For the final EIS, see <http://www.25idl.army.mil/sbcteis/feis/index.htm>; the quotation is from page 29.
3. David K. Kirkpatrick and David M. Herszenhorn, "In Battle to Cut Billions, a Spotlight on One Man," *New York Times,* May 30, 2009: A21.
4. For recent DBEDT estimates, see "Federal Economic Activities in Hawai'i, March 2009" <http://hawaii.gov/dbedt/info/economic/data_reports/federal/fed-report-2009.pdf>.
5. See Jason Ubay, "Military Spending," *HawaiiBusiness,* May 2008, May 5, 2010 <http://hawaiibusiness.com/Hawaii-Business/May-2008/Military-Spending>.
6. Karen W. F. Lee, "Impact Aid and the Establishment of United States Department of Defense Schools in Hawai'i," Report #4 (Honolulu: Legislative Reference Bureau, 1993).
7. Schofield Barracks, Hawaii (HI) Poverty Rate Data, "Information about poor and low income residents," Apr. 19, 2010 <http://www.city-data.com/poverty/poverty-Schofield-Barracks-Hawaii.htm>.
8. Jonathan Finer, "Iraq War Is Affecting Small State in a Big Way: Vermont Has Most Deaths Per Capita," *Washington Post,* Feb. 9, 2005: A01, A10.

RECOMMENDED READING
Kathy E. Ferguson and Phyllis Turnbull, *Oh, Say, Can You See? The Semiotics of the Military in Hawai'i* (Minneapolis: U of Minnesota P, 1999).

JOHN P. ROSA, RACE / ETHNICITY

1. Jonathan Y. Okamura, *Ethnicity and Inequality in Hawai'i* (Philadelphia: Temple UP, 2008): 6–7.
2. For more information on race categories for federal data collection, see <http://factfinder.census.gov/home/en/epss/race_ethnic.html>, and the U.S. Office of Management and Budget Web site <http://www.whitehouse.gov/omb/fedreg/1997standards.html>.
3. Robert C. Schmitt, ed., *Hawai'i Data Book: A Statistical Reference to Hawai'i's Social, Economic and Political Trends* (Honolulu: Mutual, 2002): 2, Table 1.01—Population of Counties, 1831 to 2000. A conservative estimate of 250,000 and a more generous one of 800,000 to 1 million for Hawai'i's pre-contact population was used in calculating the 75–95 percent drop in population that was reached by 1872. For more on population debates, see David E. Stannard, *Before the Horror: The Population of Hawai'i on the Eve of Western Contact* (Honolulu: Social Science Research Institute, University of Hawai'i, 1989), which includes comments sections by Eleanor C. Nordyke, of the East-West Center's Population Institute, and Robert C. Schmitt, State Statistician of the State of Hawai'i Department of Business, Economic Development, and Tourism.
4. See Beth Bailey and David Farber, *The First Strange Place: The Alchemy of Race and Sex in World War II Hawaii* (New York: Free Press, 1992).
5. For local identity, see John P. Rosa, "Local Story: The Massie Case Narrative and the Cultural Production of Local Identity in Hawai'i," *Amerasia Journal* 26.2 (2000): 93–115, and Jonathan Y. Okamura, "Aloha Kanaka Me Ke Aloha 'Aina: Local Culture

and Society in Hawaii," *Amerasia Journal* 7.2 (1980): 119–37. For the Massie case, see also David E. Stannard, *Honor Killing: How the Infamous "Massie Affair" Transformed Hawaii* (New York: Viking, 2005).

6.   For an account of this election, see Tom Coffman, *Island Edge of America: A Political History of Hawai'i* (Honolulu: U of Hawai'i P, 2003): 148–53.

7.   See Schmitt 16, Table 1.29—Ranking of Races, for the State of Hawaii: 2000.

8.   Joe Balaz, "Da Mainland To Me," *Electric Laulau,* CD (Honolulu: Hawai'i Dub Music 1998).

9.   Census 2000 recorded a total resident population of 1,211,537 for Hawai'i; 476,162 indicated that they were White (either alone or in combination with another race), thus accounting for 39.3 percent of the islands' population. Though not a majority (over fifty percent), Whites are by far the largest racial/ethnic group. By comparison, 296,674—or 24.5 percent of the islands' population—indicated that they were part of the second largest racial/ethnic group: Japanese and part-Japanese. Filipinos and part-Filipinos make up 22.8 percent of Hawai'i's population; Native Hawaiians and part-Native Hawaiians make up 19.8 percent. For more information, see <http://hawaii.gov/dbedt/info/economic/databook/db2008/section01.pdf>.

10.   George R. Ariyoshi, *Hawai'i: The Past Fifty Years, The Next Fifty Years* (Honolulu: Watermark, 2009): 16–18.

LOWELL CHUN-HOON, LABOR

1.   For Hawai'i's early labor history, see "CLEAR Timeline of Hawai'i Labor History," Center for Labor Education and Research, University of Hawai'i at West O'ahu <http://clear.uhwo.hawaii.edu/Timeline.html>; and Lowell Chun-Hoon, "Teaching the Asian American Experience," *Teaching Ethnic Studies: Concepts and Strategies,* ed. James Banks (Washington, D.C.: National Council for Social Studies, 1973): 125.

2.   *Lexington Observer and Reporter,* July 12, 1869, qtd. in *Bitter Strength: A History of the Chinese in the United States,* by Gunther Barth (Cambridge: Harvard UP, 1964): 187.

3.   Qtd. in *Cane Fires: The Anti-Japanese Movement in Hawaii, 1865–1945,* by Gary Okihiro (Philadelphia: Temple UP, 1991): 17.

4.   Qtd. in *Margins and Mainstreams: Asians in American History and Culture,* by Gary Okihiro (Seattle: U of Washington P, 1996): 157.

5.   Qtd. in Okihiro, *Cane Fires* 74.

6..   Transcript of the "Report of the Grand Jury, September 20, 1938" in the Circuit Court of the Fourth Judicial Circuit, Territory of Hawaii, qtd. in *The Hilo Massacre: Hawaii's Bloody Monday, August 1st, 1938,* by William J. Puette (Honolulu: Center for Labor Education and Research, U of Hawai'i, 1988): 56.

7.   Qtd. in *A Spark is Struck! Jack Hall and the ILWU in Hawaii,* by Sandord Zalburg (Honolulu: U of Hawai'i P, 1979): 40.

8.   See U.S. Department of Labor, Bureau of Labor Statistics, News Release, BLS 10–32, "Union Membership in Hawaii—2009," Mar. 9, 2010, May 5, 2010 <http://www.bls.gov/ro9/unionhi.pdf>.

9.   Jacob Hacker, *The Great Risk Shift: The New Economic Insecurity and the Decline of the American Dream* (New York: Oxford UP, 2008): 68.

KARL KIM, TRANSPORTATION

1. Howard Frumpkin, Lawrence D. Frank, and Richard Jackson, *Urban Sprawl and Public Health: Designing, Planning, and Building for Healthy Communities* (Washington, D.C.: Island Press, 2004).

2. David Gartman, *Auto Opium: A Social History of American Automobile Design* (London: Routledge, 1994).

3. US Department of Transportation, Bureau of Transportation Statistics, *Hawaii Transportation Profile* (Washington, D.C.: Bureau of Transportation Statistics, 2002).

4. Heidi Worley, "Road Traffic Accidents Increase Dramatically, Worldwide," *Population Reference Bureau*, Apr. 6, 2010 <http://www.prb.org/Articles/2006/RoadTrafficAccidentsIncreaseDramaticallyWorldwide.aspx>.

5. Elisabeth Rosenthal, "Ban calls climate change defining challenge of our age," *New York Times* 17 Nov. 2007, Apr. 6, 2010 <http://www.nytimes.com/2007/11/17/world/europe/17iht-climate.1.8372066.html?_r=1>.

6. United Nations Intergovernmental Panel on Climate Change, 2007, *Climate Change 2007: Synthesis Report,* Adopted at IPCC Plenary XXVII, Valencia, Spain, Nov. 2007 (New York: United Nations, 2007).

7. US Department of the Interior, North American Bird Conservation Initiative, "State of the Birds Report—2010 Report on Climate Change" (Washington, D.C.: U.S. Department of the Interior, 2010).

8. Ian L. McHarg, *Design with Nature* (New York: Wiley, 1969).

9. Joan Roelofs, *Greening Cities: Building Just and Sustainable Communities* (New York: Bootstrap, 1996).

10. J. H. Crawford, *Carfree Cities* (Utrecht: International Books, 2002).

11. Bernard Rudolfsky, *Streets for People: A Primer for Americans* (Garden City: Doubleday, 1969).

12. *National Complete Streets Coalition,* Apr. 6, 2010 <http://www.completestreets.org>.

13. "America's Top 50 Bike-Friendly Cities," *Bicycling Magazine,* 2010, Apr. 6, 2010 <http://www.bicycling.com/tourdefrance/article/0,6802,s1-3-583-21901-1,00.html>.

14. Gerda R. Wekerle and Carolyn Whitzman, *Safe Cities: Guidelines for Planning, Design, and Management* (New York: Van Nostrand Reinhold, 1995).

15. P. J. O'Rourke, "The End of Our Love Affair with Cars," *Wall Street Journal,* May 30, 2009, Apr. 6, 2010 <http://online.wsj.com/article/SB10001424052970203771904574173401767415892.html>.

CHAD BLAIR, GOVERNMENT

Recommended Reading

Benjamin J. Cayetano, *Ben: A Memoir, From Street Kid to Governor* (Honolulu: Watermark, 2009).

Gavan Daws, *Shoal of Time: A History of the Hawaiian Islands* (Honolulu: U of Hawai'i P, 1989).

Hawaii State Legislature <http://capitol.hawaii.gov>.

Hawaii Office of Elections <http://hawaii.gov/elections>.

Hawaii Campaign Spending Commission <http://hawaii.gov/campaignspending>.

Honolulu Civil Beat <http://www.civilbeat.com>.

Samuel P. King and Randall W. Roth, *Broken Trust: Greed, Mismanagement, and Political Manipulation at America's Largest Charitable Trust* (Honolulu: U of Hawai'i P, 2006).

"Laws, rules and opinions on Sunshine Law," Hawaii Office of Information Practice <http://hawaii.gov/oip/sunshinelaw.html>.

Richard C. Pratt and Zachary A. Smith, *Hawai'i Politics and Government: An American State in a Pacific World* (Lincoln: U of Nebraska P, 2000).

Jim Shon, *Inside Hawaii's Capitol: Lessons in Legislative Democracy* (Honolulu: Waikiki Health Center, 2002).

Chad Blair, *Money, Color and Sex in Hawaii Politics* (Honolulu: Mutual, 1998).

MELODY KAPILIALOHA MACKENZIE, LAW AND THE COURTS

1. ABA Spirit of Excellence Award Acceptance Speech (Miami, Florida, Feb. 10, 2007).
2. P.L. 103-150, 107 Stat. 1510 (Nov. 23, 1993).
3. HCDCH, 117 Hawai'i 174, 195, 177 P.3d 884, 905 (2008) (citation omitted).
4. HCDCH, 117 Hawai'i 174, 213, 177 P.3d 884, 923 (2008).
5. Id. at 214, 177 P.3d at 924 (2008) citing the trial court (citation omitted) (emphasis in the original).
6. Haw. Rev. Stat. § 5.75(b) (2009).
7. Haw. Rev. Stat. § 5.75(a) (2009). The law incorporates the words to an Oli Aloha, or chant of Aloha, composed by Pilahi Paki, a Hawaiian chanter, composer, and writer. The oli assigns important Hawaiian cultural values to each of the letters of Aloha.
8. Id.

MARI MATSUDA, PUBLIC EDUCATION

1. This article is a deliberate allusion to, and is dedicated to, the parents, students, and community supporters in Save Our Schools, a grassroots organization that held a sit-in at the Governor's office in April of 2010 to end Furlough Fridays. While the ideas expressed here are the author's, the fortitude of the sit-in veterans is my inspiration. Thank you to Abigail Fee and Mishelle Kim for research assistance, and to Charles Lawrence, Jane Iijima Dickson, Craig Howes, Jon Goldberg-Hiller, Robert Perkinson, and Sonny Ganaden for comments on earlier drafts.
2. Is the DOE "too big?" Managed properly, size itself can generate net gains in quality and cost containment. If identifiable waste is the problem, across-the-board defunding is not the solution. It is politically expedient to flatten public funding generally, avoiding the hard choice of culling underperformers. This increases government inefficiency when it destroys the incentive and ability to create modern systems of, for example, payroll management, and it drives out people who know how to run a tight ship when they see that cuts are unrelated to performance. Furthermore, a single school district for all of Hawai'i has huge potential to avoid the wealth inequality that plagues schools on the continent. Similarly, the myth that a private firm model is more "efficient" than government is not

supported by economic analysis. For-profit and non-profit entities all have the "same problem of inducing their employees to work toward the organizational goals." See Herbert Simon, "Organizations and Markets," *Journal of Economic Perspectives* 5.2 (1991): 28, as cited in Joseph E. Stiglitz, *Freefall: America, Free Markets, and the Sinking of the World Economy* (New York: Norton, 2010): 198.

3. The best model may be a strong undergraduate degree in a subject other than education, combined with a graduate degree in education. This model, used for doctors and lawyers, creates a public expectation of excellence, and justifies salary increases as well as increased demands on teachers. I dedicate this suggestion to the hundreds of gifted law students who have told me that they would rather be teachers, if only teachers could make what lawyers make.

4. Principals are the pivot point that could turn around the entire system. We need leaders who are willing to fire bad teachers, who will create energized school cultures. Credible leaders in neighborhood schools will capture the amazing alchemy of Hawai'i's generous talent pool. The baby boomers looking for meaning in the next chapter of their lives are waiting for a strong principal to put them to work as volunteers.

5. This is not a ridiculous dream. The children who come from families in distress are typically failing in school. To teach them, we have to provide what their families cannot. The Maya Angelou public charter school in Washington, D.C. has beds for children who have no safe place to go home to on any given night. Using the philosophy that it is the school's job to provide students with what they need to keep learning, the Maya Angelou school has taken children from the juvenile justice system and sent them on to college.

6. For discussion of studies supporting early childhood education and wrap-around social services, see Mari Matsuda, "On Causation," *Columbia Law Review* 100.8 (Dec. 2000).

7. Consider tax incentives and college scholarships for public school families, and creation of class-integrated magnet schools along the model of the successful UH laboratory school. Studies show that class integration brings up performance of low-income students without harming performance of high-income students.

8. Pushing through all of these demands requires organizing parents, students, and teachers together to fight for them. That is an unbeatable coalition, using the same formula that won Hawai'i's democratic revolution: there are more of us who are hurt by lousy public schools, and we vote.

9. Evaluation models exist that ask whether the school culture is supporting the development of critical thinking, and whether the students exhibit actual competencies measured by what they can do, not how they perform in time pressure tests.

10. Start with public recognition. Publicize and celebrate our public school successes: the students who have gone on to excel at the top colleges, the stunning poetry slams, history day entries, Hawaiian language accomplishments, professional May Day performances, and the many hidden moments of brilliance in our public school lives. We should also reward master teachers and model schools, and have others visit them to see what they are doing right.

FURTHER READING

Charles R. Lawrence III, "Forbidden Conversations: On Race, Privacy, and Community," *Yale Law Journal* 114 (2005): 1353.

Sara Lawrence-Lightfoot, *The Good High School: Portraits of Character and Culture* (New York: Basic Books, 1983).

Mari Matsuda, "My Teacher Loves Me But She Hates Mice; An Existential Lamentation on the Collapse of Public Education," *Journal of Race, Ethnicity & Education* 9.1 (2006): 117–28.

Deborah Meier, *In Schools We Trust: Creating Communities of Learning in an Era of Testing and Standardization* (Boston: Beacon, 2003).

Ann Shea Bayer, *Going Against the Grain: When Professionals in Hawai'i Choose Public Schools Instead of Private Schools* (Honolulu: U of Hawai'i P, 2009).

NEAL MILNER, UNIVERSITY OF HAWAI'I

1. "Trends in College Spending," Report of the Delta Cost Project (Washington, D.C.: Delta Cost Project on Postsecondary Education Costs, Productivity and Accountability, 2009).

2. David Yount, *Who Runs the University?: The Politics of Education in Hawaii, 1985–1992* (Honolulu: U of Hawai'i P, 1996).

3. Helen Altonn, "2 UH Faculty Reports: Close Medical School," *Honolulu Star-Bulletin,* Sept. 14, 1998.

4. Randall J. Roth, "Public Education in Hawaii: Past, Present and Future," Aug. 21, 2009, Apr. 30, 2010 <http://www.law.hawaii.edu/sites/_files/rroth/Essay.pdf.

5. Anthony Grafton, "The Marketplace of Ideas," *New Republic,* Mar. 11, 2010: 32–36.

6. "Final Report of the WASC Visiting Team Capacity and Preparatory Review" (Oakland, CA: WASC, 2010).

7. Peter S. Adler, "Hawaii Leadership Boards"; for a copy e-mail padler@ketstone.org.

MEDA CHESNEY-LIND AND KAT BRADY, PRISONS

1. Sentencing Project, *Facts about Prisons and Prisoners* (Washington, D.C.: Sentencing Project, 2010).

2. Pew Center on the States, "One in a Hundred: Behind Bars in America" (Washington, D.C.: Pew Center, 2008).

3. Adam Liptak, "U.S. prison population dwarfs that of other nations," *New York Times,* Apr. 23, 2008, Apr. 30, 2010 <http://www.nytimes.com/2008/04/23/world/americas/23iht-23prison.12253738.html>.

4. Jim Webb, "Why We Must Fix Our Prisons," *Parade Magazine,* Mar. 29, 2009, Apr. 30, 2010 <http://www.parade.com/news/2009/03/why-we-must-fix-our-prisons.html>.

5. For the data in this paragraph, see Randall G. Shelden, and William B. Brown, *Criminal Justice in America: A Critical View* (Boston: Allyn and Bacon, 2004).

6. Paula M. Ditton and Doris James Wilson, "Truth in Sentencing in State Prisons" (Washington, D.C.: U.S. Dept. of Justice, Bureau of Justice Statistics, 1999).

7. Jeremy Travis and Sarah Lawrence, "Beyond the Prison Gates: The State of Parole in America," Research Report (Washington, D.C.: Urban Institute. Nov. 2002): 22–23.

8. William J. Sabol, Heather West, and Matthew Cooper, *Prisoners in 2008* (Washington, D.C.: Bureau of Justice Statistics, National Institute of Justice, 2009).

9. Crime Prevention Statistics Division, "Crime in Hawai'i" (Honolulu: Dept. of the Attorney General, 2009).

10. Sabol, West, and Cooper 18.

11. Marc Mauer, "Racial Disparities in the Criminal Justice System" (Washington, D.C.: Sentencing Project. 2009), Apr. 18, 2010 <http://www.sentencingproject.org/doc/publications/rd_mmhousetestimonyonRD.pdf?>; see also Sentencing Project, "Racial Disparity" (Washington, D.C.: 2010) <http://www.sentencingproject.org/template/page.cfm?id=122>.

12. Clayton Frank, "Statistics on Hawaiian and Part Hawaiian Prison Inmates," Letter to Senator Will Espero, 2008.

13. Gene Kassebaum and Janet Davidson, "Parole Decision Making in Hawaii" (Honolulu: Dept. of the Attorney General, 2001).

14. Richard Yen, Memo to Senator Will Espero, Jan. 8, 2009.

15. Travis and Lawrence 23.

16. "Preliminary Report Classification—Systematic Approach to Sound Correctional Management," Criminal Justice Institute, Inc., Middletown, CT: 2008.

17. Tom Lengyel, "Emerging Issues for Children of Incarcerated Parents," Presentation to the State Task Force on Children of Incarcerated Parents, Sept. 21, 2005.

18. Meda Chesney-Lind, "Testimony on House Concurrent Resolution 35 House Resolution 22," presented to the House Committee on Public Safety and the House Committee on Judiciary and Hawaiian Affairs, Feb. 1, 1999.

19. Travis and Lawrence.

20. Ian Urbina, "Hawaii To Remove Inmates Over Abuse Charges," *New York Times,* Aug. 25, 2009, Apr. 30, 2010 <http://www.nytimes.com/2009/08/26/us/26kentucky.html>.

21. Cited in Rebecca Tuhus-Dubrow, "Prison Reform Talking Points," *The Nation,* Jan. 5, 2004, Apr. 30, 2010 <http://www.thenation.com/doc/20040105/tuhusdubrow>.

22. Pew Center on the States, "One in a Hundred: Behind Bars in America."

23. Kat Brady, *Smart Justice* (Honolulu: Community Alliance on Prisons, 2010).

24. Pew Center on the States, "One in a Hundred: Behind Bars in America."

25. Philip Reese, "Higher Education vs. Prisons: See where California's money goes," *Sacramento Bee,* Jan. 7, 2010, Apr. 30, 2010 <http://www.sacbee.com/2010/01/06/2442430/higher-education-vs-prisons-see.html>.

26. Arnold Schwarzenegger, "State of the State Address" (Sacramento: Office of the Governor, 2010), Mar. 30, 2010, Apr. 30, 2010 <http://gov.ca.gov/index.php?/fact-sheet/14128>.

27. Mary Sprect, "Tuition Increases Moderate?," *USA Today,* Aug. 30, 2006, Apr. 30, 2010 <http://www.usatoday/com/news/education/2006-08-30-tuition-increases_x.htm>.

28. Nicole P Porter, *The State of Sentencing, 2009* (Washington, D.C.: Sentencing Project, 2010).

29. Sabol, West, and Cooper.

30. Susan Essoyan, "Signs of Hope," *Honolulu Star-Bulletin,* Mar. 28, 2010, Apr. 30, 2010 <http://www.starbulletin.com/news/20100328_Signs_of_HOPE.html>.

SUSAN CHANDLER, SOCIAL SERVICES

1. Gretchen Rowe and Linda Giannarelli, "Getting On, Staying On, and Getting Off Welfare" (Washington, D.C.: Urban Institute, 2006).
2. Debbie Shimizu, personal communication.
3. "Hawaii 2050 Update Report to the Legislature," University of Hawai'i at Mānoa Public Policy Center <http://www.publicpolicycenter.hawaii.edu/sustainability.html>.

For FURTHER INFORMATION . . .

Gregory Acs and Pamela J. Loprest, "TANF Caseload Composition and Leavers Synthesis Report" (Washington, D.C.: Urban Institute, 2007).

Julie Cooper Altman and Gertrude Schaffner Goldberg, "Rethinking Social Work's Role in Public Assistance," *Journal of Sociology & Social Welfare* 35.4 (Dec. 2008): 71–94.

Joel Blau and Mimi Abramovitz, *The Dynamics of Social Welfare Policy* (Oxford: Oxford UP, 2010).

Diana M. DiNitto and Linda K. Cummins, *Social Welfare: Politics and Public Policy,* 6th ed. (Boston: Allyn and Bacon, 2007).

Younghee Lim, Claudia J. Coulton, and Nina Lalich, "State TANF Policies and Employment Outcomes among Welfare Leavers," *Social Service Review* 83.4 (Dec. 2009): 526–55.

Harrell R. Rodgers, Jr. and Lee Payne, "Child Poverty in the American States: The Impact of Welfare Reform, Economics, and Demographics," *Policy Studies Journal* 35.1 (Feb. 2007): 1–22.

TRISHA KEHAULANI WATSON, HOMELESSNESS

1. Donald D. Kilolani Mitchell, *Resource Units in Hawaiian Culture,* rev. ed., 3rd printing (Honolulu: Kamehameha Schools P, 2007).
2. Howard Thurman, "Community and the Self," Speech given at Marsh Chapel, Boston University, Boston, MA, Apr. 16, 1961, reprinted in *Say It Plain: A Century of Great African American Speeches,* ed. Catherine Ellis and Stephen Drury Smith (New York: NYU Press, 2005): 36–37.
3. E. S. Craighill Handy and Mary Kawena Pukui, *The Polynesian Family System in Ka'u, Hawai'i,* 1958, 7th printing (Rutland: VT: Charles E. Tuttle, 1988): 40.
4. University of Hawai'i Center on the Family, "Homeless Service Utilization Report" (Honolulu: U of Hawai'i, 2008), Apr. 30, 2010 <http://uhfamily.hawaii.edu/publications/brochures/HomelessServiceUtilization2008.pdf>.
5. Ann M. Pobutsky, Lee Buenconsejo-Lum, Catherine Chow, Neal Palafox, and Gregory G. Maskarinec, "Micronesian Migrants in Hawaii: Health Issues and Culturally Appropriate, Community-Based Solutions," *California Journal of Health Promotion* 3.4 (Dec. 2005): 59–72.
6. Legislative Reference Bureau Systems Office, Bills Passed by the Hawai'i State Legislature Regular Session of 2004 (Honolulu, 2004): 10.
7. National Coalition for the Homeless and the National Law Center on Homelessness and Poverty, "A Dream Denied: The Criminalization of the Homeless in U.S. Cities," Jan. 2006, Apr. 30, 2010 <http://www.nationalhomeless.org/publications/crimreport/2006_index.html>.

8.   American Civil Liberties Union of Hawai'i, "Joint Statement by the ACLU of Hawai'i, The Interfaith Alliance Hawai'i and Kokua Council Groups Urge Legislature to Heed Community's Demand to Repeal Act 50 'The Squatter's Law,'" Apr. 21, 2005, Apr. 30, 2010 <http:// www.acluhawaii.org/news.php?id=165 1>.

9.   B. J. Reyes, "Proposals to repeal squatter law delay lawsuit," *Honolulu Star-Bulletin,* Apr. 21, 2005, Apr. 30, 2010 <http://www.starbulletin.com/2005/04/21/news/index12. html>.

10. The Women's Support Group of the Wai'anae Coast, *A Time for Sharing: Women's Stories from the Wai'anae Coast* (Honolulu: Women's Support Group of the Wai'anae Coast, 1982): 33.

11. Will Hoover, "Hawaii homeless shelter's beds empty," *Honolulu Advertiser,* Aug. 13, 2007, Apr. 30, 2010 <http://the.honoluluadvertiser.com/article/2007/Aug/13/ln/hawaii708130353.html>.

12. University of Hawai'i Center on the Family, "Homeless Service Utilization Report."

SUSAN HIPPENSTEELE, DOMESTIC VIOLENCE

1.   Rob Perez, "Crossing the Line: Abuse in Hawaii Homes," *Honolulu Advertiser,* Dec. 2008, Apr. 30, 2010 <http://www.honoluluadvertiser.com/DOMESTICVIOLENCE>.

2.   See the "State of Hawaii Strategic Plan for S.T.O.P. Violence Against Women Formula Grant FY 2008–2011," Department of the Attorney General, Crime Prevention and Justice Assistance Division, Oct. 2007, May 5, 2010 <http:// hawaii.gov/ag/cpja/main/ gp/State%20of%20Hawaii%20Strategic%20Plan%20for%20VAWA%20Grant.pdf>, and the Judiciary State of Hawai'i 2009 Annual Report Statistical Supplement, May 5, 2010 <http:// www.courts.state.hi.us/docs/news_and_reports_docs/annual_reports/ Jud_Statistical_Sup_2009.pdf>.

3.   See the "State of Hawaii Strategic Plan for S.T.O.P. Violence Against Women."

4.   See p. 4, "Domestic Violence in Hawaii: Impact on Mothers and their Children," Pacific Behavioral Health Sciences Corporation, Department of Psychology, University of Hawai'i at Mānoa, and Department of the Attorney General, State of Hawai'i, Oct. 2000 (Honolulu: Hawaii Correctional Industries), Apr. 30, 2010 <http://hawaii.gov/ ag/cpja/main/rs/Folder.2006-02-06.3414/dvrpr00.pdf>

5.   National Network to End Domestic Violence, "Census 2009 Report," Apr. 30, 2010 www.nnedv.org/resources/census/2009-census-report.html

INFORMATION AND RESOURCES

For a county by county listing of service providers and contact information, see the Hawai'i State Coalition Against Domestic Violence <http://www.hscadv.org>.

DEANE NEUBAUER, HEALTH AND HEALTHCARE

1.   See Deane Neubauer, "Hawaii: A Pioneer in Health System Reform," *Health Affairs* 12.2 (Summer 1993): 31–39.

2.   For the development of healthcare in Hawai'i from the 1970s to the 1990s, see Neubauer, "Hawaii: A Pioneer in Health System Reform"; see also Annette Gardner and Deane Neubauer, "Hawaii's Health Quest," *Health Affairs* 14.1 (Spring 1995): 300– 303; and Deane Neubauer, "Health Care and Money," *The Unfinished Health Agenda:*

Lessons from Hawai'i, ed. Robert Grossman and James Shon (Honolulu: Hawaii State Primary Care Association, 1994)

3. For Kānaka Maoli health statistics, see Esther Figueroa, "Native Hawaiian Healthcare: Hawaiian Health History," Apr. 23, 2010 <www.nativehawaiianhealth.net/history. cfm>; and Kekuni Blaisdell, "Update on Kanaka Maoli (Indigenous Hawaiian) Health," *Motion Magazine*, Nov. 16, 1997, Apr. 30, 2010 < www.inmotionmagazine.com/kekuni3.html>.

4. For budget data, see the "2008 Hawaii State Data Book," State of Hawai'i Department of Business, Economic Development, and Tourism, May 6, 2010 <http://hawaii.gov/dbedt/info/economic/databook/db2008>.

5. Gerald Russo, Sang-Hyop Lee, and Jaclyn Lindo, "Hawaii's Uninsured Population: Estimates from the Current Poulation Survey 1997–2008," Draft Report, Prepared for the State of Hawai'i Department of Health, Family Health Services Division, June 30, 2009.

6. For information on the new health reform laws, see Kaiser Family Foundation, "Side-by-Side Comparison of Major Health Care Reform Proposals," Apr. 21, 2010, Apr. 30, 2010 <http://www.kff.org/healthreform/sidebyside.cfm>.

7. For data on Hawai'i's health status and system, see Hawaii Health Information Corporation, "Health Trends in Hawaii," Apr. 23, 2010 <http://www.healthtrends.org>.

8. See Greg Wiles, "Hawai'i's Shortage of Doctors May Double or Triple Over Next Decade," *Honolulu Advertiser,* Mar. 28, 2010, Apr. 23, 2010 <http://www.honoluluadvertiser.com/article/20100328/NEWS01/3280389/Hawaii%E2%25>.

MARILYN CRISTOFORI, ARTS

1. The National Endowment for the Arts is the public agency dedicated to supporting excellence in the arts, bringing the arts to all Americans and providing leadership in arts education. It is the nation's largest annual funder of the arts. For its programs and resources, see <http://arts.endow.gov>; for its history, see <arts.endow.gov/pub/nea-history-1965-2008.pdf>. See also <http://www.kennedy-center.org> for information on the John F. Kennedy Center for the Performing Arts, our national cultural center, which offers splendid performances in every arts form, and leads a national network for arts education.

2. Americans for the Arts, the nation's nonprofit organization for advancing the arts in America, has a wealth of information on arts in the economy, arts education, and the national arts index 2009. Please visit <http://www.artsusa.org>.

3. For information on HFSCA programs, history, and budgets, see Hawai'i State Foundation on Culture and the Arts <www.state.hi.us/sfca>.

4. Arts Education Partnership (AEP), a collaboration between education, business, philanthropic, and government organizations to promote educational policies supportive of arts education, publishes leading research about the impact of all arts on learning; see <http://www.aep-arts.org>.

5. Arts with Aloha provides a helpful overview of art and cultural institutions, performances, and events on O'ahu; see <http://www.artswithaloha.com>.

6. *Learning, Arts, and the Brain: The Dana Consortium Report on Arts and Cognition*, ed. Carolyn Asbury and Barbara Rich (New York: Dana, 2008), which includes the report

on the University of Oregon Study by Michael Posner, Mary K. Rothbart, Brad E. Sheese, and Jessica Kieras, "How Arts Training Influences Cognition," 1–10.

7.   See Richard Florida, *The Rise of the Creative Class: And How Its Transforming Work, Leisure, Community, and Everyday Life* (New York: Basic Books, 2002): Preface.

8.   Hawaii Community Foundation, "A Report on Charitable Giving in Hawaii," Aug. 2009, Apr. 30, 2010 <http://www.hawaiicommunityfoundation.org/doc_bin/studies/HCF_09GivingStudy-complete.pdf>.

9.   For more on Kanu Hawaii and its programs, see <http://www.kanuhawaii.org/kanu>.

IAN LIND, JOURNALISM

1.   Rick Daysog, "Star-Bulletin Annual Sales at 17.4 Million," *Honolulu Advertiser,* Mar. 19, 2010.

2.   Ian Lind, "Hawaii Newspaper Guild lost nearly 25% of members in past three years," Mar. 6, 2010 <http://www.iLind.net>; for industry-wide information about newspaper layoffs, see Erica Smith, "Paper Cuts" <http://newspaperlayoffs.com>.

3.   Jim Shon, Testimony on SCR193 and SR92 before the Senate Committee on Judiciary and Government Operations, Hawai'i State Legislature, Mar. 29, 2010.

4.   John Leibowitz, "'Creative Destruction' or Just 'Destruction', How Will Journalism Survive the Internet Age?," Opening Remarks for the Federal Trade Commission News Media Workshop, Washington, D.C., Dec. 1–2, 2009.

5.   Robert W. McChesney, "Rejuvenating American Journalism: Some tentative policy proposals," Presentation to Workshop on Journalism, Federal Trade Commission, Washington, D.C., Mar. 10, 2010.

6.   Geoffrey Cowan and David Westphal, "Public Policy and Funding the News," Annenberg School for Communication and Journalism, U of Southern California, Jan. 2010.

7.   Media Council Hawaii, "Raycom-HITV Seek to Silence Community Voices," *Hawaii Reporter,* Nov. 19, 2009.

8.   Clay Shirky, "Newspapers and Thinking the Unthinkable," Mar. 13, 2009, May 6, 2010 <http:// www.shirky.com/weblog/2009/03/newspapers-and-thinking-the-unthinkable/>.

PATRICIA TUMMONS, TERRESTRIAL ECOSYSTEMS

1.   Animal Species Advisory Committee, "Reviews of the Five-Year Forest Planting Plan for the State of Hawaii, Fiscal Years 1972–1976," Jan. 1974, prepared in response to Senate Resolution No. 303, 1973.

2.   State of Hawai'i, Department of Land and Natural Resources, Division of Fish and Game, "Public Hunting Areas," Oct. 1977: Appendix D-2.1 to the *DLNR Recreation Program Handbook,* Mar. 1978.

3.   "Vandals Damage Rare Plant Enclosure at Laupahoehoe Natural Area Reserve," *Environment Hawai'i* 5.11 (May 1995).

RECOMMENDED READING

Sherwin Carlquist, *Hawai'i: A Natural History,* 3rd printing (Honolulu: National Tropical Botanical Garden, 1992).

Linda W. Cuddihy and Charles P. Stone, *Alteration of Native Hawaiian Vegetation: Effects of Humans, Their Activities, and Introductions* (Honolulu: Cooperative National Park Resources Studies Unit, U of Hawai'i, 1990).

Thane K. Pratt, Carter T. Atkinson, Paul C. Banko, James D. Jacoby, and Bethany L. Woodworth, eds., *Conservation Biology of Hawaiian Forest Birds* (New Haven: Yale UP, 2009).

Charles P. Stone and J. Michael Scott, eds., *Hawai'i's Terrestrial Ecosystems: Preservation and Management* (Honolulu: Cooperative National Park Resources Studies Unit, U of Hawai'i. 1985).

Charles P. Stone, Clifford W. Smith, and J. Timothy Tunison, eds., *Alien Plant Invasions in Native Ecosystems of Hawai'i* (Honolulu: Cooperative National Park Resources Studies Unit, U of Hawai'i, 1992).

P. Quentin Tomich, *Mammals in Hawai'i: A Synopsis and Notational Bibliography*, Rev. ed. (Honolulu: Bishop Museum, 1986).

Patricia Tummons and Teresa Dawson, *Cattle in Hawaiian Forests: Two Centuries of Loss*, bound reprint of three issues of *Environment Hawai'i* (Sept.-Nov. 2002) <http://www.environment-hawaii.org>.

Alan Ziegler, *Hawaiian Natural History, Ecology, and Evolution* (Honolulu: U of Hawai'i P, 2002).

CHIP FLETCHER, CLIMATE CHANGE

AUTHOR'S NOTE: This essay is a contribution of the Center for Island Climate Adaptation and Policy, University of Hawai'i Sea Grant College Program.

1. T. W. Giambelluca, H. F. Diaz, and M. S. A. Luke, "Secular Temperature Changes in Hawai'i," *Geophysical Research Letters* 35 (2008): L12702.

2. G. A. Meehl, C. Tebaldi, G. Walton, D. Easterling, and L. McDaniel, "Relative Increase of Record High Maximum Temperatures Compared to Record Low Minimum Temperatures in the U.S.," *Geophysical Research Letters* 36 (2009): L23701.

3. D. Easterling and M. Wehner, "Is the Climate Warming or Cooling?" *Geophysical Research Letters* 36 (2009): L08706; see also the NASA website on this study, last accessed Jan. 16, 2010 <http://climate.nasa.gov/news/index/cfm?FuseAction+ShowNews&NewsID=175>.

4. L. L. Loope and T. W. Giambelluca, "Vulnerability of Island Tropical Montane Cloud Forests to Climate Change, with Special Reference to East Maui, Hawai'i," *Climate Change* 39 (1998): 503–517.

5. G. A. Vecchi, B. J. Soden, A. T. Wittenberg, I. M. Held, A. Leetmaa, and M. J. Harrison, "Weakening of Tropical Pacific Atmospheric Circulation due to Anthropogenic Forcing," *Nature* 441 (2006): 73–76.

6. O. Timm and H. Diaz, "Synoptic-Statistical Approach to Regional Downscaling of IPCC Twenty-First Century Climate Projections: Seasonal Rainfall over the Hawaiian Islands," *Journal of Climate* 22.16 (2009): 4261–80.

7. P. S. Chu and H. Chen, "Interannual and Interdecadal Rainfall Variations in the Hawaiian Islands," *Journal of Climate* 18 (2005): 4796–4813; see also H. F. Diaz, P. S. Chu, and J. K. Eischeid, "Rainfall Changes in Hawai'i during the Last Century," 16th

Conference on Climate Variability and Change, American Meteorological Society, Boston, MA, 2005; cited in *Global Climate Change Impacts in the United States*, ed. T. R. Karl, J. M. Melillo, and T. C. Peterson (Cambridge: Cambridge UP, 2009).

8. D. Oki, "Trends in Streamflow Characteristics at Long-term Gauging Stations, Hawai'i," U.S. Geological Survey Scientific Investigations Report 2004–5080.

9. P. Ya. Groisman, R. W. Knight, T. R. Karl, D. R. Easterling, B. Sun, and J. H. Lawrimore, "Contemporary changes of the hydrological cycle over the contiguous United States, trends derived from in situ observations," *Journal of Hydrometeorology* 5.1 (2004): 64–85; cited in *Global Climate Change Impacts in the United States*.

10. IPCC, *Climate Change 2007, Synthesis Report, Contribution of Working Groups I, II and III to the Fourth Assessment Report of the Intergovernmental Panel on Climate Change* [Core Writing Team, R. K. Pachauri, and A. Reisinger, eds.], IPCC, Geneva, 2007, 104 pp.

11. S.-P. Xie, K. Hu, J. Hafner, H. Tokinaga, Y. Du, G. Huang, T. Sampe, "Indian Ocean Capacitor Effect on Indo-western Pacific Climate during the Summer Following El Niño," *Journal of Climate* 22.3 (2009): 730–47.

12. Timm and Diaz, see note 6.

13. See the Honolulu tide record at National Oceanographic and Atmospheric Administration, Sea Levels Online, last accessed Jan. 16, 2010 <http://tidesandcurrents.noaa.gov/sltrends/sltrends.html>.

14. Y. Firing and M. A. Merrifield, "Extreme Sea Level Events at Hawai'i: Influence of Mesoscale Eddies," *Geophysical Research Letters* 31 (2004): L24306.

15. C. H. Fletcher, R. A. Mullane, and B. M. Richmond, "Beach Loss along Armored Shorelines of Oahu, Hawaiian Islands," *Journal of Coastal Research* 13 (1997): 209–215.

16. C. H. Fletcher, J. Rooney, M. Barbee, S.-C. Lim, and B. M. Richmond, "Mapping shoreline change using digital orthophotogrammetry on Maui, Hawai'i," *Journal of Coastal Research* Special Issue 38 (2003): 106–124.

17. M. A. Merrifield, S. T. Merrifield, and G. T. Mitchum, "An anomalous recent acceleration of global sea level rise," *Journal of Climate* 22 (2009): 5772–81.

18. Global sea level rise is measured by satellite detection of the ocean surface; see NASA, "Rising Water: new map pinpoints areas of sea level increase," last accessed Jan. 16, 2010 <http://climate.nasa.gov/news/index/cfm?FuseAction=ShowNews&NewsID=16>.

19. M. Vermeer and S. Rahmstorf, "Global sea level linked to global temperature," *Proceedings of the National Academy of Sciences,* PNAS Early Edition, 2009 <http://www.pnas.org_cgi_coi_10.1073_pnas.0907765106>; see also C. H. Fletcher, "Sea Level by the End of the 21st Century: A Review," *Shore and Beach* 77.4 (2009): 1–9.

20. K. S. Casey and P. Cornillon, "Global and Regional Sea Surface Temperature Trends," *Journal of Climate* 14.18 (2001): 3801–818.

21. P. Jokiel and E. Brown, "Global Warming, Regional Trends and Inshore Environmental Conditions Influence Coral Bleaching in Hawai'i," *Global Change Biology* 10 (2004): 1627–41; see also P. L. Jokiel and S. L. Coles, "Response of Hawaiian and other Indo-Pacific Reef Corals to Elevated Temperature," *Coral Reefs* 8 (1990): 1155–62.

22. A. Friedlander, G. Aeby, R. Brainard, E. Brown, K. Chaston, A. Clark, P. McGowan, T. Montgomery, W. Walsh, I. Williams, and W. Wiltse, with contributions from J.

Asher, S. Balwani, E. Co, E. DeCarlo, P. Jokiel, J. Kenyon, J. Helyer, C. Hunter, J. Miller, C. Morshige, J. Rooney, H. Slay, R. Schroeder, H. Spalding, L. Wedding, and T. Work, *The State of Coral Reef Ecosystems of the Main Hawaiian Islands,* National Oceanographic and Atmospheric Administration, 2008, last accessed Nov. 16, 2009 <http://ccma.nos.noaa.gov/ecosystems/coralreef/coral2008/pdf.Hawaii.pdf>.

23. J. E. Dore, R. Lukas, D. W. Sadler, M. J. Church, and D. M. Karl, "Physical and Bio-geochemical Modulation of Ocean Acidification in the Central North Pacific," *Proceedings of the U.S. National Academy of Sciences* 106 (2009):12235–40; see also R. H. Byrne, S. Mecking, R. A. Feely, and X. Liu, "Direct Observations of Basin-wide Acidification of the North Pacific Ocean," *Geophysical Research Letters* 37 (2010): L02601.

HENRY CURTIS, ENERGY

1. United Nations Environment Programme and New Energy Finance Ltd., "Global Trends in Sustainable Energy Investment 2009: Analysis of Trends and Issues in the Financing of Renewable Energy and Energy Efficiency," 2009, May 3, 2010 <http://www.unep.org/pdf/Global_trends_report_2009.pdf>.

RECOMMENDED READING: GENERAL ISSUES AND DATA

Henry Curtis, "Big Wind, Geothermal & Inter-island Transmission Lines," 2009, May 3, 2010 <http://vimeo.com/10452417>.

Enterprise Honolulu, "Imports, Exports and Economic Development," Aug. 28, 2003 <http://www.enterprisehonolulu.com/html/pdf/EHeseries10.pdf>.

———. "Export Enhancement and Import Substitution—Key Strategies for Hawaii's Prosperity," Sept. 4, 2003 <www.enterprisehonolulu.com/html/pdf/EHeseries11.pdf>.

Thomas L. Friedman, *The Lexus and the Olive Tree* (New York: Anchor, 2000).

———. *Hot, Flat and Crowded: Why We Need a Green Revolution—and How It Can Renew America* (New York: Farrar, Straus, and Giroux, 2008).

Horace Herring, "Does energy efficiency save energy? The debate and its consequences," The Open University, *Applied Energy* 63.3 (July 1999): 209–226, May 3, 2010 <http://www.sciencedirect.com/science/article/B6V1T-3X05FPD-B/1/ae95e991e81b00-f5a379eca9958641d3>.

Thomas Kemper Hitch, *Islands in Transition: The Past, Present and Future of Hawaii's Economy,* ed. Robert M. Kamins (Honolulu: First Hawaiian Bank, 1992).

Kohala Center, "Analysis and Recommendations for the Hawai'i County Energy Sustainability Plan," by Michael Davies, Claire Gagne, Zeke Hausfather, and Dawn Lippert, Kamuela, Hawai'i, Oct. 3, 2007, May 3, 2010 <http://www.co.hawaii.hi.us/rd/hiesp_full.pdf>.

———, "Hawaii County Baseline Energy Analysis," by Jeremiah Johnson, Dan Leistra, Jules Opton-Himmel, Mason Smith, and advisors Marian Chertow, Arnulf Grübler, and Derek Murrow, Kamuela, Hawai'i, Feb. 19, 2007, May 3, 2010 <http://www.kohalacenter.org/pdf/hawaii_county_baseline_energ.pdf>.

Hunter Lovins, Natural Capitalism Solutions, "The Future of Industry in Asia," Presented at the International Conference on Green Industry in Asia, Manila, Philippines, Sept. 9–11, 2009, May 3, 2010 <www.unido.org/fileadmin/user_media/UNIDO_Header_Site/Subsites/Green_Industry_Asia_Conference__Maanila_/Ind_Resource.pdf>.

Carl Myatt, *Hawaii: The Electric Century. A History of HECO* (Honolulu: Signature, 1991).

Robert Rapier, "Energy Blog: objective discussions on energy and environmental issues" <http://www.consumerenergyreport.com/blogs/rsquared>.

E. F. Schumacher, *Small Is Beautiful: Economics as if People Mattered* (New York: Harper and Row, 1973).

State of Hawai'i, Dept. of Business, Economic Development, and Tourism, *Hawaii Data Book, 2008*, Aug. 12, 2009, May 3, 2010 <http://hawaii.gov/dbedt/info/economic/databook/db2008>.

———, "Hawaii Energy Strategy," 2000 <http://hawaii.gov/dbedt/info/energy/planning/hes/hes2000.pdf>.

State of Hawai'i, Dept. of Business, Economic Development, and Tourism, and U.S, Department of Energy, "Hawaii Clean Energy Initiative," Mar. 1, 2010, May 3, 2010 <http://www.hawaiicleanenergyinitiative.org>.

University of Hawai'i, "Sustainable Saunders," May 3, 2010 <http://sustainablesaunders.hawaii.edu>.

Daniel Yergin, *The Prize: The Epic Quest for Oil, Money, and Power* (New York: Simon and Schuster, 1991).

RECOMMENDED READING: BIOFUELS

Kristina J. Anderson-Teixeira, Sarah C Davis, Michael D Masters, and Evan H Delucia, "Changes in soil organic carbon under biofuel crops," *GCB Bioenergy* 1.1 (2009): 75–96, Feb. 25, 2009, May 3, 2010 <http://www3.interscience.wiley.com/journal/122217824/abstract>.

Juliette Budge et al., "Biofuels in Hawai'i: A Case Study of Hāmākua," Report by the Department of Urban Regional Planning Master's Practicum, Spring 2009, May 3, 2010 <http://www.kohalacenter.org/pdf/Biofuels.pdf>.

Winnie Gerbens-Leenesa, Arjen Y. Hoekstraa, and Theo H. van der Meerb, "The water footprint of bioenergy," ed. David Pimentel, June 3, 2009, May 3, 2010 <http://www.pnas.org/content/early/2009/06/03/0812619106.full.pdf+html>.

Life of the Land, Testimony re Palm Oil before the Public Utilities Commission, June 23, 2008, May 3, 2010 <http://www.lifeofthelandhawaii.org/Bio_Documents/2007.0346/LOL%20Testimony%20and%20Exhibits.pdf>.

Dr. Tad Patzek, "Biofuel Testimony before the Public Utilities Commission," Aug. 14, 2006, May 3, 2010 <http://www.lifeofthelandhawaii.org/Proposed-2009-plant/Patzek.pdf>.

Robert Rapier, "How Reliable are those USDA Ethanol Studies?," Mar. 30, 2006, May 3, 2010 <http://www.lifeofthelandhawaii.org/doc2/Rapier_Reliability_USDA_Ethanol_Studies_2006.pdf>.

Rocky Mountain Institute, "Hawaii Biofuels Summit Briefing Book," Aug. 8, 2006, May 3, 2010 <http://www.lifeofthelandhawaii.org/Bio_Documents/Hawaii_Biofuels_Summit_Briefing_Book_2006.pdf>.

State of Hawai'i, Dept. of Business, Economic Development, and Tourism, "Hawaii Bioenergy Master Plan," Dec. 2009, May 3, 2010 <http://hawaii.gov/dbedt/info/energy/publications/bemp-09.pdf/download>.

RECOMMENDED READING: OCEAN AND WATER ENERGY

Reb Bellinger, "Testimony re Sea Water Air Conditioning before the Public Utilities Commission," Makai Ocean Engineering, May 3, 2010 <www.lifeofthelandhawaii.org/Proposed-2009-plant/Bellinger.pdf>.

Dr. David Rezachek, "Testimony re Sea Water Air Conditioning before the Public Utilities Commission," May 3, 2010 http://www.lifeofthelandhawaii.org/Proposed-2009-plant/Rezachek.pdf>.

Dr. Tom Denniss, "Testimony re Blowhole Wave Energy before the Public Utilities Commission, Energetech (Oceanlinx)," May 3, 2010 <http://www.lifeofthelandhawaii.org/Proposed-2009-plant/Denniss.pdf>.

Electric Power Research Institute (EPRI)/Electricity Innovation Institute, "Economic Assessment Methodology for Offshore Wave Power Plants," Nov. 30, 2004, May 3, 2010 <http://www.lifeofthelandhawaii.org/doc2/EPRI_Wave_Economic_Modeling.pdf>.

———. "Offshore Wave Power in the US: Environmental Issues," Dec. 21, 2004, May 3, 2010 <http://www.lifeofthelandhawaii.org/doc2/EPRI%20_Wave_Environmental_Issues.pdf>.

———. "Survey and Characterization of Potential Offshore Wave Energy Sites in Hawaii," June 15, 2004, May 3, 2010 <http://www.lifeofthelandhawaii.org/doc2/EPRI_Wave_Hawaii_Site_Report.pdf>.

———. "System Level Design, Performance and Costs—Hawaii State Offshore Wave Power Plant," Jan. 12, 2005, May 3, 2010 <http://www.lifeofthelandhawaii.org/doc2/EPRI_Hawaii_Wave_System.pdf>.

———. "Wave Energy Devices, June 16, 2004, May 3, 2010 <http://www.lifeofthelandhawaii.org/doc2/EPRI_Wave_Energy_Devices.pdf>.

———. "Wave Power in the U.S: Permitting and Jurisdictional Issues," Dec. 21, 2004, May 3, 2010 <http://www.lifeofthelandhawaii.org/doc2/EPRI_Wave_Permitting_Issues.pdf>.

Carolyn Elefant, "RenewablesOffshore," attorney focusing on helping ocean energy, offshore wind, and other marine renewables and hydro developers get projects funded, permitted and built <http://carolynelefant1.typepad.com/renewablesoffshore>.

Dr. Hans Krock, "Testimony re Ocean Thermal Energy Conversion before the Public Utilities Commission," Hawaii PUC Docket 2005-0145, May 3, 2010 <http://www.lifeofthelandhawaii.org/Proposed-2009-plant/Krock.pdf>.

US Department of Energy, OTEC, May 3, 2010 <http://www.lifeofthelandhawaii.org/doc2/US_DOE_EERE_OTEC.pdf>.

RECOMMENDED READING: SOLAR POWER

Donald W. Aitken, Ph.D., "Transitioning to a Renewable Energy Future," 2003, May 3, 2010 <http://www.donaldaitkenassociates.com/transitioning_daa.pdf>.

Thomas E. Hoff and Richard Perez, "Quantifying PV Power Output Variability Clean Power Research," May 2, 2009, May 3, 2010 < www.cleanpower.com/Content/Documents/research/capacityvaluation/QuantifyingPVPowerOutputVariability.pdf >.

National Renewable Energy Laboratories, "Solar Energy Technology Programs Overview," May 3, 2010 <http://www.nrel.gov/programs/solar.html >.

Sopogy: SopoHow, Episode 1: How it Works <http://www.youtube.com/watch?v=rus3qkHdAk4>.

D. KAPUA'ALA SPROAT, WATER

1. Excerpts from "He Mele nō Kāne" in Nathaniel B. Emerson, *Unwritten Literature of Hawaii, the Sacred Songs of Hula* (diacritical marks added) (Rutland, VT: Tuttle, 1964): 257–59.
2. Emerson 258.
3. E. S. Craighill Handy and Elizabeth Green Handy, with the Collaboration of Mary Kawena Puku'i, *Native Planters in Old Hawai'i, Their Life, Lore, & Environment,* 3rd ed. (Honolulu: Bishop Museum, 1991): 64 (kahakō added).
4. *McBryde Sugar Co. v. Robinson,* 54 Haw. 174, 185–87, 504 P.2d 1330, 1338–39 (1973).
5. Haw. Const. of 1840, reprinted in *The Fundamental Law of Hawaii,* ed. Lorrin A. Thurston (Honolulu: Hawaiian Gazette, 1904): 3.
6. For a more in-depth discussion of the Commission of Private Ways and Water Rights, see Antonio Perry, "Hawaiian Water Rights," *Hawaiian Almanac and Annual for 1913,* ed. Thomas G. Thrum (Honolulu: Thos. Thrum): 96–99; the quotation is from 97.
7. See, for example, Hawai'i Revised Statutes § 1–1 (adopting English common law except as established by Hawaiian usage).
8. *McBryde Sugar Co. v. Robinson,* 54 Haw. 174, 504 P.2d 1330 (1973).
9. *McBryde Sugar Co. v. Robinson,* 54 Haw. 174, 186–87, 504 P.2d 1330, 1338–39 (1973).
10. For more information on Hawai'i's water resources, see generally <http://hi.water.usgs.gov> and <http://www.state.hi.us/dlnr/cwrm>.
11. For more information on increasing chloride (salt) levels in various Maui wells, see <http://hi.water.usgs.gov/recent/iao/chloride.html>.
12. See *In re Waiāhole Combined Contested Case,* 94 Haw. 97 (2000) (the Hawai'i Supreme Court's first decision in this case that strongly reaffirmed the public trust doctrine), and *In re Waiāhole Combined Contested Case,* 105 Haw. 1 (2004) (the Hawai'i Supreme Court's decision on the second appeal in this case).
13. For more information on the legal framework regarding Hawai'i's water resources, including legal tools and other resources for more proactive management, see D. Kapua'ala Sproat, *Ola I Ka Wai: A Legal Primer for Water Use and Management in Hawai'i* (Honolulu: Ka Huli Ao Center for Excellence in Native Hawaiian Law, 2009).

DANA NAONE HALL, SOVEREIGN GROUND

1. For more information and a copy of the law, see State of Hawai'i, Office of Information Practices, "Sunshine Law" <http://www.state.hi.us/oip/sunshinelaw.html>.
2. Lee Cataluna, "Furlough Sit-In Lifts Mother's Profile," *Honolulu Advertiser,* Apr. 18, 2010.
3. Sean Hao, "Hawaii Audit Calls for Ouster of Economic Development Director," *Honolulu Advertiser,* Jan. 30, 2010: 1, May 3, 2010 <www.honoluluadvertiser.com/article/20100130/NEWS01/1300332/Hawaii-audit-calls-for-ouster-of-economic-development-director>.

SARA L. COLLINS, HISTORIC PRESERVATION

SOURCES ON FEDERAL HISTORIC PRESERVATION LAW AND PRACTICE:

Thomas F. King, *Saving Places that Matter: A Citizen's Guide to the National Historic Preservation Act* (Walnut Creek, CA: Left Coast, 2007), and *Cultural Resource Laws and Practice*, 3rd ed. (Lanham: MD: Altamira, 2008); he also blogs on preservation-related issues: <http:crmplus.blogspot.com>.

The National Park Service's main portal to historic preservation matters: <http://www.nps.gov/history/index.htm>.

The President's Advisory Council on Historic Preservation: <http://www.achp.gov>.

SOURCES ON STATE HISTORIC PRESERVATION MATTERS:

The Hawaiian Historical Society's website: <http://www.hawaiianhistory.org>.

The State Historic Preservation Division's website: <http://hawaii.gov/dlnr/hpd>.

Stacy L. Kamehiro, *The Arts of Kingship: Hawaiian Art and National Culture of the Kalākaua Era* (Honolulu: U of Hawai'i P, 2009).

DAVIANNA PŌMAIKA'I MCGREGOR, SUSTAINABILITY

1. For its vision statement and additional information on Ke Aupuni Lōkahi, see "Molokai Enterprise Community <http://www.molokaiec.org>.
2. Lanaians for Sensible Growth and Hawaii Alliance for Community-Based Economic Development (HACBED), Lana'i Strategic Vision and Development Framework, Mar. 2010.
3. Kailua Historical Society, *Kailua: In the Wisps of the Malanai Breeze / Kailua ia ke oho o ka Malanai* (Kailua: Kailua Historical Society, 2009).
4. State of Hawai'i, Department of Economic Development and Tourism, Community-Based Economic Development, "Overview," May 3, 2010 <hawaii.gov/dbedt/business/info/cbed/Overview/view?searchterm=community-based%20economic%20development%20program>.

RECOMMENDED READING

Carlos Andrade, *Hā'ena: Through the Eyes of the Ancestors* (Honolulu: U of Hawai'i P, 2008)

E. S. Craighill Handy and Mary Kawena Pukui, *Polynesian Family System in Ka'u, Hawai'i*, 1958 (Honolulu: Mutual 1998).

"The Health of Native Hawaiians," Special Issue of *Pacific Health Dialog, Journal of Community Health and Clinical Medicine for the Pacific* 5.2 (Sept. 1998).

Wayne Levin, Rowland Reeve, Franco Salmoiraghi, and David Ulrich, *Kaho'olawe: Nā Leo o Kanaloa* (Honolulu: 'Ai Pohaku, 1995).

Jon Matsuoka, Davianna McGregor, and Luciano Minerbi, "Hawaiian Subsistence and Community Sustainability," *Here! Urbanism, Design and Planning, Moloka'i*, U of Hawai'i Dept. of Urban and Regional Planning, Winter 2007: 40–67.

Davianna McGregor, "A Community-Based Master Land Use Plan for Moloka'i Ranch? This effort deserves serious reflection," *Here! Urbanism, Design and Planning, Moloka'i*, U of Hawai'i Dept. of Urban and Regional Planning, Winter 2007: 68–87.

———. *Na Kua'āina: Living Hawaiian Culture* (Honolulu: U of Hawai'i P, 2007).

Lawrence H. Miike, *Water and the Law in Hawai'i* (Honolulu: U of Hawai'i P, 2004).

Mary Kawena Pukui, *'Ōlelo No'eau: Hawaiian Proverbs and Poetical Sayings* (Honolulu: Bishop Museum, 1983).

Mary Kawena Pukui, Samuel H. Elbert, and Esther T. Mookini, *Place Names of Hawaii* (Honolulu: U of Hawai'i P, 1966).

Robert H. Stauffer, *Kahana: How the Land Was Lost* (Honolulu: U of Hawai'i P, 2004).

CARLOS ANDRADE, HĀ'ENA

Carlos Andrade, *Hā'ena: Through the Eyes of the Ancestors* (Honolulu: U of Hawai'P, 2008).

Nā Pali's recording of "Aloha Hā'ena" appears on the album *Nā Pali* (Awapuhi Productions, 2005).

CONTRIBUTORS

Carlos Andrade is Associate Professor and Director at Kamakakūokalani Center for Hawaiian Studies at the University of Hawai'i at Mānoa. He returned to university at age forty-three, earned a BA in Hawaiian Studies (1989), a MEd in Educational Counseling (1993), and finally a doctorate in Geography (2001). He is a father of three, grandfather of five, has lived as a subsistence fisherman and farmer, and worked as a musician and professional boat captain. A former crewmember aboard *Hōkūle'a* on two voyages in 1985 and 1993, he is a recording artist, a composer of songs, a practitioner of kī hō'alu (slack key guitar), and an author.

Chad Blair reports on state issues for *Honolulu Civil Beat*. He previously reported for *Pacific Business News, Hawai'i Public Radio,* and *Honolulu Weekly*. Blair holds a PhD in American Studies from the University of Hawai'i at Mānoa (1996), and has taught political science, communications, journalism, English, and other disciplines at the University of Hawai'i at Mānoa, Hawai'i Pacific University, Chaminade University of Honolulu, and Honolulu Community College. He is author of *Money, Color and Sex in Hawaii Politics* (Mutual, 1998), and was a Racial Justice Fellow 2005–2006, at the Institute for Justice and Journalism, University of Southern California Annenberg School for Communication.

Kat Brady is Coordinator of Community Alliance on Prisons, a community initiative promoting smart justice strategies for Hawai'i's lawbreakers for more than a decade.

Susan M. Chandler is the Director of the College of Social Sciences Public Policy Center and a Professor of Public Administration at the University of Hawai'i at Mānoa. From 1995 to 2002 she served in Governor Benjamin J. Cayetano's administration as the Director of Human Services. From 1976 to 2006 she was a Professor in the UHM School of Social Work. She teaches in the areas of public policy, network governance, community and organizational change, and policy implementation. She recently completed a book with Richard Pratt, *Backstage in the Bureaucracy: Politics and Public Services* (U of Hawai'i P, 2010).

Meda Chesney-Lind is Professor of Women's Studies at the University of Hawai'i at Mānoa, and the author of numerous books on imprisonment in the United States, including *Invisible Punishment: The Collateral Consequences of Mass Incarceration* (New Press, 2003), and most recently, *Beyond Bad Girls: Gender, Violence and Hype* (Routledge, 2009), with Katherine Irwin.

Lowell Chun-Hoon is a Honolulu labor lawyer, and the former editor and co-founder of the *Amerasia Journal.*

Tom Coffman is an independent researcher, writer, and documentary producer. He moved to Hawai'i in 1965, and began his work as a newspaper reporter, first for the *Honolulu Advertiser* and then the *Honolulu Star-Bulletin.* He also worked as a field coordinator for the Honolulu Community Action Program. Books by Tom Coffman include *Catch A Wave, Nation Within,* and *The Island Edge of America.* Films include *O Hawai'i, Nation Within,* and *First Battle: The Battle for Equality in Wartime Hawai'i.* A written biography of the labor lawyer Ed Nakamura, *And Justice for All,* is soon to be released by the University of Hawai'i Press, and a new documentary film, *Ninoy Aquino and the Rise of People Power,* is being distributed nationally by PBS.

Sara L. Collins worked as a regulatory archaeologist at SHPD for ten years. Her areas of responsibility included Maui and Kaua'i Counties and the City and County of Honolulu. She has also taught Historic Preservation at the University of Hawai'i at Mānoa. Her professional and research interests include Hawaiian archaeology, human and faunal osteology, forensic anthropology, and historic preservation law and practice.

Marilyn Cristofori is Chief Executive Officer of the Hawai'i Arts Alliance. Earlier in her career she was a professional dancer, directed national Summer Arts Festivals, and produced award-winning PBS documentaries. She is Professor Emeritus, California State University, and serves as Affiliate Graduate Faculty at the University of Hawai'i at Mānoa. From 2005 to 2008 she served on the National Leadership Committee for National Partnerships at the John F. Kennedy Center for the Performing Arts. In 2008 she was recognized by Hawai'i Community Foundation with the Ho'okele Award for executive leadership.

Henry Curtis has been Executive Director of Life of the Land since 1995, and has a BA in Economics from Queens College, City University of New York. He is a community organizer, videographer, director, producer, peer reviewer, moot court judge, community facilitator, and provides expert testimony on ocean power, biofuels, energy, and externalities at the Public Utilities Commission, where he has represented Life of the Land in over twenty regulatory proceedings. He is committed to Hawai'i's energy self-reliance and well-being, and is motivated by the values of aloha 'āina, mālama 'āina, and his love for Hawai'i nei.

Kathy E. Ferguson is Professor of Political Science and Women's Studies at the University of Hawai'i at Mānoa. She is co-author of *Oh, Say, Can You See? The Semiotics of the Military in Hawai'i* (U of Minnesota P, 1999). She is currently writing a book on Emma Goldman.

Chip Fletcher is Professor and past Chair of the Department of Geology and Geophysics at the University of Hawai'i at Mānoa. He and his wife have raised three children in Kailua, O'ahu.

Dana Naone Hall is a former member of the Maui-Lāna'i Island Burial Council, and has been involved with cultural, environmental, and historic preservation issues for twenty-five years. She lives in Haiku, Maui.

Susan Hippensteele is a faculty member in the Women's Studies Program at the University of Hawai'i at Mānoa, and a licensed attorney who has represented victims of domestic violence in Hawai'i courts. She has studied aspects of violence and discrimination in Hawai'i and worked in various capacities with victims since 1987.

Craig Howes has been Director of the Center for Biographical Research at the University of Hawai'i at Mānoa since 1997, Editor and Co-Editor of the journal *Biography: An Interdisciplinary Quarterly* since 1994, and a faculty member in the Department of English since 1980. The co-producer and principal scholar for the television documentary series *Biography Hawai'i*, he has also been active in Hawai'i's arts and humanities communities. A past President of the Hawai'i Literary Arts Council and a former board member of Kumu Kahua Theatre, he currently serves as President of Monkey Waterfall Dance Theatre Company and as a member of the board for the Hawaiian Historical Society.

Karl Kim is Professor of Urban and Regional Planning at the University of Hawai'i at Mānoa, where he is currently serving as the Executive Director of the National Disaster Preparedness Training Center. He was educated at Brown University and the Massachusetts Institute of Technology, and has been a Fulbright Scholar to Korea and the Russian Far East.

Sumner La Croix is Professor of Economics and Research Fellow in the University of Hawai'i Economic Research Organization, University of Hawai'i at Mānoa. He is co-author of *Government and the American Economy* (Chicago, 2007), and a co-editor of *Institutional Change in Japan* (Routledge, 2006), and *Challenges to the Global Trading System* (Routledge, 2007). La Croix is an associate editor of *Asian Economic Journal,* and a member of the editorial board of the *Journal of Economic History.*

Ian Lind writes a daily blog on Hawai'i politics and media (www.iLind.net). He was previously an award-winning investigative reporter for the *Honolulu Star-Bulletin,* served as executive director of Common Cause Hawaii, and is a past chair of the Honolulu Community-Media Council, now known as Media Council Hawaii.

Melody Kapilialoha MacKenzie is an Associate Professor and Director of Ka Huli Ao Center for Excellence in Native Hawaiian Law, William S. Richardson School of Law, University of Hawai'i at Mānoa. After serving as a law clerk to Hawai'i Supreme Court Chief Justice William S. Richardson, she joined the staff of the Native Hawaiian Legal Corporation, a public interest law firm advancing Native Hawaiian rights. Prof. MacKenzie is chief editor for the second edition of the *Native Hawaiian Rights Handbook,* and has litigated cases dealing with Hawaiian lands, asserting traditional and customary rights, and defending the constitutionality of Hawaiian programs.

Mari Matsuda is author of two of the hundred most-cited law review articles in the United States. She is a founder of Critical Race Theory, a professor of law, and a proud product of Hawai'i public schools, including Mānoa Elementary, Stevenson Intermediate, Roosevelt High School, and the William S. Richardson School of Law. She is the author, with Charles Lawrence, of a forthcoming book entitled *The Last Public Place: Essays on Race, Education, and Democracy.*

Davianna Pōmaika'i McGregor is a Professor and founding member of Ethnic Studies at the University of Hawai'i at Mānoa. Dr. McGregor is a historian of Hawai'i and the Pacific. She lives in Kaiwi'ula, O'ahu and Ho'olehua, Moloka'i, and helps steward Kanaloa Kaho'olawe as a member of the Protect Kaho'olawe 'Ohana. Her book, *Nā Kua'āina: Living Hawaiian Culture* (U of Hawai'i P, 2007) focuses on Hawaiian cultural customs, beliefs, and practices in cultural kīpuka.

Neal Milner is Professor of Political Science at the University of Hawai'i at Mānoa. He is also a political analyst. He headed the UH Mānoa Ombuds Office from its beginning in 2006 until the office was shut down in 2009.

Deane Neubauer is Professor Emeritus of Political Science at the University of Hawai'i at Mānoa. He also currently serves as Senior Consultant to the International Forum for Education 2020 Program of the East-West Center, and as Senior Research Fellow for the Globalization Research Center, UHM. His research focus is on policy and globalization, with particular interests in health and educational policy.

Jonathan Kay Kamakawiwo'ole Osorio, PhD, is Professor of Hawaiian Studies at the University of Hawai'i at Mānoa, a historian of the Hawaiian Kingdom, and a practicing musician and composer. He has been an advocate for the restoration of Hawai'i's political independence, and writes about the sovereignty movement in Hawai'i. He and his wife Mary live in Pālolo, and have sent all of their children to public schools and Kamehameha High School.

Charles Reppun was born and raised in Hawai'i, and has been farming with his brother Paul for thirty-plus years. They grow all kinds of food, with taro as a central focus. He also helped to draft the state water code.

John P. Rosa is Assistant Professor of Modern Hawai'i History at the University of Hawai'i at Mānoa. He previously taught U.S. history at Kamehameha Schools–Kapālama (2006–2008), and was Assistant Professor of Asian Pacific American Studies at Arizona State University, Tempe (2000–2006), and Visiting Assistant Professor at Loyola Marymount University (1998–1999). His book, *Local Story: The Massie-Kahahawai Case and the Politics of History,* is under contract with University of Hawai'i Press. If you really must know, he wen grad in '86 from Damien Memorial High School in Kalihi-Pālama.

D. Kapua'ala Sproat is an Assistant Professor at the University of Hawai'i at Mānoa's William S. Richardson School of Law, where she teaches courses and provides program support for Ka Huli Ao Center for Excellence in Native Hawaiian Law and the Environmental Law Program. Ms. Sproat has spent over a decade working on water issues on O'ahu, Maui, Moloka'i, and Hawai'i Island, both in her capacity as UH's Environmental Law Clinic Director and as an attorney with Earthjustice, a public interest environmental litigation firm. She hails from the Island of Kaua'i and is a member of the Akana and Sproat 'ohana.

Ramsay Remigius Mahealani Taum is President of the Hawai'i-based Life Enhancement Institute (LEI) of the Pacific LLC. He lectures on host cultural values in the workplace at the University of Hawai'i School of Travel Industry Management (TIM), is on the Hawaii Visitors and Convention Bureau Board of Trustees, HVCB Marketing Advisory Committee, and the Hawaii Tourism Authority Hawaiian Cultural Program Advisory Group. Taum works with travel, leisure, retail, and development industries integrating cultural values and principles into contemporary business, and is a sought after keynote speaker, lecturer, trainer, and facilitator. His work promoting sustainable place-based Hawaiian cultural stewardship principles and practices is acknowledged locally, nationally, and internationally.

Patricia Tummons is a career journalist. She has written for *Environment Hawai'i* since 1990, winning many awards for her hard-hitting reports on Hawai'i's environmental problems. She was awarded a BA in philosophy and history from the University of Buffalo, and an MA in philosophy from the same institution. She makes her home in Hilo.

Phyllis Turnbull is retired from teaching in the Political Science Department at the University of Hawai'i at Mānoa. She is co-author of *Oh, Say, Can You See? The Semiotics of the Military in Hawai'i* (U of Minnesota P, 1999).

Trisha Kehaulani Watson, JD, PhD, earned her degrees from Washington State University and the University of Hawai'i at Mānoa. A lifelong Mānoa resident, she works as a community advocate and private consultant. She particularly enjoys working with Hawaiian nonprofit organizations and other cultural organizations. She is President of Honua Consulting. and specializes in environmental issues, historic preservation, fundraising/grant-writing, evaluation, research, and policy matters. She is a member of numerous community organizations, including 'Ahahui Ka'ahumanu, the Hawaiian Civic Club of Honolulu, the Daughters of Hawai'i, and the Native Hawaiian Bar Association.